The PLAN *of*
SALVATION

Understanding Our Divine Origin and Destiny

The PLAN of SALVATION

Understanding Our Divine Origin and Destiny

MATTHEW B. BROWN

Covenant Communications, Inc.

For my siblings
Richard, Alan, and Kristen

Cover Painting *The Grand Council* © Robert T. Barrett

Cover design copyrighted 2002, 2007 by Covenant Communications, Inc.

Published by Covenant Communications, Inc.
American Fork, Utah

Printed in the United States of America
First Printing: October 2002

13 12 11 10 09 08 07   10 9 8 7 6 5 4 3 2 1

ISBN 978-159811-346-4

CONTENTS

Introduction 1

SECTION ONE: *Where Did I Come From?* 5

CHAPTER 1: Sons and Daughters of God 7

CHAPTER 2: The Grand Council 31

SECTION TWO: *Why Am I Here?* 55

CHAPTER 3: Creation, Fall, and Atonement 57

CHAPTER 4: The Purpose of Mortality 87

CHAPTER 5: Ordinances of Salvation 103

SECTION THREE: *Where Am I Going?* 139

CHAPTER 6: The Spirit World 141

CHAPTER 7: Resurrection and Judgment 171

CHAPTER 8: Rewards of Darkness and Glory 201

Appendix I: The Salvation of Children 235

Appendix II: Covenant Status and Salvation 245

Appendix III: Salvation and Grace 251

Selected Bibliography 259

Index 265

ABBREVIATIONS

In citing works in the notes, short titles have generally been used. Works frequently cited have been identified by the following abbreviations:

AGQ	*Answers to Gospel Questions*
BYUS	*BYU Studies*
CD	*Collected Discourses*
CR	Conference Report
D&C	Doctrine and Covenants
DNTC	*Doctrinal New Testament Commentary*
DS	*Doctrines of Salvation*
EM	*Encyclopedia of Mormonism*
GD	*Gospel Doctrine*
HC	*History of the Church*
IE	*Improvement Era*
JD	*Journal of Discourses*
JST	Joseph Smith Translation
MD	*Mormon Doctrine*
MS	*Millennial Star*
NWAF	*New Witness for the Articles of Faith*
TPJS	*Teachings of the Prophet Joseph Smith*
T&S	*Times and Seasons*
WJS	*Words of Joseph Smith*

INTRODUCTION

Those people who contemplate the miracle and mystery of their existence often ask themselves three fundamental, but profoundly important, questions: Where did I come from? Why am I here on the earth? What will happen to me after I die? The scriptures reveal that humanity is not on this planet by blind chance, but is, in fact, the focal point of a grand "plan" that was "laid from the foundation of the world" (Alma 12:25, 30). It is referred to in these sacred writings as the "great plan of the Eternal God" (Alma 34:9), the "plan of deliverance" (2 Ne. 11:5), and the "plan of salvation" (Alma 24:14).

This plan, said President Brigham Young, is a "system of laws and ordinances, by strict obedience to which the people who inhabit this earth are assured that they may return again into the presence of the Father and the Son."[1] In this light, it is easy to understand why the Prophet Joseph Smith would maintain that the "plan of salvation is a theme which ought to occupy our strict attention."[2] And this attention will be amply repaid, said President Hugh B. Brown, for "an open-minded and courageous study of [God] and His divine plan with respect to our salvation will be the most interesting and permanently rewarding of all ventures."[3]

The purpose of this book is to bring together information from the scriptures, LDS Church leaders, and respected gospel scholars that will help to facilitate the kind of study that was envisioned by President Brown. This volume has been arranged in such a way that it addresses the three fundamental questions of existence in their logical sequence.

WHERE DID I COME FROM? Two chapters are found in this portion of the book. The first, entitled "Sons and Daughters of God," addresses issues such as the origin of God, the creation of spirit children, and the nature of the premortal existence. The second chapter is called "The Grand Council." On these pages the reader will find discussions of the origin of the plan of salvation, the nature of the Father's foreknowledge, the premortal status of Lucifer, and the extent of foreordination.

WHY AM I HERE? This section of the book contains a series of three chapters. The first one covers the "Creation, Fall, and Atonement." It begins by dealing with the formation of the heavens and the earth and then moves on to the creation of mankind's primordial parents. This chapter then provides a series of questions and answers about the Fall. Here the reader will find information on what happened to the bodies of Adam and Eve when they partook of the forbidden fruit, the absolute necessity of the Fall, and why the Lord did not create a fallen world to begin with. The same question-and-answer format is utilized in examining the Atonement of the Lord Jesus Christ. These pages include discussions on the meaning of the word "redeemer," the operation and application of the Atonement, and the need for the Savior to shed His blood.

The next chapter focuses on "The Purpose of Mortality." Subjects covered in this portion of the book include the need for a physical body (and the advantages gained by obtaining one), the development of godly attributes while in the mortal sphere, and some reasons for human tribulations and suffering.

The last chapter deals with the "Ordinances of Salvation." Here the reader will learn of divinely ordained ceremonies that have been designed to prepare individuals for life beyond the veil. They will also find answers to questions such as, Why does the officiator at a baptism raise his right arm to the square? Does partaking of the sacrament cause one's sins to be remitted? Do any of the ordinances of the gospel pertain to the terrestrial or telestial kingdoms? and Why is it necessary for children to be sealed to their parents?

WHERE AM I GOING? The final portion of this volume begins with a chapter about "The Spirit World." Through these pages the reader will become acquainted with the stratified levels of existence within the realm of the departed. They will also read an eyewitness account of paradise related by a member of the First Presidency of the LDS Church and learn of the greatly increased abilities of righteous spirits. The second half of this chapter presents substantial information on salvation for the dead. Some of the questions that are answered in this section of the book include, Why must living proxies stand in for the deceased? Do proxy ordinances need to be performed for everyone? and Is proxy temple work a second chance at salvation?

Next, this section deals with the doctrines of "Resurrection and Judgment." Some Latter-day Saints may not be aware that Joseph Smith included these doctrines among the "first principles" of the gospel, and the missionaries of his day were instructed to teach them as such. Questions that receive attention in the first half of this chapter include, What does the word "First Resurrection" mean? How many resurrections will take place? Will a person's resurrected body appear the same as when they died? The second half of this chapter addresses inquiries such as, Why did God the Father commit all judgment unto His Son? How will the Judgment be administered? and Why is the Judgment necessary?

The final chapter in this group, which is entitled "Rewards of Darkness and Glory," deals with the eternal destinations of all of God's children. This chapter includes a discussion on the sons of perdition and the nature of the unpardonable sin. It also takes a careful look at the criteria for entering into each of the three degrees of glory and the highest realm of the celestial world.

Three appendices have been included at the back of this book. Appendix I is on "The Salvation of Children." Here the reader will find answers to questions such as, What is the nature of a child before it is born? Will those who die as children need to receive any of the ordinances of the gospel? What will be the state of children after they have been resurrected? Appendix II is entitled "Covenant Status and Salvation." It examines the historical and doctrinal context of a statement made by Joseph Smith on family sealings and eternal rewards. Appendix III includes statements on the LDS view of "Salvation and Grace" and a short bibliography of LDS sources on this issue.

On a final note, the reader should be made aware that some of the quotations in this book have been standardized to reflect modern spelling, punctuation, capitalization and grammar. They have been carefully modified, however, to ensure that their proper content and context have been preserved.

NOTES: INTRODUCTION

1. George D. Watt, comp., *Journal of Discourses* (London, England: F. D. and S. W. Richards and Sons, 1854–1886), 13:233, hereafter cited as *JD*.

2. B. H. Roberts, ed., *History of the Church,* rev. ed. (Salt Lake City: The Church of Jesus Christ of Latter-day Saints, 1932–1951), 2:23. Joseph Smith taught the Latter-day Saints about the frame of mind that is needed for a study of the principles of salvation. Said he, "The things of God are of vast importance, and [it] requires time and experience as well as deep and solemn thought to find them out; and if we would bring souls to salvation it requires that our minds should rise to the highest heavens, search into and contemplate the lowest abyss, expand wide as eternity and hold communion with Deity" (Times and Seasons, vol. 1, no. 7, May 1840, 102). Even though the Lord's plan is "wide as eternity" President Brigham Young offers the assurance that "there is no mystery throughout the whole plan of salvation, only to those who do not understand [it]" *(JD,* 3:367).

3. Conference Report, October 1962, 42. For articles that present a broad overview of the plan of salvation see Richard G. Scott, "The Plan for Happiness and Exaltation," *Ensign*, November 1981, 11–12; Neal A. Maxwell, "The Great Plan of the Eternal God," *Ensign*, May 1984, 21–23; Dallin H. Oaks, "The Great Plan of Happiness," *Ensign*, November 1993, 72–75; M. Russell Ballard, "Answers to Life's Questions," *Ensign*, May 1995, 22–24; Robert England Lee, "Teaching Our Children the Plan of Salvation," *Ensign*, September 2001, 32–39; Parley P. Pratt, "Four Kinds of Salvation," *Millennial Star,* vol. 2, no. 2, June 1841, 21–22.

SECTION 1

WHERE DID
I COME FROM?

CHAPTER 1

SONS AND DAUGHTERS OF GOD

One of the most cherished of all Latter-day Saint hymns begins with the simple yet profound phrase: "I am a child of God" *(Hymns, no. 301)*. President Marion G. Romney informs us that this "is the most important knowledge available to mortals."[1] It is of primary importance because it lies at the very heart of the Lord's plan of salvation. Those who encounter this idea for the first time may well ask themselves, "Is God my Father? Am I indeed His son? Am I indeed His daughter? Do I belong to the family of God? Is this literally true?" President George Q. Cannon answers, "Yes. God has revealed it, that we are literally His children, His offspring; that we are just as much His children as our offspring are our children; that He begot us; and that we existed with Him in the family relationship as His children" before we came to the earth.

Not only does the truth about human origins provide its possessors with enlightenment and hope, but, as President Cannon states, it also gives them "an immensity of vision" and "a field of reflection" like no other. It is both humbling and ennobling "to think that the Being under whose direction this earth was organized, who governs the planets and controls the universe, who causes the rotation of the seasons and makes this earth so beautiful and such a delightful place of habitation, is our Father, and that we are His children, descended from Him!"[2]

The enormous potential of each of God's offspring was referred to in an official statement made by the First Presidency of The Church of Jesus Christ of Latter-day Saints. This statement, which was prepared in 1909, reads in part: "Man is the child of God, formed in the divine image and endowed with divine attributes, and even as the infant son of an earthly father and mother is capable in due time of becoming a man, so the undeveloped offspring of celestial parentage is capable, by experience through ages and eons, of evolving into a god."[3] Even though the doctrine of exaltation or godhood is taught throughout the scriptures (see Gen. 3:5, 22; Deut. 10:17; Ps. 82:1; John 10:34–36; 1 Cor. 8:5–6; D&C 76:58; 132:17–20, 37) it is somewhat easier for mortals to comprehend it if they first understand something of the origin and nature of God Himself.

THE ORIGIN AND NATURE OF GOD

In the sixth chapter of the book of Moses it is revealed that in the Adamic language God the Father is called "Man of Holiness" and Jesus Christ is called the "Son of Man" (v. 57). A literal reading of this scriptural passage suggests that God the Father is an exalted man. The Prophet Joseph Smith publicly taught this concept on 7 April 1844 in what has become known as the King Follett discourse. The Prophet told the Saints who had gathered before him that "if men do not comprehend the character of God they do not comprehend themselves." He then asked them, "What kind of Being is God?"[4] He answered with the following words:

> God Himself, who sits enthroned in yonder heavens, is a man like unto one of yourselves.[5] That is the great secret. If the veil was rent today and the great God who holds this world in its sphere or its orbit—[and all] the planets [also]—if you were to see Him today you would see Him in all the person, image, [and] very form of man, for Adam was created in the very fashion of God.[6]

Not very much is known about the origin of God the Father, but an examination of the scriptures and the teachings of His authorized representatives can yield various valuable insights.

God Had a Progenitor

On 16 June 1844 the Prophet Joseph Smith presented a lecture on the plurality of gods. After referring to the first chapter and sixth verse of the book of Revelation, the Prophet stated his desire to "preach the doctrine [of] there being a God above the Father of our Lord Jesus Christ." The Prophet acknowledged his agreement with the Apostle Paul who said that even though "there are Gods many and Lords many . . . to us [there is] only one, and we are in subject[ion] to that one" (see 1 Cor. 8:5–6). The Prophet then told his audience that he wanted to "reason" with them concerning the plurality of divine beings. He related that while he was translating the papyrus roll that contained the text of the book of Abraham he learned that "intelligences" exist one above another in the eternal worlds, just like mortal men who have differing degrees of worldly wisdom (see Abr. 3:19). He then said:

> If Abraham reasoned thus, [and] if Jesus Christ was the Son of God, and John [the Revelator] discovered that God the Father of Jesus Christ had a Father [see Rev. 1:5–6] you may suppose that He had a Father also. Where was there ever a son without a father? Wherever did [a] tree or anything spring into existence without a progenitor? And everything comes in this way. Paul says "that which is earthly is in likeness of that which is heavenly" [see 1 Cor. 15:46–49]. Hence, if Jesus had a Father can we not believe that He had a Father also?[7]

Elder Orson Pratt taught this very same doctrine. He said, "We were begotten by our Father in Heaven; the person of our Father in Heaven was begotten on a previous heavenly world by His Father; and again, He was begotten by a still more ancient Father; and so on, from generation to generation, from one heavenly world to another still more ancient."[8] After pondering the question of "how many Gods there are" President Brigham Young said, "I do not know. But there never was a time when there were not Gods and worlds, and when men were not passing through the same ordeals that we are now passing through. This course has been from all eternity, and it is and will be to all eternity."[9]

Some Latter-day Saints may be confused by the idea that God the Father had a beginning when several scriptures declare that He is "everlasting," "eternal," and "from eternity to eternity." Elder Charles W. Penrose helped to clarify the meaning of these expressions by posing the following questions. He asked, "If God is an individual spirit and dwells in a body . . . 'Is He the Eternal Father?' Yes, He is the Eternal Father. 'Is it a fact that He never had a beginning?' In the *elementary particles* of His organism, He did not. But if He is an organized Being, there must have been a time when that Being was organized."[10] Elder Bruce R. McConkie provides further enlightenment on this issue by defining what "eternity" means. He says that:

> Eternity is the name of that infinite duration of existence when we lived as the spirit children of the Eternal Father. It contrasts with time, which is our temporal or mortal existence. Eternity is also that existence gained by exalted beings who gain eternal families of their own that are patterned after the family of God the Father. When our revelations say of Christ, "From eternity to eternity He is the same, and His years never fail" (D&C 76:4), they mean that from one preexistence to the next He does not vary, His course is one eternal round. They mean, for instance, that from our premortal or preexistent state to the day when the exalted among us provide a preexistence for our spirit children, He is the same.
>
> Those who enter the order of celestial marriage have the potential of being "from everlasting to everlasting" (D&C 132:20).[11]

God Has Experienced Mortality

Joseph Smith told the Saints in Nauvoo, Illinois, "[I am] going to tell you how God came to be God. We have imagined that God was God from all eternity. These [concepts] are incomprehensible to some but are the first principle[s] of the gospel—to know that we may converse with Him as one man with another and that He was once as one of us and was on a planet as Jesus was in the flesh."[12] The Prophet was even more specific when he declared that "God the Father took life unto Himself precisely as Jesus did."[13] A statement made by President Joseph F. Smith is the most explicit to be found on this topic. He said, "The Son, Jesus Christ, grew and developed into manhood the same as you or I, as likewise did God, His Father, grow and develop to the Supreme Being that He now is. Man was born of woman; Christ, the Savior, was born of woman; and God, the Father, was born of woman."[14]

According to President Brigham Young, the great Parent of the human race took part in mortal circumstances that are similar to our own. He "has passed the ordeals we are now passing through; He has received an experience, has suffered and enjoyed, and knows all that we know regarding the toils, sufferings, life and death of this mortality, for He has passed through the whole of it, and has received His crown and exaltation."[15] President Joseph F. Smith expressed the same idea and also pointed out that God's children take bodies upon themselves in mortality so that they can become like Him.

> It is absolutely necessary that we should come to the earth and take upon us tabernacles; because if we did not have tabernacles we could not be like God, nor like Jesus Christ. God has a tabernacle of flesh and bone. He is an organized Being just as we are, who are now in the flesh. Jesus Christ . . . [also] had a fleshly tabernacle. . . . and His body was raised from the dead. . . . You and I have to do the same thing. We must go through the same ordeal in order to attain to the glory and exaltation which God designed we should enjoy with Him in the eternal worlds. In other words, we must become like Him; peradventure to sit upon thrones, to have dominion, power, and eternal increase. God designed this in the beginning. We are the children of God. He is an eternal Being, without beginning of days or end of years. He always was, He is, He always will be. We are precisely in the same condition and under the same circumstances that God our Heavenly Father was when He was passing through this, or a similar ordeal.[16]

Wilford Woodruff was in agreement with all that has been said thus far. It was his teaching that "whoever goes back into the presence of God our Eternal Father, will find that He is a noble man, a noble God, tabernacled in a form similar to ours, for we are created after His own image." In addition, said President Woodruff, they will learn that God "has placed us here that we may pass through a state of probation and experience, the same as He Himself did in His day of mortality."[17]

God Has Received Temple Ordinances

When Latter-day Saints go to the House of the Lord and receive the ordinances that are administered there they are following an exceedingly ancient pattern. Wilford Woodruff informed the Latter-day Saints of his day that God the Father "had His endowments long ago; it is thousands and millions of years since He received His blessings."[18]

When certain revelations in the Doctrine and Covenants and Pearl of Great Price are placed next to each other one can see a connection between the ordinances of the temple, godhood, and the ongoing work of the Almighty. These confirm the following:

- Those who become "gods" will receive the same "fullness, and . . . glory" that the Lord Himself possesses (D&C 76:56, 58).
- The temple is the place where the Lord's disciples can obtain His "fullness" (D&C 124:28) and its attendant "glory" (v. 34).
- It is necessary for men and women to be sealed to each other in an eternal marriage covenant so that they can inherit "the fullness of [the Lord's] glory" (D&C 132:6; see also vv. 16, 18, 21).
- Those who become "gods" in the celestial kingdom (D&C 132:17, 20) will receive "exaltation and glory in all things . . . which glory shall be a fullness and a continuation of the seeds [i.e., children] forever and ever" (v. 19).
- Eternal marriage provides the means whereby God the Father is "glorified" and the way by which His "works" are continued throughout eternity (D&C 132:31, 63).
- "And as one earth shall pass away, and the heavens thereof even so shall another come, and there is no end to my works, neither to my words. For behold, this is my work and my glory—to bring to pass the immortality and eternal life of man" (Moses 1:38–39).

A careful consideration of the last two points, in conjunction with all the others, leads one to the conclusion that God the Father has a divine Spouse. Elder Erastus Snow taught that "there can be no God except He is composed of the man and woman united, and there is not in all the eternities that exist, nor ever will be, a God in any other way. . . . There never was a God, and there never will be in all [the] eternities, except they are made of these two component parts; a man and a woman, the male and the female."[19] Indeed, it is an established doctrine of The Church of Jesus Christ of Latter-day Saints that mortals not only have a Heavenly Father but also a Heavenly Mother.[20] President Spencer W. Kimball told the sisters of the Church, "God made man in His own image and certainly He made woman in the image of His wife-partner. You [women] are daughters of God. You are precious. You are made in the image of our Heavenly Mother."[21]

God Has Been Resurrected

On 2 April 1843 the Prophet Joseph Smith proclaimed that God the Father "has a body of flesh and bones as tangible as man's" (D&C 130:22).[22] During a discourse on 16 June 1844 the Prophet elaborated on this idea, stating that Jesus Christ "laid down His life and took it up, [the] same as His Father had done before."[23] President Brigham Young alluded to this same precept:

> [T]he Father, after He had once been in the flesh, and lived as we live, obtained His exaltation, attained to thrones, gained the ascendancy over principalities and powers, and had the knowledge and power to create—to bring forth and organize the elements upon natural principles. This He did after His ascension, or His glory, or His eternity, and was actually classed with the Gods, with the Beings who create, with those who have *kept the celestial law while in the flesh, and again obtained their bodies.* Then He was prepared to commence the work of creation, as the scriptures teach.[24]

A document that was issued jointly by the First Presidency of the LDS Church and the Quorum of the Twelve Apostles, dated 30 June

1916, affirms the doctrine of a resurrected God. This paper certifies that the Lord Jesus Christ has a "unique status in the flesh as the offspring of a mortal mother and . . . an immortal, or *resurrected* and glorified, Father."[25]

Even though information on the origin and nature of God is only available in limited amounts, there is enough at hand to construct a fascinating and familiar picture. This picture provides an insightful perspective on the purpose of the plan of salvation, and it also gives added meaning to the idea that "the course of the Lord is one eternal round" (1 Ne. 10:19). Indeed, the Father's children were created for the express purpose of following in His holy footsteps.

SPIRIT CHILDREN

There are several passages in the Bible that provide an important insight on the origin and nature of mankind. These writings reveal that "there is a spirit in man" (Job 32:8) and that God is "the Father of spirits" (Heb. 12:9; cf. Num. 16:22; 27:16). Men and women are "the children of God" (Rom. 8:16) or, to use a more precise term, they are "the *offspring* of God" (Acts 17:29, emphasis added).

Ancient scriptural texts that were restored through the Prophet Joseph Smith teach that the spirit children of God were brought into existence through an act of creation. In Moses chapter 3 verse 5, for instance, the Lord says, "I, the Lord God, . . . *created* all the children of men; . . . [I]n heaven *created* I them" (emphasis added). And in Moses chapter 6 verse 51 God speaks these words: "I *made* . . . men before they were in the flesh" (emphasis added). In 1909 the First Presidency of The Church of Jesus Christ of Latter-day Saints (consisting of Joseph F. Smith, John R. Winder, and Anthon H. Lund) issued a statement that sheds some light on the nature of the spirit creation.

> The doctrine of the preexistence, revealed so plainly, partic-
> ularly in latter days, pours a wonderful flood of light upon
> the otherwise mysterious problem of man's origin. It shows
> that *man, as a spirit, was begotten and born of heavenly
> Parents,* and reared to maturity in the eternal mansions of

the Father, prior to coming upon the earth in a temporal body to undergo an experience in mortality. . . . Jesus, however, is the firstborn among all the sons of God—*the first begotten in the spirit,* and the Only Begotten in the flesh. He is our elder brother, and we, like Him, are in the image of God. *All men and women are in the similitude of the universal Father and Mother, and are literally the sons and daughters of Deity.*[26]

Elder Orson Pratt made some remarks that tie in with those made by the First Presidency. He took the method of creating spirit children into consideration, and it was his belief that both the Father and His divine Spouse acted together in this enterprise.

If we were born in heaven before this world was made, the question might arise as to the nature of that birth. Was it by command that the spiritual substance, scattered through space, was miraculously brought together, and organized into a spiritual form, and called a spirit? Is that the way we were born? Is that the way that Jesus, the firstborn of every creature, was brought into existence? Oh no; *we were all born there after the same manner that we are here, that is to say, every person that had an existence before he came here had a literal Father and a literal Mother,* a personal Father and a personal Mother; . . . [E]very man and woman that have ever come here on this globe, or that ever will come, . . . [had] a Father and Mother in the heavens by whom their spirits were brought into existence.[27]

Spirits Are Made of Matter

Many of the religious leaders that lived during Joseph Smith's day were of the opinion that spirits are immaterial. But the Prophet insisted that "there is no such thing as immaterial matter." He maintained that "all spirit is matter, but is more fine or pure, and can only be discerned by purer eyes. We cannot see it; but when our bodies are purified we shall see that it is all matter" (D&C 131:7–8).[28] Thus, people with physical bodies cannot see spirit beings (except when permitted) because their tabernacles are not of the same nature; they also do not have the ability to touch a spirit body. President Brigham Young said, however, that "spirits are just as familiar with spirits [in a tactile way] as bodies are with bodies, though spirits are composed of matter so refined as to not be tangible to this coarser organization."[29]

Where did the matter come from that was utilized in the creation of spirit entities? There seems to be an abundant supply of these particles, elements or atoms scattered throughout the universe. According to Brigham Young "the matter composing our . . . spirits has been organized from the eternity of matter that fills [the] immensity" of space.[30] Elder Bruce R. McConkie explains that "the bodies of Deity's spirit children were created from the existing spirit element just as the spirit bodies of the progeny of future exalted beings will be organized from the same substance." But Elder McConkie was adamant in his view that the birth of a spirit personage "constitute[s] the beginning of the human ego as a conscious identity."[31] He refutes the belief that there is any type of individual consciousness prior to this point.

> Any notion or theory that life, or ego, or agency, existed for each individual prior to the time of the spirit birth is *pure speculation,* wholly unsupported by any correctly understood and properly interpreted scripture. Life began for man and for all created things at the time of their respective spirit creations. Before that there were only the spirit elements from which the Almighty would in due course create life. In the sense that spirits never die or go out of existence, life is unending or eternal.[32]

Spirits Resemble Mortal Bodies

Verse 2 in Doctrine and Covenants section 77 says, "that which is spiritual [is] in the likeness of that which is temporal; and that which is temporal [is] in the likeness of that which is spiritual; the spirit of man [is] in the likeness of his person."[33] Elder Orson Pratt echoed this idea when he said that "the spirits that occupy [our] tabernacles have form and likeness similar to the human tabernacle. Of course there may be deformities existing in connection with the outward tabernacle which do not exist in connection with the spirit that inhabits it." He went on to say that even though accidents might happen to the human body, the resultant deformities do not distort the spirit in any degree.[34]

An excellent illustration of the close correspondence between the body and the spirit can be seen in the account of the premortal Savior appearing to the brother of Jared. In the scriptural passage that records this theophany the Savior teaches:

> Seest thou that ye are created after mine own image? Yea, even all men were created in the beginning after mine own image. Behold, this body, which ye now behold, is the body of my spirit; and man have I created after the body of my spirit; and even as I appear unto thee to be in the spirit will I appear unto my people in the flesh (Ether 3:15–16).[35]

Elder Parley P. Pratt reports that the spirit is "in the likeness and after the pattern of the fleshly tabernacle" to such a great degree that it "possesses, in fact, all the organs and parts exactly corresponding to the outward tabernacle."[36] The extent of differentiating features among the premortal masses is unknown, but President David O. McKay inferred from a reading of Abraham 3:23 that "there were no national distinctions among those spirits such as Americans, Europeans, Asiatics, Australians, etc. Such 'bounds of habitation' would have to be 'determined' when the spirits entered their earthly existence or second estate."[37]

THE PREMORTAL REALM

There is not a great deal of information available on the activities and environment of the premortal realm, but there is just enough to provide students of the gospel with a generalized view.

Environment
What kind of an environment are premortal spirits born into? It is evident from the scriptures that the spirit children of God begin their existence in a place of glory, innocence, and agency.

Glory: In verses 6 and 7 of section 130 of the Doctrine and Covenants it is revealed that "the angels do not reside on a planet like this earth; but they reside in the presence of God, on a globe like a sea of glass and fire, where all things for their glory are manifest, past, present, and future, and are continually before the Lord." Elder Orson Pratt reports that as premortal spirits "we dwelt in the presence of our Father . . . in the celestial world . . . [It was] a world that had passed through its stages, its ordeals, the same as this world is passing through [cf. D&C 88:17–20, 25–26; 130:9]. . . . That celestial world from whence we came, is more perfect than this earth. It is organized after a celestial order, a higher order, and glorified by the presence of immortal, glorified, celestial beings."[38]

Innocence: In Doctrine and Covenants 93:38, it is stated that "every spirit of man was innocent in the beginning." The Savior informed His mortal disciples that in order for them to return to "the kingdom of heaven" they would need to "become as little children" (Matt. 18:2–4; see also 19:13–14; Mark 10:13–16), meaning that they would need to become humble, submissive, and innocent. President Joseph Fielding Smith pointed out that "when Lucifer rebelled because of his agency, [and] he persuaded others to follow him, then their innocence came to an end, for they were in rebellion before God."[39]

Agency: The scriptures plainly teach that God bestowed the gift of agency upon His spirit children. It is said in the book of Moses chapter 4 verse 3 that in premortal times Satan "sought to destroy the agency of man, which . . . the Lord God had given him." And again, Doctrine and Covenants 29:36 relates that "a third part of the hosts of heaven turned . . . away from [God] because of their agency." President Charles W. Penrose confirms that "in the spirit birth" the Father's offspring obtained "power and intelligence by which [they could] determine and understand light from darkness, truth from error, and choose between that which is right and that which is wrong." It is precisely because these spirits were granted the great "power of choice" that they are held responsible before God and will be obliged to answer for all of their actions on the Day of Judgment.[40]

Organization

President Brigham Young reported that he had seen Joseph Smith in a vision a few years after the Prophet's death. During this manifestation President Young requested that his predecessor give him a few words of instruction on the sealing ordinances of the temple. The Prophet's response was most interesting:

> "Be sure to tell the people to keep the Spirit of the Lord; and if they will, they will find themselves just as they were *organized by our Father in Heaven before they came into the world.* Our Father in Heaven organized the human family, but [now] they are all disorganized and in great confusion."
>
> Joseph then showed me the *pattern, how they were in the beginning.* This I cannot describe, but I saw it.[41]

Some of the leaders of The Church of Jesus Christ of Latter-day Saints feel that a formal ecclesiastical structure can be found in the premortal world. Joseph Fielding Smith, for instance, said that "it is reasonable to believe that there was a Church organization there. The heavenly beings were living in a perfectly arranged society. Every person knew his place."[42] The idea of a pre-earth Church corresponds well with Elder Bruce R. McConkie's declaration that all premortal spirits are "taught the gospel."[43]

Authority

On 16 February 1832 the Lord showed Joseph Smith and Sidney Rigdon a vision about the sons of perdition. During this otherworldly experience they learned that Lucifer had held "*authority* in the presence of God" before he was cast out for rebellion (D&C 76:25, emphasis added). The Prophet subsequently taught that "the Priesthood is an everlasting principle and existed with God from eternity and will to eternity, without beginning of days or end of years."[44] President Wilford Woodruff provides some insight into some of the Prophet's other teachings on this topic:

> [T]he Prophet Joseph taught us that Father Adam was the first man on the earth to whom God gave the keys of the Everlasting Priesthood. He held the keys of the Presidency,

and was the first man who did hold them. Noah stood next to him. These keys were given to Noah, he being the father of all living in his day, as Adam was in his day. These two men were the first who received the Priesthood in the eternal worlds, before the worlds were formed.[45]

"Priesthood, without any question, had been conferred" in the pre-earthly state, said Joseph Fielding Smith, and "leaders were chosen to officiate. Ordinances pertaining to that preexistence were required."[46] When Elder Smith was serving in the First Presidency and also as President of the Quorum of the Twelve Apostles he said the following: "In regard to the holding of the Priesthood in [the] preexistence, I will say that there was an organization there just as well as an organization here, and men there held authority. *Men chosen to positions of trust in the spirit world held the Priesthood.*"[47]

Achievement
According to Elder Bruce R. McConkie the spirit progeny of God live in "a sphere governed by laws, laws ordained by the Father to enable them to advance and progress like Him."[48] Progression seems to be facilitated in this realm by a teaching system of some kind. Section 138 of the Doctrine and Covenants says that "lessons" are taught in the pre-earthly "world of spirits" (v. 56). As a result of this educational process, a stratification of intellect occurs among the Lord's offspring; "one being more intelligent than the other; . . . [and] another more intelligent than they" (Abr. 3:19).

Our spirits, said President Howard W. Hunter, "have had an extensive period of growth and development in the spirit world, where we came to know God and to comprehend the nature of spiritual realities. Some of our Father's sons developed spiritual talents to a marked degree, and they were foreordained to spiritual callings in mortality whereby their talents would be utilized to administer salvation to our Father's children."[49] Elder McConkie expanded upon this theme. He said that the characteristics, attributes, and abilities of mortals are directly connected to the growth that they experienced prior to their arrival in the temporal sphere.

Being subject to law, and having their agency, all the spirits of men, while yet in the Eternal Presence, developed aptitudes, talents, capacities, and abilities of every sort, kind, and degree. During the long expanse of life which then was, an infinite variety of talents and abilities came into being. As the ages rolled, no two spirits remained alike. Mozart became a musician; Einstein centered his interest in mathematics; Michelangelo turned his attention to painting. Cain was a liar, a schemer, a rebel who maintained a close affinity to Lucifer. Abraham and Moses and all of the prophets sought and obtained the talent for spirituality. Mary and Eve were two of the greatest of all the spirit daughters of the Father. The whole house of Israel, known and segregated out from their fellows, was inclined toward spiritual things. And so it went through all the hosts of heaven, each individual developing such talents and abilities as his soul desired.[50]

One of the premortal children of God surpassed all of the others in their progression and achievement; this was Jesus Christ, the firstborn spirit (see D&C 93:21).[51] Elder McConkie makes note of the fact that it was "by obedience to law [that] the Firstborn advanced and progressed and became like the Father in power and intelligence, and became, under the Father, the Creator of all things, meaning that He was the Executive Officer who brought to pass the Father's creative enterprises."[52] The opportunity to become like God is available to all of His children, but such a task can only be accomplished through the laws that are laid out in the plan of salvation.

NOTES: CHAPTER 1

1. Conference Report, April 1973, 136, hereafter cited as CR.

2. *The Contributor,* vol. 11, no. 12, October 1890, 476. Elder Parley P. Pratt taught that "Gods, angels, and men are all of one species, one race, one great family, widely diffused among the planetary systems as colonies, kingdoms, nations, etc. The great distinguishing difference between one portion of this race and another consists in the varied grades of intelligence and purity and

also in the variety of spheres occupied by each in the series of progressive being" (Parley P. Pratt, *Key to the Science of Theology* [Salt Lake City: Deseret Book, 1978], 21).

3. *Improvement Era,* November 1909, 81, hereafter cited as *IE.* President John Taylor stated that "man is a dual being, possessed of body and spirit, made in the image of God, and connected with Him and with eternity. He is a god in embryo and will live and progress throughout the eternal ages, if obedient to the laws of the Godhead, as the Gods progress throughout the eternal ages" (George D. Watt, comp., *Journal of Discourses* [London, England: F. D. and S. W. Richards and Sons, 1854–1886], 23:65, hereafter cited as *JD).*

4. Andrew F. Ehat and Lyndon W. Cook, eds., *The Words of Joseph Smith: The Contemporary Accounts of the Nauvoo Discourses of the Prophet Joseph* (Orem, Utah: Grandin Book, 1991), 340, hereafter cited as *WJS.* Thomas Bullock recorded that at this point in the speech the Prophet said, "There are very few who understand rightly the char[acter] of God. They do not comprehend anything that is *past* or that which is to *come"* (ibid., 348, emphasis added). The William Clayton notes say there are "few beings in the world who under- stand the character of God and do not comprehend their own character. They cannot compre[hend] the *beginning* nor the *end* neit[her] *their own relation"* to them (ibid., 356, emphasis added). It appears that the Prophet was trying to help his audience understand the "one eternal round" principle of existence (see 1 Ne. 10:19; Alma 7:20; 37:12; D&C 3:2; 35:1)—Gods create men and women in their image, some of those men and women become Gods; those Gods create men and women in their image, some of those men and women become Gods, etc., etc., etc.

5. *WJS,* 349. Readers should be aware that the King Follett discourse—as found in the *History of the Church* and *The Teachings of the Prophet Joseph Smith*—is an amalgamated text that has been pieced together from several different sources. The portion of the Prophet's discourse that is reported here comes from the notes made by Thomas Bullock.

6. Ibid., 357. This portion of the King Follett discourse is from the William Clayton report. Joseph Fielding Smith said, "God is an exalted man. Some people are troubled over the statements of the Prophet Joseph Smith as found in the King Follett sermon delivered in Nauvoo in 1844. The matter that seems such a mystery is the statement that our Father in heaven at one time passed through a life and death and is an exalted man. This is one of the mysteries" (Joseph Fielding Smith, *Doctrines of Salvation* [Salt Lake City: Bookcraft, 1999], 1:10, hereafter cited as *DS*).

7. *WJS,* 378–80.

8. *The Seer,* vol. 1, no. 9, September 1853, 132. Compare this concept with W. W. Phelps's hymn "If You Could Hie to Kolob" *(Hymns,* no. 284).

9. *JD,* 7:333.

10. Ibid., 26:23, emphasis added. Elder Penrose goes on to say that wherever we may travel throughout the universe we will "find space, and also inexhaustible material. And the elements, whether they be spiritual or what we call natural (we use these terms to distinguish them), never had a beginning—the primal particles never had a beginning. They have been organized in different shapes; the organism had a beginning, but the elements or atoms of which it is composed never had. You may burn this book, but every atom of which the book was composed, every particle of substance that entered into its composition, still exists; they are indestructible. When you go right down to the primary elements, they never had a beginning, they will never have an end. For in their primal condition they are not 'created.' They did not come from nothing; they were organized into different forms, but the elementary parts of matter as well as of spirit, using ordinary terms, never had a beginning, and never will have an end" (ibid., 26:27).

11. Bruce R. McConkie, *The Promised Messiah* (Salt Lake City: Deseret Book, 1981), 166. According to President Joseph Fielding Smith the phrase *"from eternity to eternity means from the spirit existence through the probation which we are in, and then back again to the eternal existence which will follow.* Surely this is everlasting, for when we receive the resurrection, we will never die. We all existed in the first eternity. I think I can say of myself and others, we are *from eternity;* and *we will be to eternity everlasting, if we receive the exaltation"* (DS, 1:12, emphasis in original).

12. *WJS,* 357. The Samuel W. Richards record of the King Follett discourse reports the Prophet as saying, "God: a man like one of us, even like Adam. Not God from all eternity. Once on a planet with *flesh and blood,* like Christ" (ibid., 361, emphasis added). Brigham Young likewise taught that "God, . . . the Father of our spirits, . . . was once a man in mortal flesh as we are, and is now an exalted Being" *(JD,* 7:333). On another occasion President Young said, "Our Father in heaven is exalted and glorified. . . . While He was in the flesh, as we are, He was as we are" (ibid., 4:54). President Lorenzo Snow's oft repeated couplet applies here. "As man now is, God once was" (Clyde J. Williams, ed., *The Teachings of Lorenzo Snow* [Salt Lake City: Bookcraft, 1996], 2). Bishop Orson F. Whitney said, "Mormonism teaches that God was once just like ourselves; that the eternal part of Him was enshrined in mortal flesh, subject to mortal

ills and earthly pains and toils. I do not now refer to the experience of the Savior in the meridian of time. I mean that in the far away eons of the past God once dwelt upon an earth like this, and that through its trials and vicissitudes and the experience they afforded He became a more intelligent being than before, ascending finally by obedience to certain principles, ennobling and exalting in their nature, to the plane which He now occupies" (Brian H. Stuy, ed., *Collected Discourses* [Burbank, California: B. H. S. Publishing, 1989], 3:45, hereafter cited as *CD*). Gospel scholar Stephen E. Robinson writes in the *Encyclopedia of Mormonism* that "the Father became the Father at some time before 'the beginning' as humans know it, by experiencing a mortality similar to that experienced on earth" (Daniel H. Ludlow, ed., *Encyclopedia of Mormonism* [New York: Macmillan, 1992], 2:549, hereafter cited as *EM*).

13. *WJS*, 60.

14. *Deseret Evening News*, 27 December 1913, section III, 7. Elder Orson Hyde said, "Remember that God, our Heavenly Father was perhaps once a child, and mortal like we ourselves, and rose step by step in the scale of progress, in the school of advancement; has moved forward and overcome, until He has arrived at the point where He now is" (*JD*, 1:123).

15. *JD*, 11:249.

16. Joseph F. Smith, *Gospel Doctrine* (Salt Lake City: Deseret Book, 1986), 64, hereafter cited as *GD*.

17. *JD*, 18:32. President Daniel H. Wells of the First Presidency said that "[God] is a Being of agency, and has passed along the path which He wishes us to tread, and has attained to His exaltation just as He desires us to attain to ours" (*Millennial Star*, vol. 26, no. 50, 10 December 1864, 786, hereafter cited as *MS*).

18. *JD*, 4:192. President Gordon B. Hinckley stated during a temple dedicatory prayer that "the initiatory ordinances, the endowments, [and] the sealings are all eternal in their very nature" (*Church News*, 8 November 1997, 4).

19. *JD*, 19:270.

20. See *EM*, 2:961; Bruce R. McConkie, *Mormon Doctrine*, 2d ed. (Salt Lake City: Bookcraft, 1966), 516–17, hereafter cited as *MD;* Joseph Fielding Smith, *Answers to Gospel Questions* (Salt Lake City: Deseret Book, 1998), 3:142–44, hereafter cited as *AGQ*. For further reading see Matthew B. Brown, *All Things Restored: Confirming the Authenticity of LDS Beliefs* (American Fork, Utah: Covenant Communications, 2000), 113–14.

21. Edward L. Kimball, ed., *The Teachings of Spencer W. Kimball* (Salt Lake City:

Bookcraft, 1982), 25. President Gordon B. Hinckley has stated that "in light of the instruction we have received from the Lord Himself, I regard it as inappropriate for anyone in the Church to pray to our Mother in Heaven. . . . The fact that we do not pray to our Mother in Heaven in no way belittles or denigrates her" (*Ensign*, November 1991, 100).

22. President Joseph Fielding Smith clarifies this idea. "Our *Father* in heaven and our Savior and all those who have *passed through the resurrection* have physical bodies of flesh and bones, but their bodies are quickened by spirit and not by blood, hence they are spiritual bodies and not blood bodies" *(DS,* 1:76–77, emphasis added). "Let me ask, are we not taught that we as sons of God may become like Him? Is not this a glorious thought? Yet we have to pass through mortality and *receive the resurrection* and then go on to perfection *just as our Father did before us.* The Prophet [Joseph Smith] taught that our Father had a Father and so on. Is not this a reasonable thought, especially when we remember that the promises are made to us that we may become like Him?" (ibid., 1:12, emphasis added).

23. *WJS,* 380.

24. *JD,* 4:217, emphasis added.

25. *The Relief Society Magazine,* vol. 57, no. 9, September 1970, 703, emphasis added. President Thomas S. Monson has also taught this doctrine. "God Himself is a soul, composed of a spirit and of a body of flesh and bones, as tangible as man's. He is a resurrected, glorified, exalted, omniscient, omnipotent person and is omnipresent in spirit and power and influence, the ruler of the heavens and the earth and all things therein" (Thomas S. Monson, *An Invitation to Exaltation* [Salt Lake City: Deseret Book, 1997], 2–3). Elder James E. Talmage wrote that "the Father . . . passed through the experiences of mortal life, including death and resurrection" (James E. Talmage, *Jesus the Christ* [Salt Lake City: Deseret Book, 1979], 39). Bruce R. McConkie said, "No man can conceive of the glory that may be attained through the resurrection. God Himself, the Father of us all, is a glorified, exalted, immortal, *resurrected Man" (MD,* 643, emphasis in original).

26. *EM,* 4:1667–68, emphasis added. The two parts of this quotation have been reversed for the sake of clarity. Elder Bruce R. McConkie taught that "by the ordained procreative process our exalted and immortal Father begat His spirit progeny in [the] preexistence" *(MD,* 84).

27. *JD,* 15:246, emphasis added.

28. On another occasion the Prophet noted that "the spirit by many is thought to be immaterial, without substance. With this . . . statement we should beg leave

to differ—and state that spirit is a substance; that it is material, but that it is more pure, elastic, and refined matter than the body . . . [and] it existed before the body" (*Times and Seasons,* vol. 3, no. 11, 1 April 1842, 745).

When Joseph Smith gave the funeral sermon for Brother King Follett on 7 April 1844 he made some remarks on the eternal nature of spirits which call for commentary. It is important to note that he prefaced his entire sermon by saying, "I shall . . . offer you *my ideas* so far as *I* have ability." After declaring that God created the earth out of elements or "materials" that "had an existence from the time [God] had [existed]," the Prophet used "logic" and "reason"— and possibly D&C 93:29 and Abraham 3:18—to conclude that the "spirit" or "mind" or "intelligence" of man "does not have a beginning or end" but is "self existing." He said, "We say that God Himself is a self-existing God. Who told you so? How did it get into your head? Who told you that man did not exist in like manner?" He then asked, "Is it logic[al] to say the spirit of man had a beginning and yet had no end?" It was the Prophet's view that if "man has a beginning [it] proves that he must have an end" and he used the imagery of making a cut in his wedding band to illustrate this point (Donald Q. Cannon and Larry E. Dahl, *The Prophet Joseph Smith's King Follett Discourse: A Six Column Comparison of Original Notes and Amalgamations* [Provo, Utah: BYU Religious Studies Center, 1983], 12–13, 46–51, emphasis added). It should be noted that the Prophet was propounding these ideas at least as early as August of 1839. At this time he said, "The spirit of man is not a created being; it existed from eternity and will exist to eternity. Anything created cannot be eternal. And earth, water, etc.—all these had their existence in an *elementary state* from eternity" (*WJS,* 9, emphasis added). On 5 February 1840 the Prophet "contended . . . that everything which had a *beginning* must have an *ending*" (including "God" and the "spirit" of man). These concepts, his audience understood, were "according to his logic and belief" (ibid., 33, emphasis in original; see also ibid., 60).

In 1845, just one year after the King Follett discourse had been delivered, Joseph Lee Robinson reported that the Nauvoo Saints were perplexed by the portion of the Prophet's sermon that dealt with the eternal nature of spirits. Robinson wrote: "[T]he question arose then, 'How is God the Father of our spirits?' I wondered, studied and prayed over it for I did want to know how it could be. I inquired of several of the brethren how that could be—a father and son and the son as old as the father. There was not a person that could or that would even try to explain that matter. But it came to pass that in time a vision was opened, the voice of the Spirit came to me saying: that all matter was eternal, that it never had a beginning and that it should never have an end and that the spirits of all men were organized of a pure material or matter upon the principle of male and female so that there was a time when my immortal spirit, as well as every other man's spirit that was ever born into the world—that is to say, there was a moment when the spirit was organized or begotten or born so that the spirit has a [F]ather, and the material or matter that our tabernacles are composed of is eternal and, as we understand, are organized upon the principles of male and female" (Joseph Lee Robinson Journal, 21, cited in Charles R. Harrell, "The Development of the Doctrine of Preexistence, 1830–1844," *BYU Studies,* vol. 28, no. 2, Spring 1988, 87).

Students of the scriptures who interpret Abraham 3:18 and D&C 93:29 in a strictly literal sense might take the following points into consideration. The Lord says in Abraham 3:18 that "spirits . . . have no beginning . . . [and] they shall have no end . . . for they are . . . eternal," but He also uses the same type of language in D&C 29:33, where He says, "unto myself my works have no end, neither beginning." Despite the language in this latter verse, Latter-day Saints understand that there was indeed a moment when the Lord received His exaltation and commenced the processes of creation and salvation (see Milton R. Hunter, *The Gospel Through the Ages* [Salt Lake City: Stevens and Wallis, 1945], 104–105). In the case of Abraham 3:18 it would seem prudent to recall that the Lord sees things from a different perspective than mortals do—"all is as one day with God, and time only is measured unto men" (Alma 40:8). Joseph Smith said, "God dwells in eternity, and He does not view things as we do" *(WJS,* 346). Commentators on D&C 93:29 typically take "man" and "intelligence" to be synonyms and they therefore conclude that man "was not created or made, neither indeed can be." They do this despite the fact that the sentence structure clearly indicates that "intelligence" is synonymous with "the light of truth." This idea is closely matched in verse 36 where "intelligence" is synonymous with "light and truth." Since verse 24 states that "truth is knowledge of things as they are, and as they were, and as they are to come" it may naturally be concluded that it is *truth* that is eternal—it "was not created or made, neither indeed can be" (v. 29). Indeed, Bishop Orson F. Whitney stated that the "truths" which lead to "celestial heights . . . are self-existent and eternal. God did not create them. Intelligence, the light of truth, cannot be created" *(CD,* 3:45).

29. *JD,* 3:371–72.

30. Ibid., 7:285. Brigham Young also taught that "there is an eternity of matter, and it is all acted upon and filled with a portion of divinity. . . . Eternity is without bounds, and is filled with matter. . . . And matter is capacitated to receive intelligence" (ibid., 7:2).

31. *MD,* 84.

32. Ibid., 442, emphasis added. For articles that discuss the various theories about "intelligence" and "intelligences" see *EM*, 2:692–93; Brent L. Top, *The Life Before* (Salt Lake City: Bookcraft, 1988), 39–51; Kenneth W. Godfrey, "The History of Intelligence in Latter-day Saint Thought," in H. Donl Peterson and Charles D. Tate, Jr., eds., *The Pearl of Great Price: Revelations From God* (Provo, Utah: BYU Religious Studies Center, 1989), 213–35. In this latter source note especially the writer's comments on page 216. They read: "It is not entirely clear whether intelligence is something individual or collective, or an attribute or principle. In fact, it is not clear what [D&C 93:29] means when the Lord says, 'Man was also in the beginning with God.'"

In addition, the reader should pay particular attention to the letter by Elder Bruce R. McConkie found on page 232 of this same source which addresses the issue of men and women having some type of existence before their birth as the Father's spirit children. It says, "I do know that this matter has arisen perhaps six or eight times in the years that I have been here and have been involved in reading and approving Priesthood and auxiliary lessons. In each of these instances, the matter was ordered deleted from the lesson. In each case it was expressly stated that we have no knowledge of any existence earlier than our existence as the spirit children of God. The views in this field were described *as pure speculation.* President Joseph Fielding Smith personally, on more than one occasion, directed this material not be published and said that he did not believe it . . . I do not believe it either" (emphasis added). Dr. Sidney B. Sperry makes a similar point. "Section 93 certainly challenges our minds concerning the origin of man in the preexistence, especially verses 23, 29, 30, and 33. For a long time a theory has gone about in the Church to the effect that men existed originally as intelligent egos or entities who were later permitted to make a distinct step in their progression by each having his ego clothed with a spirit body by celestial Parents. I understand that *our leading brethren consider this teaching to be speculation and should under no circumstances be taught.* At any rate, no such teaching has been permitted in the lesson materials issued to auxiliary organizations in recent years" (Sidney B. Sperry, *Doctrine and Covenants Compendium* [Salt Lake City: Bookcraft, 1960], 476–77, emphasis added).

33. Spirits are like mortal beings in that they possess emotions such as joy (see Job 38:4–7) and sorrow (see D&C 76:26). They are also free to develop their own character traits. Jesus Christ developed the godly attribute of humility (see Moses 4:2) while Lucifer developed a rebellious attitude (see D&C 76:28) and cultivated anger (see Abr. 3:28).

34. *JD*, 15:242–43. The close correspondence between the spirit and the physical body is hinted at in Luke 24:36–39. When the Savior appeared to His apostles

after the Resurrection they "suposed that they had seen a spirit," but the Lord said to them, "Behold my hands and my feet, that it is I myself: handle me, and see; for a spirit hath not flesh and bones, as ye see me have." Joseph Smith's brother, Patriarch Hyrum Smith, brought attention to the fact that "the spirit of Jesus Christ was full-grown before He was born into the world [see Ether 3:6–16]; and so our children were full-grown and possessed their full stature in the spirit before they entered mortality, the same stature that they will possess after they have passed away from mortality, and as they will also appear after the resurrection, when they shall have completed their mission" *(GD,* 455).

35. The mention of premortal "sons" of God in Job 38:7 brings up the question of sexual identity before mortal birth. Elder James E. Talmage writes, "We affirm as reasonable, scriptural, and true, the eternity of sex among the children of God. The distinction between male and female is no condition peculiar to the relatively brief period of mortal life; it was an essential characteristic of our pre-existent condition, even as it shall continue after death, in both disembodied and resurrected states. . . . [The] scriptures attest a state of existence preceding mortality, in which the spirit children of God lived, doubtless with distinguishing personal characteristics, including the distinction of sex" *(MS,* vol. 84, no. 34, 24 August 1922, 539).

36. Pratt, *Key to the Science of Theology,* 79.

38. *JD,* 20:75.

39. Joseph Fielding Smith, *Church History and Modern Revelation* (Salt Lake City: Deseret News Press, 1947), 2:163.

40. CR, October 1914, 40. Similar comments are made by Elder Bruce R. McConkie. "An all-wise Father endowed His spirit children with agency—the freedom and ability to choose good or evil—while they yet dwelt in His presence. Unless there are opposites—good and evil, virtue and vice, right and wrong—and unless intelligent beings are free to choose; free to obey or disobey; free to do good and work righteousness, or to walk in evil paths—unless this freedom exists, there can be no advancement and progression; no joy as contrasted with sorrow; no talents of one kind or another as contrasted with their absence; no eternal salvation as contrasted with eternal damnation. There can be no light unless there is darkness. . . . Opposites and agency are essential to existence and to progression. Without them there would be nothing" (Bruce R. McConkie, *The Mortal Messiah* [Salt Lake City: Deseret Book, 1981], 1:22–23).

41. Journal History, 23 February 1847, LDS Church Archives, Salt Lake City, Utah, emphasis added. The following remarks by Joseph Smith seem, in

context, to be speaking of the premortal world. "I would just remark, that the spirits of men are eternal, that they are governed by the same Priesthood that Abraham, Melchizedek, and the apostles were: that they are *organized according to that Priesthood which is everlasting,* 'without beginning of days or end of years,'—that they all move in their respective spheres, and are governed by the law of God; that when they appear upon the earth they are in a probationary state" (Joseph Fielding Smith, comp., *Teachings of the Prophet Joseph Smith* [Salt Lake City: Deseret Book, 1976], 208, emphasis added).

42. Joseph Fielding Smith, *The Way to Perfection* (Salt Lake City: Genealogical Society of Utah, 1949), 51.

43. Bruce R. McConkie, *The Millennial Messiah* (Salt Lake City: Deseret Book, 1982), 12.

44. *WJS,* 8.

45. *CD,* 1:215–16. President Woodruff is evidently referring to a lecture that was given by Joseph Smith in Nauvoo in the summer of 1839. Notes from this lecture can be found in *WJS,* 8.

46. Smith, *The Way to Perfection,* 51.

47. CR, October 1966, 84, emphasis added. Another confirmation of this concept comes from President Ezra Taft Benson who said that "the calling of men to sacred office is not confined to earth life only. There is organization, direction, and assignment in pre-earth life and in post-earth life also" (Ezra Taft Benson, *The Teachings of Ezra Taft Benson* [Salt Lake City: Bookcraft, 1988], 21).

48. McConkie, *The Millennial Messiah,* 12.

49. Clyde J. Williams, ed., *The Teachings of Howard W. Hunter* (Salt Lake City: Bookcraft, 1997), 12.

50. McConkie, *The Mortal Messiah,* 1:23.

51. Elder Orson Pratt asked, "Now, who is Jesus? He is only our brother, but happens to be the firstborn. What, the firstborn in the flesh? Oh no, there were millions and millions born in the flesh before He was. Then how is He the firstborn? Because He is the eldest—the first one born of the whole family of spirits and therefore He is our elder brother" *(JD,* 14:241).

52. McConkie, *The Mortal Messiah,* 1:35.

CHAPTER 2

THE GRAND COUNCIL

At some time in the far distant past a Grand Council was convened in the heavenly world to discuss the progression of the Lord's spirit children (see D&C 121:32; cf. Ps. 82:1). The principles that were discussed during this meeting were not at all new but had been in existence for untold eons of time. "The gospel is infinite in scope, eternal in nature, and everlasting in duration," said Elder Bruce R. McConkie. "It is the system that saves men on this world and all of the worlds of the Lord's creating. It is like unto God in beauty, glory, and perfection. It has existed from all eternity and will continue through all ages without end."[1] Elder Orson Pratt of the Quorum of the Twelve Apostles offered the same expansive view of the gospel's antiquity.

> The dealing of God towards His children from the time that they are first born in heaven, through all their successive stages of existence, until they are redeemed, perfected, and made gods, is a pattern after which all other worlds are dealt with. . . . The creation, fall, and redemption of all future worlds with their inhabitants will be conducted upon the same general plan. . . .
>
> The Father of our spirits has only been doing that which His Progenitors did before Him. Each succeeding generation of gods follow the example of the preceding ones. . . . [Their offspring] are redeemed after the pattern by which

more ancient worlds have been redeemed. . . . Thus will
worlds and systems of worlds . . . be multiplied in endless
succession through the infinite depths of boundless space;
some telestial, some terrestrial, and some celestial, differing
in their glory.[2]

President Joseph Fielding Smith was another Church authority
who spoke of the primeval nature of the gospel. He assures us that
"the plan of salvation is the same today as it was in the days of Adam.
It is the same plan that has been adopted in other worlds, because this
plan is eternal, therefore, members of the Church are subject to
eternal regulations, laws, rules, and decrees that were instituted before
the foundation of the world for the government of the Church and
for the salvation of men."[3]

Latter-day Saints are accustomed to speaking of the universal laws
of redemption as *the gospel of Jesus Christ,* but it is rightly stated that
"the Father, not the Son, is the author of the plan of salvation." This
plan, said Elder Bruce R. McConkie, "embodies the Father's doctrine,
the Father's laws, [and] the Father's gospel. He ordained and
announced the whole plan of creation, redemption, salvation, and
exaltation, and He chose one of His spirit offspring to be born into the
world as His Son to work out the infinite and eternal Atonement—all
in accordance with His will." However, the laws of redemption are
appropriately spoken of as *the gospel of Jesus Christ* because the Savior
"conformed to them perfectly" and "worked out the atoning sacrifice,
by means of which they gained full force and validity."[4]

Place and Purpose

Joseph Smith taught the Saints in Nauvoo that "the head one of
the gods [i.e., the Father] . . . called the gods together in Grand
Council to bring forth the world."[5] An inquiry might be made into
where this council took place. One of the revelations in the Doctrine
and Covenants indicates that God and His angels reside somewhere
in the universe "on a globe like a sea of glass and fire" (D&C 130:7).
The book of Abraham also reveals that there is an enormous planet
called "Kolob" which is nearby this glorified orb (Abr. 3:3, 9, 16). In
February of 1843 Joseph Smith published a poetic rendition of

section 76 of the Doctrine and Covenants, and in parallel with verse 7—where the Lord speaks of revealing the "hidden mysteries . . . from days of old"—the Prophet speaks of "the council in Kolob."[6] Elder Orson F. Whitney, in his epic poem *Elias*, likewise writes, "In solemn council sat the Gods / From Kolob's height supreme / Celestial light blazed forth afar / O'er countless kokaubeam."[7]

An unsigned article that was published in the *Times and Seasons* during Joseph Smith's lifetime says that the Grand Council was convened in heaven because the Lord desired "to promote His purposes and to advance His glory." This article relates that the creation of the heavens, the earth, the animals, and mankind were all discussed during this momentous meeting. "Their organization, habits, propensities, the object of their creation, the position they would take in the order of that creation, and how, and by what means they would be made happy, and increase [God's] glory, was fully understood by Him" at this time.[8]

The main focus of the Grand Council was on the creation of mankind. God promised eternal life to His children "before the world began," says Titus chapter 1 verse 2 (cf. 1 Jn. 2:24–25). But in order for the Father to raise His progeny to the level of glory and perfection that He Himself had attained, He needed to supply them with physical bodies. "All beings who have bodies have power over those who have not," said the Prophet Joseph Smith.[9] The "spirits of the eternal world" are as diverse from each other in their dispositions as mortals are on the earth. Some of them are aspiring, ambitious, and even desire to bring other spirits into subjection to them. "As man is liable to [have] enemies [in the spirit world] as well as [on the earth] it is necessary for him to be placed beyond their power in order to be saved. This is done by our taking bodies (keeping our first estate) and having the power of the resurrection pass upon us whereby we are enabled to gain the ascendancy over the disembodied spirits."[10] It might be said, therefore, that "the express purpose of God in giving [His spirit children] a tabernacle was to arm [them] against the power of darkness."[11]

Laws and Ordinances
In premortal times God "saw proper to institute laws" so that His spirit children "could have [the] privilege to advance like Himself."[12]

He also established laws that would pertain to life on the earth. "If men would acquire salvation," said Joseph Smith, "they have got to be subject to certain rules and principles which were fixed by an unalterable decree before the world was."[13] In addition to laws, said the Prophet, "the order and ordinances of the kingdom were instituted by the Priesthood in the Council of Heaven before the world was."[14] On 10 March 1845 William Clayton made the following notation in his journal. He wrote, "It has been a doctrine taught by this Church that we were in the Grand Council amongst the Gods when the organization of this world was contemplated and that the laws of government were all made and sanctioned by all present and all the ordinances and ceremonies decreed upon."[15] Some of these foreordained ordinances are listed in sections 124 and 132 of the Doctrine and Covenants. They include baptism for the dead (see D&C 124:33),[16] temple endowment ceremonies (see D&C 124:40–41), and eternal marriage (see D&C 132:5, 11, 28).

Laws were also enacted during premortal times to govern the administration of earthly ordinances. For instance, Joseph Smith said that it was proposed in the mind of God "before the world was" that the higher ordinances pertaining to the "glories of His kingdom" and the "ways of salvation" would need to be practiced in a "place or house built for that purpose," meaning that they could only be performed in a temple or other dedicated space.[17]

The Risk of Mortal Experience

Even though the Lord promised that those who adhered to the plan of salvation would have "glory added upon their heads forever and ever" (Abr. 3:26), the harsh reality remained that mortality carried a great deal of risk for a great many people. President Lorenzo Snow believed that "in the spirit world, when it was proposed to us to come into this probation, and pass through the experience that we are now receiving, it was not altogether pleasant and agreeable; the prospects were not so delightful in all respects as might have been desired."[18] Why not? Because, said Brigham Young, it had "been decreed by the Almighty that spirits, upon taking bodies, [would] forget all they had known previously, or they could not have a day of trial—could not have an opportunity for proving themselves [worthy] in darkness and temptation, in unbelief and wickedness."[19] Elder John A. Widtsoe elaborated upon this doctrine:

> One condition of the plan [of salvation] is that the spirits transferred to the earth shall remain here in forgetfulness of an earlier existence. . . . A veil has been drawn over the past; and, without the aid of memory, man fights his battle with the world of gross matter. This forgetfulness seems reasonable. The spirit of man accepted the earth-plan in detail, and if he remembered every step that led to the acceptance, and every detail of the plan itself, there would not be much need for the exercise of will in adhering to it. Left as he is, with little memory to steady him, he must exercise all his power to compel surrounding forces to serve him in searching out the past and in prophesying of the future. By such vigorous exercise of his will he develops a more intimate acquaintanceship with the things of the earth.[20]

President Joseph Fielding Smith writes that when the plan of salvation was presented "the spirits of men were informed that only by passing through this mortal probation, where they would come in contact with temptation and all manner of evil as well as the good, and by passing through death and the resurrection, could the exaltation come so that they could be like our glorious Father. We were informed, and the matter was made very clear, that we would have to walk by faith, not by sight." Moreover, it became apparent that "many would yield to temptation and sin and would refuse to accept the divine law of the gospel which should be given us for our guidance and by means of which we could come back into the presence of the Father and the Son." But, continued President Smith, "we understood the dangers and the risk of failure in making the journey through the mortal life, yet we rejoiced and were glad to have the opportunity to come and receive all that mortality offered. What we accepted there, without doubt, was accepted by all with eyes open and with understanding of the dangers and advantages fully understood."[21] Elder Neal A. Maxwell is in agreement with these thoughts. He reminds us that "our memories of the first estate will eventually be fully restored; and, upon regaining our premortal perspectives, we will acknowledge that we did indeed come here under certain conditions to which we earlier agreed—with the risks and rewards adequately explained beforehand."[22]

Elder Hugh B. Brown makes note of the fact that "free agency is prerequisite to any character-building plan, and while with free agency any plan is inevitably crammed with risk, we, with all the sons of God, accepted that risk and shouted for joy at the prospect of earth life"[23] (cf. Job 38:4–7). Why did we shout for joy with so much at stake, with the knowledge that we would live in a fallen state, understanding that we might not be able to return again to the presence of God? After all, one-third of the Father's spirit children were not willing to take such a chance! Joseph Fielding Smith and John A. Widtsoe offer two perspectives that may be helpful in answering these questions. President Smith says that "celestial glory could never have come to us without a period of time in mortality. . . . We are in the mortal life to get an experience, a training that we couldn't get any other way. And in order to become gods, it is necessary for us to know something about pain, about sickness, and about the other things that we partake of in this school of mortality."[24] Elder Widtsoe points out, on the other end of the spectrum, that even "the lowest glory to which man is assigned is so glorious as to be beyond the understanding of man. It is a doctrine fundamental in Mormonism that the meanest sinner, in the Final Judgment, will receive a glory which is beyond human understanding, which is so great that we are unable to describe it adequately."[25] Thus, it may be concluded that regardless of the outcome, a spirit being would benefit immensely from living a mortal life.

WAR IN HEAVEN

The risk inherent in the plan of salvation was intolerable for some of the Father's spirit children, chief among which was Lucifer. Not only was Lucifer "a son of God" (Moses 5:13) but he was also "a son of the morning" (D&C 76:26–27). Some LDS commentators believe that "just as Jesus was the 'first-born' spirit child of our Father (see

D&C 93:21), so Lucifer appears to be one of those who was an early born spirit child, 'a' son of the morning."[26] At the time of the Grand Council Lucifer held a high station; he stood "in authority in the presence of God" (D&C 76:25). Joseph Smith's poetic version of section 76 of the Doctrine and Covenants discloses that before his rebellion Lucifer was "an angel of light" who had such "great" authority that he was in a "godified state."[27] The Prophet also explains that "Lucifer being *the next heir* [to Jesus Christ] . . . had allotted to him great power and authority, even [as the] prince of [the power of] the air"[28] (cf. Eph. 2:2).

Lucifer's Bid for Power

After God the Father proposed the plan of salvation to His children they became aware that because of the fallen nature of mortality they would all become—to one degree or another—"carnal, sensual, and devilish" (Alma 42:10; see also Mosiah 16:3; Moses 5:13; 6:49). Because their sinful natures would place them in a state of uncleanliness (see 1 Jn. 1:8), a Savior would be needed to purify them and thus enable them to return to the Lord's holy presence. The Father asked for a volunteer to fill the vital role of the Redeemer. "Whom shall I send?" He asked. "And one answered like unto the Son of Man [i.e., Jesus Christ]: 'Here am I, send me'" (Abr. 3:27). Jesus Christ presented Himself "to come and redeem this world as *it was His right by inheritance*," said the Prophet Joseph Smith.[29] But then "another answered [i.e., Lucifer] and said: 'Here am I, send me'" (Abr. 3:27). The book of Moses supplies more of the dialogue that was spoken on this important occasion. In that source the Lord says, Satan "came before me, saying—'Behold, here am I, send me, I will be thy son, and *I will redeem all mankind, that one soul shall not be lost, and surely I will do it*; wherefore give me thine honor.' But, behold, my Beloved Son, which was my Beloved and Chosen from the beginning, said unto me—'Father, thy will be done, and the glory be thine forever'" (Moses 4:1–2, emphasis added).

It is evident from this last scriptural passage that Lucifer desired to modify the Father's plan of redemption by guaranteeing the return of all of His children.[30] But by making such a proposition Satan was also offering the following:

- "Satan . . . sought to destroy the agency of man, which . . . the Lord God, had given him" (Moses 4:3). In this thing the "devil . . . sought that which was evil before God" (2 Ne. 2:17).[31]
- "Satan sought . . . to redeem . . . all [the Father's children] *in their sins*," said Elder Orson Pratt.[32] President Brigham Young pointed to the fact that "if you undertake to save *all*, you must save them in unrighteousness and corruption."[33]
- "Satan . . . sought . . . that [God] should give unto him [His] own power, by the power of [the] Only Begotten" (Moses 4:3). One scripture relates that Satan said on this occasion, "Give me thine honor, which is my power" (D&C 29:36). Marion G. Romney made the interesting remark that "it now is and has always been the objective of Satan to destroy the Priesthood of God. As long ago as the war in heaven, he sought to usurp the power of the Priesthood."[34]

After the Father had considered the offer of His two sons to act in the role of the Redeemer, He made a decision and announced, "I will send the first [i.e., Jesus Christ]. And the second [i.e., Lucifer] was angry, and kept not his first estate; and, at that day, many followed after him" (Abr. 3:27–28). How many? In symbolic language the book of Revelation portrays a dragon's tail drawing together a "third part of the stars of heaven" (Rev. 12:4). A latter-day revelation confirms this staggering number, stating that Lucifer turned "a third part of the hosts of heaven . . . away from [God] because of their agency" (D&C 29:36).

The adversary and his faction of dissenters came out in open rebellion against the Father and His Beloved Son (see D&C 76:25; Moses 4:3) and "sought to take [their] kingdom" (D&C 76:28). This resulted in a "war in heaven: Michael and his angels fought against the dragon; and the dragon fought and his angels, and prevailed not" (Rev. 12:7–8). Elder Orson Pratt offered a few thoughts on this conflict that are worthy of consideration:

> It is not likely that the final decision of the contending armies took place immediately. Many, no doubt, were unsettled in their views, unstable in their minds, and undecided as to which force to join: there may have been, for

[all] we know, many deserters from both armies: and there may have been a long period before the division line was so strictly drawn as to become unalterable. Laws, without doubt, were enacted, and penalties affixed, according to the nature of the offences or crimes: those who altogether turned from the Lord, and were determined to maintain the cause of Satan, and who proceeded to the utmost extremities of wickedness, placed themselves without the reach of redemption: therefore, such were prohibited from entering into a second probationary state, and had no privilege of receiving bodies of flesh and bones. . . .

Among the two-thirds who remained, it is highly probable that there were many who were not valiant in the war, but whose sins were of such a nature that they could be forgiven through faith in the future sufferings of the Only Begotten of the Father, and through their sincere repentance and reformation. We see no impropriety in Jesus offering Himself as an acceptable offering and sacrifice before the Father to atone for the sins of His brethren, committed not only in the second, but also in the first estate. Certain it was that the work which Jesus was to accomplish was known in the Grand Council where the rebellion broke out; it was known that man would sin in his second estate: for it was upon the subject of his redemption that the assembly became divided, and which resulted in war.[35]

After Lucifer failed in his futile attempt to seize control of the Father's kingdom he was "thrust down from the presence of God and the Son, and was called Perdition [Greek *apoleia*—loss, ruin], for the heavens wept over him" (D&C 76:25–26). He "was cast out [of heaven], and his angels were cast out with him" (Rev. 12:9). They were cast down "to the earth" (Rev. 12:4) and into a region prepared especially for them; a place called "hell" (D&C 29:37–38).

Because their sin was unpardonable, the fallen spirits were forever denied the ability to become like the Father by receiving a physical body. On this point the Prophet Joseph Smith remarked, "When Lucifer was hurled from heaven the decree was that he should not

obtain a tabernacle—no[r] those that were with him—but go abroad
upon the earth exposed to the anger of the elements, naked and bare.
But oftimes he lays hold upon men, binds up their spirits, enters their
habitations, laughs at the decree of God and rejoices in that he ha[s] a
house to dwell in. By and by he is expelled by authority and goes
abroad mourning [and] naked upon the earth like a man without a
house; exposed to the tempest and the storm."[36]

FOREORDINATION

According to the *Encyclopedia of Mormonism* foreordination is
"the premortal selection of individuals to come forth in mortality at
specified times, under certain conditions, and to fulfill predesignated
responsibilities. In LDS interpretation, 'foreordained' does not mean
predetermined. . . . Foreordination does not preclude the exercise of
agency. Foreordination is a *conditional* preappointment to or bestowal
of certain blessings and responsibilities." The Church of Jesus Christ
of Latter-day Saints, unlike some other Christian denominations,
rejects the notion that God predetermines the salvation or damnation
of each individual.[37]

The Apostle Peter makes a brief reference to the foreordination of
the Messiah in 1 Peter chapter 1 verse 20.[38] Sometime after this
appointment took place the Godhead was formed—consisting of the
Father, the Son, and the Holy Ghost. The Prophet Joseph Smith
reveals that an "everlasting covenant was made between [these] three
personages before the organization of this earth, and relates to their
dispensation of things to men on the earth. These personages
according to Abraham's record are called God the first, the Creator;
God the second, the Redeemer; and God the third, the Witness or
Testator."[39]

Leadership Positions
On 12 May 1844 Joseph Smith informed a group of Latter-day
Saints that "at the general and Grand Council of heaven, all those to
whom a dispensation was to be committed, were set apart and
ordained at that time, to that calling. The Twelve [apostles] also, as
witnesses, were ordained."[40] He then remarked, "I suppose that I was

ordained to this very office in that Grand Council."[41] President Joseph F. Smith observed in his canonized vision of the spirit world that "the Prophet Joseph Smith, . . . Hyrum Smith, Brigham Young, John Taylor, Wilford Woodruff, and other choice spirits" were "among the noble and great ones who were chosen in the beginning to be rulers in the Church of God" (D&C 138:53, 55; cf. Abr. 3:22–23). Wilford Woodruff also mentioned some of the other persons who were appointed beforehand to perform earthly tasks.

> In every dispensation the Lord has had those who were foreordained to do a certain work. We all dwelt in the presence of God before we came here, and such men as Abraham, Isaac, Jacob, the ancient prophets, Jesus and the apostles received their appointments before the world was made. They were ordained before the foundation of the world to come and tabernacle here in the flesh and to work for the cause of God, and this because of their faith and faithfulness.[42]

Elder Parley P. Pratt tied these ideas together with Abraham 3:22–23 and "the election before the foundation of the world, of certain individuals to certain offices." He explained:

> [C]ertain individuals, more intelligent than the others, were chosen by the Head, to teach, instruct, edify, improve, govern, and minister truth and salvation to others, and to hold the delegated powers or keys of government in the several spheres of progressive being.
>
> These were not only chosen, but were set apart by a holy ordinance in the eternal worlds, as ambassadors, foreign ministers, priests, kings, apostles, etc., to fill the various stations in the vast empire of the Sovereign of all.[43]

Earthly Circumstances

In the book of Acts chapter 17 verse 26 the Apostle Paul says that before men and women are born on the earth God determines "the times" of their mortal experience and also "the bounds of their habitation." What criteria does the Lord use in determining who goes where and when they go there? It was President Heber J. Grant's belief that "we have been placed upon this earth because of our faithfulness in having kept our first estate. The labors that we performed in the sphere that we left before we came here have had a certain effect upon our lives here, and to a certain extent they govern and control the lives that we lead here, just the same as the labors that we do here will control and govern our lives when we pass from this stage of existence."[44] President Harold B. Lee thought along similar lines. He said that it is "reasonable to believe that what we have received here in this earth [life] was given to each of us according to the merits of our conduct before we came here."[45]

Some of the leaders of The Church of Jesus Christ of Latter-day Saints hold the view that those who were to be born through the lineage of the Patriarchs constituted a distinct group during premortal times. Elder Melvin J. Ballard, for instance, said that "there was a group of souls tested, tried, and proven before they were born into the world, and the Lord provided a lineage for them. That lineage is the house of Israel, the lineage of Abraham, Isaac, and Jacob and their posterity."[46] Joseph Fielding Smith provided scriptural support for such a belief. He said, "We learn from the word of the Lord to Moses that the Lord selected a place for the children of Israel, even before they were born, thus He indicated the number of spirits who were assigned to become the descendants of Jacob"[47] (see Deut. 32:8–9). President Smith concluded from the passage of scripture just referenced, and also from Acts chapter 17 verse 26, that "there must have been a division of the spirits of men in the spiritual world, and those who were appointed to be the children of Israel were separated and prepared for a special inheritance."[48] On another occasion he wrote, "Through this covenant people [i.e., Israel] the Lord reserved the right to send into the world a chosen lineage of faithful spirits who were entitled to special favors based on premortal obedience."[49] Elder Bruce R. McConkie of the Quorum of the Twelve Apostles also had a few words to say on this subject. In one of his publications he wrote:

> The concept of a chosen and favored people, a concept scarcely known in the world and but little understood even

by the Saints of God, is one of the most marvelous systems ever devised for administering salvation to all men in all nations in all ages. Israel, the Lord's chosen people, were a congregation set apart in the preexistence. In large measure, the spirit children of the Father who acquired a talent for spirituality, who chose to heed the divine word then given, and who sought, above their fellows, to do good and work righteousness—all these were foreordained to be born in the house of Israel. They were chosen before they were born. This is the doctrine of election. They were true and faithful in the premortal life, and they earned the right to be born as the Lord's people and to have the privilege, on a preferential basis, of believing and obeying the word of truth. Believing blood, the blood of Abraham, flows in their veins. They are the ones of whom Jesus said: "My sheep hear my voice, and I know them, and they follow me. And I give unto them eternal life; and they shall never perish, neither shall any man pluck them out of my hand" (John 10:27–28).[50]

It can be said with absolute certainty that Jesus Christ was foreordained to be born into the House of Israel (see Ps. 132:11; Luke 1:30–33; Acts 2:29–30). It is not too difficult to imagine, then, that others would follow the same path. In Elder Mark E. Petersen's view the Lord sent His "most loyal spirits to be born in a lineage that would encourage the worship of Jehovah and help to prepare them to receive and minister in the holy Priesthood."[51]

Earthly Relationships

Some Latter-day Saints have wondered if perhaps they covenanted in the premortal world to become somebody's earthly parents, children or spouse. But the First Presidency of the Church, in a letter dated 14 June 1971, clearly stated that "we have no revealed word to the effect that when we were in the preexistent state we chose our parents and our husbands and wives."[52] In a book published in 1949, Joseph Fielding Smith wrote that "we have no scriptural justification . . . for the belief that we had the privilege of choosing our parents and our life companions in the spirit world. This belief has been advocated by some, and it is possible that in some instances it is true, but it would require too great a stretch of the imagination to believe it to be so in all, or even in the majority of cases. Most likely we came where those in authority decided to send us. Our agency may not have been exercised to the extent of making choice of parents and posterity."[53]

Earthly Events

Some people wonder if all earthly events were foreordained in the premortal Council of Heaven. It is certain that some incidents were purposefully designed to take place, such as the ministry of the Savior. But President Brigham Young did not believe that foreordination applied to every single earthly occurrence.

> [I]t is a mistaken idea, as entertained by [some religious sects], that God has decreed all things whatsoever that come to pass, for the volition of the creature is as free as air. You may inquire whether we believe in foreordination; we do, as strongly as any people in the world. We believe that Jesus was foreordained before the foundations of the world were built, and His mission was appointed Him in eternity to be the Savior of the world, yet when He came in the flesh He was left free to choose or refuse to obey His Father. Had He refused to obey His Father, He would have become a son of perdition. We also are free to choose or refuse the principles of eternal life.

> God has decreed and foreordained many things that have come to pass, and He will continue to do so; but when He decrees great blessings upon a nation or upon an individual they are decreed upon certain conditions. When He decrees great plagues and overwhelming destructions upon nations or people, those decrees come to pass because those nations and people will not forsake their wickedness and turn unto the Lord. It was decreed that Nineveh should be destroyed in forty days, but the decree was stayed on the repentance of the inhabitants of Nineveh. . . . God rules and reigns, and has made all His children as free as Himself, to choose the right or the wrong, and we shall then be judged according to our works.[54]

If mortals are truly free to determine their own actions—and consequently their eternal destinies—then what is to be made of D&C 130:6–8 which states that the "future" is "manifest" on the globe where God resides? Does this mean that even before the Father sends His children to the earth He already has an absolute knowledge of all of the events that will occur in their mortal lives and also the level of salvation that they will ultimately attain? Elder James E. Talmage offered some insightful remarks on this issue:

> Our Heavenly Father has a full knowledge of the nature and dispositions of each of His children, a knowledge gained by long observation and experience in the past eternity of our primeval childhood; a knowledge compared with which that gained by earthly parents through mortal experience with their children is infinitesimally small. By reason of that surpassing knowledge, God reads the future of child and children, of men individually and of men collectively as communities and nations; He knows what each will do under given conditions, and sees the end from the beginning. *His foreknowledge is based on intelligence and reason.* He foresees the future as a state which naturally and surely will be; not as one which must be because He has arbitrarily willed that it shall be. . . .
>
> The Father of souls has endowed His children with the divine birthright of free agency; He does not and will not control them by arbitrary force; He impels no man toward sin; He compels none to righteousness. Unto man has been given freedom to act for himself; and, associated with this independence, is the fact of strict responsibility and the assurance of individual accountability.[55]

Elder Talmage's words are in perfect accord with the text of Alma chapter 42 verse 27 which says, "[W]hosoever *will* come may come and partake of the waters of life freely: and whosoever *will not* come the same is not compelled to come; but in the last day it shall be restored unto him according to his deeds" (emphasis added). "Every soul coming into this world," said President Joseph Fielding Smith, "came here with the promise that through obedience he would receive the blessings of salvation. No person was foreordained or appointed to sin or to perform a mission of evil. No person is ever predestined to salvation or damnation. Every person has free agency."[56]

Agency is the key to the entire plan of salvation. It was granted by the Lord to every one of His offspring when they were spiritually born. It was not negated during the heavenly Council when so many chose to rebel. And, as will be demonstrated in the chapters that follow, it is at the very heart of the mortal experience and will play a critical role on the day of the Final Judgment.

NOTES: CHAPTER 2

1. Bruce R. McConkie, *A New Witness for the Articles of Faith* (Salt Lake City: Deseret Book, 1985), 135, hereafter cited as *NWAF*.

2. *The Seer*, vol. 1, no. 9, September 1853, 134–35.

3. Joseph Fielding Smith, *Seek Ye Earnestly* (Salt Lake City: Deseret Book, 1970), 407. On another occasion President Smith said, "Not only was this earth planned as an architect plans his building but its entire destiny and the destiny of its inhabitants was considered and known to the great Architect before its foundation stones were laid. Our Eternal Father was not experimenting when this world came into existence. It did not come by chance. It is not the first of His creations. Millions upon millions of worlds such as this had rolled into existence before our earth was born. Every step taken was according to the divine plan, and that plan was an eternal one, which had been followed in the construction of other worlds without number unto man. In other worlds the plan of salvation had been given. Here we are enacting familiar scenes; scenes which are new to all mortal men, but which are well known to the Father and also to the Son (see Moses 1:33, 37–38)" (Joseph Fielding Smith, *The Way to Perfection* [Salt Lake City: Genealogical Society of Utah, 1949], 35–36).

4. Bruce R. McConkie, *Doctrinal New Testament Commentary* (Salt Lake City: Bookcraft, 1965), 1:441–42, hereafter cited as *DNTC*; see also Bruce R. McConkie, *The Promised Messiah* (Salt Lake City: Deseret Book, 1981), 48; Bruce R. McConkie, *The Millennial Messiah* (Salt Lake City: Deseret Book, 1982), 334; *NWAF*, 63, 132–33. Gospel scholar Noel B. Reynolds explains in

the *Encyclopedia of Mormonism* that "the Father is the author of the gospel, but it is called the gospel of Jesus Christ because, in agreement with the Father's plan, Christ's Atonement makes the gospel operative in human lives. Christ's gospel is the only true gospel, and 'there shall be no other name given nor any other way nor means whereby salvation can come unto the children of men, only in and through the name of Christ, the Lord Omnipotent' (Mosiah 3:17; cf. Acts 4:12)" (Daniel H. Ludlow, ed., *Encyclopedia of Mormonism* [New York: Macmillan, 1992], 2:556, hereafter cited as *EM*).

5. Andrew F. Ehat and Lyndon W. Cook, eds., *The Words of Joseph Smith: The Contemporary Accounts of the Nauvoo Discourses of the Prophet Joseph* (Orem, Utah: Grandin Book, 1991), 341, hereafter cited as *WJS*.

6. Lawrence R. Flake, *Three Degrees of Glory: Joseph Smith's Insights on the Kingdoms of Heaven* (American Fork, Utah: Covenant Communications, 2000), 34–37.

7. *Improvement Era*, March 1921, 378, hereafter cited as *IE*. The word "kokaubeam" is Hebrew for "stars" (Abr. 3:13, 16).

8. *Times and Seasons*, vol. 5, no. 2, 15 January 1844, 407–408.

9. *WJS*, 60.

10. Ibid., 208. "The design of God before the foundation of the world," said Joseph Smith, "was that we should take tabernacles [so] that through faithfulness we should overcome and thereby obtain a resurrection from the dead, [and] in this wise obtain glory, honor, power, and dominion." Receiving a physical body was "needful, inasmuch as [some] spirits in the eternal world glory in bringing other spirits in[to] subjection unto them, striving continually for the mastery" (ibid., 207). "God is good and all His acts [are] for the benefit of inferior intelligences. God saw that those intelligences had not power to defend themselves against those that had a tabernacle. Therefore, the Lord call[ed] them together in Council and agree[d] to form them tabernacles so that He might gender the spirit and the tabernacle together so as to create sympathy for their fellowman. . . . [I]t is a natural thing with those spirits that [have] the most power to bore down on those of lesser power" (ibid., 68).

11. Ibid., 62.

12. Ibid., 360. "The relationship we have with God places us in a situation to advance in knowledge. God has power to institute laws to instruct the weaker intelligences, that they may be exalted [like] Himself" (ibid., 346). "God . . .

[found] Himself in the midst of spirits and . . . He saw proper to institute laws for those who were in less intelligence that they might have one glory upon another in all that knowledge, power, and glory. And so [He] took in hand to save the world of spirits" (ibid., 352).

13. Ibid., 254.

14. Ibid., 215. On another occasion the Prophet taught that "the ordinances of the gospel . . . [were] laid out before the foundation of the world" (ibid., 368).

15. Cited in *BYU Studies*, vol. 20, no. 3, Spring 1980, 269, hereafter cited as *BYUS*.

16. "Baptism . . . was ordained before the foundation of the world" (*WJS*, 159). "One of the ordinances of the House of the Lord is baptism for the dead. God decreed before the foundation of the world that that ordinance should be administered in a house prepared for that purpose" (ibid., 213).

17. Ibid., 212.

18. Clyde J. Williams, ed., *The Teachings of Lorenzo Snow* (Salt Lake City: Bookcraft, 1984), 92–93. President Joseph F. Smith asserts that "had we not known before we came the necessity of our coming, the importance of obtaining tabernacles, the glory to be achieved in posterity, the grand object to be attained by being tried and tested—weighed in the balance, in the exercise of the divine attributes, god-like powers and free agency with which we are endowed; whereby, after descending below all things, Christlike, we might ascend above all things, and become like our Father, Mother, and Elder Brother, Almighty and Eternal!—we never would have come; that is, if we could have stayed away" (Joseph F. Smith, *Gospel Doctrine* [Salt Lake City: Deseret Book, 1986], 13).

19. George D. Watt, comp., *Journal of Discourses* (London, England: F. D. and S. W. Richards and Sons, 1854–1886), 6:333, hereafter cited as *JD*.

20. John A. Widtsoe, *A Rational Theology* (Salt Lake City: Deseret Book, 1965), 41–42.

21. Joseph Fielding Smith, *The Progress of Man* (Salt Lake City: Deseret Book, 1973), 65–66.

22. Neal A. Maxwell, *We Will Prove Them Herewith* (Salt Lake City: Deseret Book, 1982), 57.

23. Conference Report, April 1956, 105, hereafter cited as CR.

24. Ibid., October 1967, 122.

25. John A. Widtsoe, *The Message of the Doctrine and Covenants* (Salt Lake City: Bookcraft, 1969), 167.

26. Hoyt W. Brewster, Jr., *Doctrine and Covenants Encyclopedia* (Salt Lake City: Bookcraft, 1988), 543. Similar statements can be found in Richard O. Cowan, *Answers to Your Questions About the Doctrine and Covenants* (Salt Lake City: Deseret Book, 1996), 86; Bruce R. McConkie, *Mormon Doctrine*, 2d ed. (Salt Lake City: Bookcraft, 1966), 192, hereafter cited as *MD*; Bruce R. McConkie, *The Mortal Messiah* (Salt Lake City: Deseret Book, 1979), 1:407; *DNTC*, 3:518.

27. Flake, *Three Degrees of Glory: Joseph Smith's Insights on the Kingdoms of Heaven*, 41.

28. *BYUS*, vol. 18, no. 2, Winter 1978, 172, emphasis added. This same source reports Brigham Young as saying in December of 1844 that "Jesus was the first-born or begotten of the Father. . . . [and] the devil . . . [was] *third in power*, prince of the air" (ibid., 178, emphasis added). W. W. Phelps wrote in December of 1844 that "Lucifer, son of the morning, *the next heir* to Jesus Christ . . . lost the glory, the honor, power, and dominion of a God [i.e., the Father]: and the knowledge, spirit, authority and keys of the Priesthood of the Son of God!" (*Times and Seasons*, vol. 5, no. 24, 1 January 1845, 758, emphasis added, hereafter cited as *T&S*).

29. *BYUS*, vol. 18, no. 2, Winter 1978, 172, emphasis added.

30. Elder Bruce R. McConkie provides the following remarks: "One of the saddest examples of a misconceived and twisted knowledge of an otherwise glorious concept is the all-too-common heresy that there were two plans of salvation; that the Father (presumptively at a loss to know what to do) asked others for proposals; that Christ offered a plan involving agency and Lucifer offered a plan denying agency; that the Father chose between them; and that Lucifer, his plan being rejected, rebelled, and then there was war in heaven. Even a cursory knowledge of the overall scheme of things reassures spiritually discerning persons that all things center in the Father; that the plan of salvation which He designed was to save His children, Christ included; and that neither Christ nor Lucifer could of themselves save anyone. As Jesus said: 'The Son can do nothing of himself. . . . I can of mine own self do nothing' (John 5:19, 30). There is, of course, a sense in which we may refer to Lucifer's proposed modifications of the Father's plan as Lucifer's plan, and Christ made the Father's plan

His own by adoption. But what is basically important in this respect is to know that the power to save is vested in the Father, and that He originated, ordained, created, and established His own plan; that He announced it to His children; and that He then asked for a volunteer to be the Redeemer, the Deliverer, the Messiah, who would put the eternal plan of the Eternal Father into eternal operation" (McConkie, *The Mortal Messiah*, 1:48–49, n. 3).

31. Joseph Smith taught that "in the [spirit] world there [are] a variety of spirits. Some . . . seek to excel and this was the case with the devil. When he fell he sought for things which were *unlawful*" (Scott G. Kenney, ed., *Wilford Woodruff's Journal* [Midvale, Utah: Signature Books, 1983], 2:230, emphasis added). The Prophet provided further details on this incident when he said that "in the beginning the great Elohim—in the Hebrew meaning 'the God of all gods'—called a Grand Council and they counseled together to form this planet on which we . . . dwell at present. They spake and earth from chaos sprang by their workmanship—chaos being matter [or] element. . . . [A]nd they spake concerning the redemption of this world and formed limited circumstances concerning the redemption. Jesus Christ . . . stated [that] He could save all those who did not sin against the Holy Ghost and they would obey the code of laws that was given. But their circumstances were that all who would sin against the Holy Ghost should have no forgiveness neither in this world nor in the world to come. For they strove against light and knowledge after they had tasted of the good things of the world to come. They should not have any pardon in the world to come because they had a knowledge of the world to come and were not willing to abide the law. Therefore they can have no forgiveness there. . . . [But] Lucifer . . . spake immediately and boasted of himself saying, 'Send me, I can save all, even those who sinned against the Holy Ghost.' And he accused his brethren [see Rev. 12:10] and was hurled from the Council for striving to break the law immediately. And there was a warfare with Satan and the Gods. And they hurled Satan out of his place and all them that would not keep the law of the Council" (*BYUS*, vol. 18, no. 2, Winter 1978, 171–72). "The contention in heaven was Jesus said there were certain m[e]n [who] would not be saved [and] the devil said he could save them. He rebelled against God and was thrust down" (*WJS*, 361; see also 353, 347, 342).

32. *JD*, 21:288, emphasis added. W. W. Phelps wrote that "Lucifer lost his [first estate] by offering to save men *in their sins* on the honor of a God, or on his Father's honor" (*T&S*, vol. 5, no. 24, 1 January 1844, 758, emphasis added).

Compare this with Helaman 5:10–11 which reads: "[Amulek] said unto [Zeezrom] that the Lord surely should come to redeem His people, but that He should not come to redeem them *in their sins*, but to redeem them *from their sins*. And He hath power given unto Him from the Father to redeem them *from their sins* because of repentance" (emphasis added).

33. *JD*, 13:282, emphasis added.

34. CR, October 1960, 74.

35. *The Seer*, vol. 1, no. 4, April 1853, 53–54. Joseph Fielding Smith emphatically declared that "there were no neutrals in the war in heaven [cf. Matt. 12:30]. *All took sides either with Christ or with Satan*. Every man had his agency there, and men receive rewards here based upon their actions there" (Joseph Fielding Smith, *Doctrines of Salvation* [Salt Lake City: Bookcraft, 1999], 1:65–66, emphasis in original, hereafter cited as *DS*; see also *MD*, 828). President Brigham Young said that "there [were] no neutral spirits in heaven. At the time of the rebellion all took sides." President Young said that he based his statement on remarks made by the Prophet Joseph Smith (Elden J. Watson, comp., *Brigham Young Addresses* [Salt Lake City: Elden J. Watson, 1979–1984], 4:196).

36. *WJS*, 207.

37. *EM*, 2:521–22, emphasis in original; see also ibid., 3:1122–23.

38. Elder Orson Pratt asked, "Why was the Lamb considered as 'slain from the foundation of the world'?" (Rev. 13:8; Moses 7:47). He then offered his opinion that "the very fact that the Atonement, which was to be made in a future world, was considered as already having been made, seems to show that there were those who had sinned, and who stood in need of the Atonement. The nature of the sufferings of Christ was such that it could redeem the spirits of men as well as their bodies. . . . All the spirits when they come here are innocent, that is, if they have ever committed sins, they have repented and obtained forgiveness through faith in the future sacrifice of the Lamb" (*The Seer*, vol. 1, no. 4, April 1853, 54, 56).

39. *WJS*, 87–88, n. #5.

40. Ibid., 371. Even though the notes that Thomas Bullock took on this same sermon report the Prophet as saying that "every man who has a calling to minister to the inhabitants of the world was ordained to that very purpose in the Grand Council" (ibid., 367), they may simply not be as specific as the Samuel W. Richards notes just cited.

41. Ibid., 367. George Laub reports that the Prophet said on this occasion that he "was chosen for the last dispensation or seventh dispensation. The time [when] the Grand Council s[a]t in heaven to organize this world [he] was chosen . . . to lay the foundation of God's work [in] the seventh dispensation" (ibid., 370). In a revelation dated 27 June 1882 the Lord told President John Taylor this very thing. "Behold, I raised up my servant Joseph Smith to introduce my gospel, and to build up my Church and establish my Kingdom on the earth. . . . He was called and ordained to this office before the world was. He was called by me, and empowered by me, and sustained by me to introduce and establish my Church and Kingdom upon the earth; and to be a Prophet, Seer, and Revelator to my Church and Kingdom; and to be a King and Ruler over Israel" (Fred E. Collier, comp., *Unpublished Revelations of the Prophets and Presidents of The Church of Jesus Christ of Latter-day Saints* [Salt Lake City: Collier's Publishing Co., 1979], 1:133).

42. *JD*, 18:114.

43. Parley P. Pratt, *Key to the Science of Theology* (Salt Lake City: Deseret Book, 1978), 40; see also D&C 138:53–56; *NWAF*, 34.

44. *IE*, February 1943, 75.

45. CR, October 1973, 8.

46. Melvin R. Ballard, ed., *Melvin J. Ballard: Crusader for Righteousness* (Salt Lake City: Bookcraft, 1966), 218–19.

47. Joseph Fielding Smith, *Answers to Gospel Questions* (Salt Lake City: Deseret Book, 1998), 4:11–12.

48. *DS*, 1:59.

49. Smith, *The Way to Perfection*, 129.

50. McConkie, *The Millennial Messiah*, 182; see also McConkie, *The Mortal Messiah*, 3:11; McConkie, *The Promised Messiah*, 507; *NWAF*, 510–11; *DNTC*, 2:284; *MD*, 216.

51. Mark E. Petersen, *Abraham: Friend of God* (Salt Lake City: Deseret Book, 1979), 56.

52. *Ensign*, June 1977, 40.

53. Smith, *The Way to Perfection*, 44–45.

54. *JD*, 10:324.

55. James E. Talmage, *The Great Apostasy* (Salt Lake City: Deseret Book, 1994), 20–21, emphasis added. Elder Talmage also writes, "The doctrine of absolute predestination, resulting in a nullification of man's free agency, has been advocated with various modifications by different sects. Nevertheless, such teachings are wholly unjustified by both the letter and the spirit of sacred writ. God's foreknowledge concerning the natures and capacities of His children enables Him to see the end of their earthly career even from the first. . . . Many people have been led to regard this foreknowledge of God as a predestination whereby souls are designated for glory or condemnation even before their birth in the flesh, and irrespective of individual merit or demerit. This heretical doctrine seeks to rob Deity of mercy, justice, and love; it would make God appear capricious and selfish, directing and creating all things solely for His own glory, caring not for the suffering of His victims. How dreadful, how inconsistent is such an idea of God! It leads to the absurd conclusion that the mere knowledge of coming events must act as a determining influence in bringing about those occurrences. God's knowledge of spiritual and of human nature enables Him to conclude with certainty as to the actions of any of His children under given conditions [cf. Moses 1:33, 35, 37–38]; yet that knowledge is not of compelling force upon the creature" (James E. Talmage, *Articles of Faith* [Salt Lake City: Deseret Book, 1984], 173). For further reading on the nature of God's knowledge of the future and its implications for individual agency and salvation see *FARMS Review of Books*, vol. 8, no. 2, 1996, 107–20; *EM*, 4:1478–79; Hyrum L. Andrus, *God, Man, and the Universe*, rev. ed. (Salt Lake City: Deseret Book, 1999), 137–42.

56. *DS*, 1:61.

SECTION 2

WHY AM I HERE?

CHAPTER 3

CREATION, FALL, AND ATONEMENT

The Book of Mormon tells the story of a prophet named Ammon who taught a king named Lamoni the core themes of the gospel. Ammon told the king about the "creation of the world," the "fall of man," and the "plan of redemption, which was prepared from the foundation of the world" and which is centered in "Christ" (Alma 18:24–39). These three foundational doctrines are conveniently encapsulated in Mormon chapter 9 verse 12, which states that God "*created* Adam, and by Adam came the *fall* of man. And because of the Fall of man came Jesus Christ . . . and because of Jesus Christ came the *redemption* of man" (emphasis added). Elder Bruce R. McConkie of the Quorum of the Twelve Apostles referred to the Creation, the Fall, and the Atonement as the three "pillars of eternity."

> The three greatest events that ever have occurred or ever will occur in all eternity are these:
>
> 1. The Creation of the heavens and the earth, of man, and of all forms of life;
> 2. The Fall of man, of all forms of life, and of the earth itself from their primeval and paradisiacal state to their present mortal state; and
> 3. The infinite and eternal Atonement, which ransoms man, all living things, and the earth also from their fallen state so that the salvation of the earth and of all living things may be completed.

> These three divine events—the pillars of eternity—are
> inseparably woven together into one grand tapestry known
> as the eternal plan of salvation. We view the Atonement of
> the Lord Jesus Christ as the center and core and heart of
> revealed religion. It brings to pass the immortality and
> eternal life of man. Salvation is in Christ.[1]

Since the Creation, the Fall, and the Atonement of Jesus Christ
are so intricately interwoven with the salvation of every person on the
earth, it would seem beneficial to understand each of them in some
detail.

THE CREATIONS OF THE GODS

In the first chapter of the book of Moses, verses 35, 37 and 38, it is
revealed that God the Father has been creating worlds for untold eons
of time. In these verses the Creator says, "For behold, there are many
worlds that have passed away by the word of my power. And there are
many that now stand, and innumerable are they unto man; but all
things are numbered unto me, for they are mine and I know them. . . .
The heavens, they are many, and they cannot be numbered unto man;
but they are numbered unto me, for they are mine. And as one earth
shall pass away, and the heavens thereof even so shall another come;
and there is no end to my works, neither to my words."

Verses 30 through 32 of section 121 of the Doctrine and
Covenants imply that a great deal of planning preceded the creation of
the earth and the astronomical bodies that surround it. They hint that
it "was ordained in the midst of the Council of the Eternal God of all
other gods before the world was" that there would be "bounds set to
the heavens [and] to the seas, [and] to the dry land, [and] to the sun,
moon, [and] stars." Such boundaries evidently included "all the times
of [the] revolutions" of the heavenly creations. These verses also suggest
that the premortal Council established "glories, laws and set times" for
"all the appointed days, months, and years" of the celestial orbs.

According to the book of Abraham in the Pearl of Great Price the
creation of the heavens and the earth took place *after* Lucifer "kept

not his first estate" and was cast out of the Lord's presence (Abr. 3:28). Chapter 4 verse 1 of this same book reads, "And *then* the Lord said: Let us go down. And they went down at the beginning, and they, that is the Gods, organized and formed the heavens and the earth" (emphasis added).

Who were the "Gods" that were involved in this creative enterprise? President Brigham Young explained that "the earth was organized by three distinct characters, namely, Elohim, [Je]hovah, and Michael, these three forming a quorum, as in all heavenly bodies, and in organizing element."[2] In Moses chapter 1 verse 33 it is indicated that the creative acts were carried out through the delegation of divine authority. God the Father says in this passage of scripture, "worlds without number have I created; and I also created them for mine own purpose; and *by the Son I created them*, which is mine Only Begotten" (emphasis added). Very little is known about the role that Michael (who was the mortal Adam—see D&C 27:11; 107:54; 128:21) played in the process of creation, but President Brigham Young taught that "he was the person who brought the animals and the seeds from other planets to this world."[3]

Abraham chapter 3 verses 22 through 24 is an especially interesting creation text because of the numerous insights that it provides. This passage reads as follows:

> Now the Lord had shown unto me, Abraham, the intelligences that were organized before the world was; and among all these there were many of the noble and great ones.
>
> And God saw these souls that they were good, and He stood in the midst of them, and He said: "These I will make my rulers;" for He stood among those that were spirits, and He saw that they were good; and He said unto me: "Abraham, thou art one of them; thou wast chosen before thou wast born."
>
> And there stood one among them that was like unto God [i.e., Jesus Christ], and He said unto those who were with Him [i.e., the noble and great ones]: We [i.e., the Gods,

see 4:1] will go down, for there is space there, and we will
take of these materials, and we will make an earth whereon
these [i.e., the intelligences or spirits] may dwell.

One of the most interesting things about this text is that it puts
forward the idea that the Creators utilized existing "materials" in the
creative process. Where did these materials come from? According to
the Prophet Joseph Smith "this earth was organized or formed out of
other planets which were broke[n] up and remodeled and made into
the one on which we live."[4] The Prophet also indicated that the
"materials" that were utilized in the creation were in the form of
"chaotic matter" or "element[s]" or particles that "may be organized
and reorganized but not destroyed."[5]

The inhabitants of the earth do not currently possess a complete
understanding of the creation, but the Lord has promised that during
His millennial reign He will provide a full accounting of these things.
"In that day when the Lord shall come, he shall reveal all things—
Things which have passed, and hidden things which no man knew,
things of the earth, by which it was made, and the purpose and the
end thereof [cf. Moses 1:31]—Things most precious, things that are
above, and things that are beneath, things that are in the earth, and
upon the earth, and in heaven" (D&C 101:32–34).[6]

Physical Bodies

Elder Bruce R. McConkie affirmed that the Lord Jesus Christ and
Michael the archangel participated in the creation of the earth. "But
when it came to placing man on earth, there was a change in
Creators. That is, the Father Himself became personally involved. All
things were created by the Son, using the power delegated by the
Father, except man. In the spirit and again in the flesh, man was
created by the Father. There was no delegation of authority where the
crowning creature of creation was concerned."[7]

Why did there need to be a change in Creators at this point? The
New Testament provides a clue. Luke chapter 3 verse 38 states that
"Adam . . . was the son of God." According to Elder McConkie "this
statement, found also in Moses 6:22, has a deep and profound significance and also means what it says."[8] Elder McConkie asked, "How

did Adam and Eve gain their temporal bodies?" He answered this intriguing question in the following manner:

> Our revelations record Deity's words in this way: "And I, God, said unto mine Only Begotten, which was with me from the beginning: 'Let us make man in our image, after our likeness'" (Moses 2:26). Man on earth—Adam and Eve and all their descendants—was to be created in the image of God; he was to be in His image spiritually and temporally, with power to convert the image into a reality by becoming like Him. Then the scripture says: "And I, God, created man in mine own image, in the image of mine Only Begotten created I him; male and female created I them" (Moses 2:27). Also: "And I, the Lord God, formed men from the dust of the ground, and breathed into his nostrils the breath of life; and man became a living soul, the first flesh upon the earth, the first man also" (Moses 3:7).
>
> For those whose limited spiritual understanding precludes a recitation of all the facts, the revealed account, in figurative language, speaks of Eve being created from Adam's rib (see Moses 3:21–25). A more express scripture, however, speaks of *"Adam, who was the son of God,* with whom God, Himself, conversed" (Moses 6:22, emphasis added). In a formal doctrinal pronouncement, the First Presidency of the Church (Joseph F. Smith, John R. Winder, and Anthon H. Lund) said that "all who have inhabited the earth since Adam have taken bodies and become souls in like manner," and that the first of our race began life as the human germ or embryo that becomes a man *(Improvement Era,* November 1909, 80).
>
> Christ is universally attested in the scriptures to be the Only Begotten. At this point, as we consider the "creation" of Adam, and lest there be any misunderstanding, we must remember that Adam was created in immortality, but that Christ came to earth as a mortal; thus our Lord is the Only Begotten in the flesh, meaning into this mortal sphere of existence. Adam came to earth to dwell in immortality until the Fall changed his status to that of mortality.[9]

President Joseph F. Smith was even more direct than Elder
McConkie in addressing the issue of mankind's origin. He said that
"man was born of woman; Christ, the Savior, was born of woman;
and God, the Father, was born of woman. Adam, our earthly parent,
was also born of woman into this world, the same as Jesus and you
and I."[10] According to President Brigham Young, God "created man
as we create our children; for there is no other process of creation in
heaven, on the earth, in the earth, or under the earth, or in all the
eternities, that [are], that were, or that ever will be. . . . There exist
fixed laws and regulations by which the elements are fashioned to
fulfill their destiny in all the varied kingdoms and orders of creation,
and this process of creation is from everlasting to everlasting."[11]

President Spencer W. Kimball taught the membership of the
Church that "the story of the rib . . . is *figurative*."[12] It would therefore
seem prudent to read the accounts of mankind's creation with that
perspective in mind. Elder Parley P. Pratt believed that the scriptural
story of Adam and Eve's formation was written for an audience that
was not spiritually mature enough to grasp "the mysteries of procreation" or accept the fact that they were literally "the offspring of
Deity."[13]

The physical, terrestrial bodies of Adam and Eve had a unique
quality to them. Joseph Fielding Smith said that when our primordial
parents were placed inside the Garden of Eden "there was no blood in
their bodies. Their lives were quickened by spirit; therefore they were
in a state where they could have lived forever."[14] Why didn't the
Father create Adam and Eve in a mortal or telestial condition? Elder
Orson Pratt explains that it would have been contrary to God's divine
nature to do so:

> Now, perhaps those who are not in the habit of reflecting
> upon this matter, may suppose that when Adam was
> placed upon the earth, and Eve, his wife, they were
> mortal, like unto us; but that was not so. God did not
> make a mortal being. It would be contrary to His great
> goodness to make a man mortal, subject to pain, subject
> to sickness, subject to death. When He made this creation,
> and when He made these two intelligent beings and

placed them upon this creation, He made them after His own likeness and His own image. He did not make them mortal, but He made them immortal, like unto Himself. If He had made them mortal, and subject to pain, there would have been some cause, among intelligent beings, to say that the Lord subjected man, without a cause, to afflictions, sorrows, death and mortality. But He could not do this; it was contrary to the nature of His attributes, contrary to the nature of that infinite goodness which dwells in the bosom of the Father and the Son, to make a being subject to any kind of pain. At the time of creation, all things that proceeded forth from His hands were considered very good.[15]

With the creation of the heavens, the earth, and mankind completed, the stage was set for a great and important drama. The events that would transpire after this point in time would affect each of the Father's children for the rest of eternity.

THE FALL OF ADAM AND EVE

Once Adam and Eve had been placed in the Garden of Eden[16] they enjoyed the presence of their Maker and conversed with Him "without a veil to separate between" them.[17] Nevertheless, Adam and Eve did not remember their premortal life and the great plan of salvation that was laid out in the Grand Council, because after they were created they had a veil of forgetfulness placed over their minds.[18] It was in this state of limited awareness that they heard the Lord issue the following directive:

> Of every tree of the garden thou mayest freely eat. But of the tree of the knowledge of good and evil, thou shalt not eat of it, *nevertheless, thou mayest choose for thyself, for it is given unto thee;* but, remember that I forbid it, for in the day thou eatest thereof thou shalt surely die (Moses 3:16–17, emphasis added).

This passage of scripture provides the valuable insight that God granted agency in relation to the tree of knowledge. President Joseph Fielding Smith says of these verses: "Just why the Lord would say to Adam that He forbade him to partake of the fruit of that tree is not made clear in the Bible account, but in the original as it comes to us in the book of Moses it is made definitely clear. It is that the Lord said to Adam that if he wished to remain as he was in the garden, then he was not to eat of the fruit, but if he desired to eat it and partake of death he was at liberty to do so."[19]

Satan eventually focused his attention on the Garden. "Because he had fallen from heaven, and had become miserable forever, he sought also the misery of all mankind" (2 Ne. 2:18). The adversary "sought to destroy the world" but he "knew not the mind of God" in relation to what was occurring in the sanctuary of Eden (Moses 4:6). The Lord knew that "it must needs be that the devil should tempt the children of men, or they could not be agents unto themselves" (D&C 29:39; see also v. 35). Therefore, as gospel scholar Victor L. Ludlow explains it, "God allowed Satan into the garden in opposition to His own glory."[20]

Once the devil had entered into the paradisiacal sanctuary he "tempted Adam" to partake of the "forbidden fruit" of the tree of knowledge (D&C 29:40), but Adam did not yield. The "father of all lies" then targeted Eve and set out to deceive her. His plan was to encourage her not to hearken unto the voice of the Lord because he knew that it was the only way that he could blind her and "lead [her] captive at his will" (Moses 4:4). After inquiring about the restriction that God had placed upon the tree of knowledge, and being informed that partaking of it would bring death, Satan lied to Eve saying, "Ye shall not surely die." But then the enemy of all righteousness mingled his lie with an important truth. He said,

> For God doth know that in the day ye eat thereof, then your eyes shall be opened, and ye shall be as gods, knowing good and evil.
>
> And when the woman saw that the tree was good for food, and that it became pleasant to the eyes, and a tree to be desired to make her wise, she took of the fruit thereof, and

did eat, and also gave unto her husband with her, and he did eat.

And *the eyes of them both were opened,* and they knew that they had been naked. And they sewed fig-leaves together and made themselves aprons (Moses 4:10–13, emphasis added).

When the Lord discovered what Adam and Eve had done He questioned them about the course that they had taken. He also reminded them of the commandment that was connected with the tree (see Moses 4:23). The Almighty then confirmed that both the man and the woman would suffer the consequence of their action. He pronounced the inevitable saying, "Thou shalt surely die" (v. 25). The Fall of mankind is a complex doctrinal issue, but one which promises to enlighten the understanding of those who delve into its depths. In the hopes of facilitating this enlightenment we will now ask and answer a series of short questions.

What happened to the bodies of Adam and Eve when they partook of the fruit?

President Joseph Fielding Smith relates that the "eating of [the] forbidden fruit subdued the power of the spirit [in their veins] and created blood in their bodies. No blood was in their bodies before the Fall. The blood became the life of the body. And the blood was not only the life thereof, but it had in it the seeds of death."[21]

Was the Fall an unfortunate and unforeseen mishap?

No. The Fall was a foreordained event. The Prophet Joseph Smith states that "the great Jehovah contemplated the whole of the events connected with the earth, pertaining to the plan of salvation, before it rolled into existence. . . . He knew of the Fall of Adam. . . . He comprehended the Fall of man, and [also] his redemption."[22] Indeed, the Apostle Peter taught the Saints of his day that Jesus Christ "was foreordained before the foundation of the world" to be the Redeemer (1 Pet. 1:20). There would have been no reason for this foreordination unless it was known in premortal times that mankind would need to be rescued from a fallen state. The Book of Mormon teaches that everything pertaining to the Fall and the Atonement was "done in the wisdom of him who knoweth all things" (2 Ne. 2:22–26).

Why did Adam and Eve break God's commandment?

The scriptural record indicates that Eve's motives for breaking the divine directive were that she "saw that the tree was good for food, and that it was pleasant to the eyes, and a tree to be desired to make her wise" (Gen. 3:6). The text of Moses 4:12 changes this slightly to read: "it *became* pleasant to the eyes" (emphasis added), possibly meaning that the evil one made it such by his enticement. Elder James E. Talmage writes that even though "Eve was fulfilling the foreseen purposes of God by the part she took in the great drama of the Fall . . . she did not partake of the forbidden fruit with that object in view, but with intent to act contrary to the divine command, being deceived by the sophistries of Satan, who also, for that matter, furthered the purposes of the Creator by tempting Eve."[23]

Elder Orson F. Whitney provides a few additional insights on this incident:

> When our First Parents partook of the forbidden fruit, it was the woman who was beguiled by the Serpent (Satan) and induced to go contrary to the divine command. The man was not deceived [see 1 Tim. 2:14]. What Adam did was done knowingly and after full deliberation. When Eve had tasted of the fruit, Adam did likewise in order to carry out another command, the first that God had given to this pair—the command to "multiply and replenish the earth" [Gen. 1:28]. Eve, by her act, had separated herself from her husband, and was now mortal, while he remained in an immortal state. It was impossible, therefore, unless he also became mortal, for them to obey the original behest. This was Adam's motive. This was his predicament. He was facing a dilemma, and must make [a] choice between two divine commands. He disobeyed in order to obey, retrieving, so far as he could, the situation resulting from his wife's disobedience. Fully aware of what would follow, he partook of the fruit of the [pro]hibited tree, realizing

that in no other way could he become the progenitor of the human race.[24]

Elder Bruce R. McConkie explains that "Eve partook *without* full understanding; Adam partook knowing that unless he did so, he and Eve could not have children and fulfill the commandment they had received to multiply and replenish the earth."[25] Thus we find Adam telling the Lord in his defense: "The woman thou gavest me, and *commandest that she should remain with me*, she gave me of the fruit of the tree and I did eat" (Moses 4:18, emphasis added).

Did Adam and Eve commit a sin when they partook of the forbidden fruit?

The Prophet Joseph Smith emphatically declared that "Adam did not commit sin in eating the fruits, for God had decreed that he should eat and fall."[26] The Lord refers in a modern revelation to Adam's act as a transgression instead of a sin. He says, "Wherefore, it came to pass that the devil tempted Adam, and he partook of the forbidden fruit and *transgressed* the commandment" (D&C 29:40–41, emphasis added). Therefore, Adam was guilty of a "*transgression*." In Moses chapter 6 verse 53 it is revealed that the Lord told Adam after the Fall, "I have forgiven thee thy *transgression* in the Garden of Eden" (emphasis added).

Elder Bruce R. McConkie tells us that "sins cannot be committed unless laws are ordained (Alma 42:17) and unless people have knowledge of those laws so that they can violate them. Adam and Eve could not commit sin while in the Garden of Eden, although laws of conduct had already been established, because the knowledge of good and evil had not been given [to] them. Unless they had partaken of the fruit of the tree of the knowledge of good and evil 'they would have remained in a state of innocence . . . for *they knew no sin*' (2 Ne. 2:23)."[27]

Elder Dallin H. Oaks clarified the difference between a sin and a transgression when he said that "some acts, like murder, are crimes because they are inherently wrong. Other acts, like operating without a license, are crimes only because they are legally prohibited. Under these distinctions, the act that produced the Fall was not a sin— inherently wrong—but a transgression—wrong because it was formally prohibited. These words [*transgression* and *sin*] are not always used to denote something different, but this distinction seems meaningful in the circumstances of the Fall."[28]

Brother Daniel H. Ludlow helps us to get a better grasp on the circumstances of our first parents when they dwelt within the boundaries of paradise. He says that "although Adam and Eve had great intellect and powers of reason in the Garden of Eden, they were without experience; although they had the opportunity of choice and the freedom of choice in the Garden of Eden, . . . they were not morally free because they did not fully understand the consequences of their choice." Even though they heard the Father speak the words, "'In the day thou eatest thereof thou shalt surely die' . . . what was death to Adam and Eve? The veil of forgetfulness had already been placed over their minds—they had never seen death nor experienced it; they could not understand it. And because they did not fully comprehend the consequences of what they did, their disobedience of the law is referred to as a transgression, not as a sin, and consequently comes under the unconditional part of the Atonement of Jesus Christ."[29]

Could the plan of salvation have gone forward if there had been no Fall?

The answer to this question is a definite, No. In the Book of Mormon we read that "if Adam had not transgressed he would not have fallen, but he would have remained in the Garden of Eden. And all things which were created must have remained in the same state in which they were after they were created; and they must have remained forever, and had no end" (2 Ne. 2:22). In other words, there would have been no progression. "Adam's Fall," said Elder Orson F. Whitney, "was a step *downward*, but it was also a step *forward*—a step in the eternal march of human progress."[30]

Elder James E. Talmage writes that "Adam and Eve could never have been the parents of a mortal posterity had they not themselves become mortal; mortality was an essential element in the divine plan respecting the earth and its appointed inhabitants; and, as a means of introducing mortality, the Lord placed before the progenitors of the race a law, knowing what would follow."[31]

President Brigham Young remarked that it was his fullest belief that it was the Lord's design for Adam to partake of the forbidden fruit in the garden. Said he, "I believe that Adam knew all about it before he came to this earth." He also said, "I believe there was no other way leading to thrones and dominions only for him to transgress, or take that position which transgression alone could place man in, to descend below all things, that they might ascend to thrones, principalities, and powers; for they could not ascend to that eminence without first descending, nor upon any other principle."[32]

Why didn't God cause the Fall to occur or simply create a fallen world to begin with?

Daniel H. Ludlow, gospel scholar and general editor of the *Encyclopedia of Mormonism*, came to the following conclusions on this question:

- It is contrary to the nature of God to create anything imperfect or unholy.
- It is contrary to the nature of God to entice men to violate law or to do evil.
- If God had created a world in which there was opposition, sin, and evil then we could hold Him responsible for such conditions.[33]

Brother Robert J. Matthews offered some thoughts on this topic that also call for consideration. He asked:

> Why didn't the Lord simply create man mortal in the first place and avoid all the trauma and experience of a Fall brought to pass through transgression and seemingly conflicting commands?
>
> There are in the scriptures no one-sentence answers to this question, but we have been given enough knowledge concerning God's plan to think through a possible response. In the plan of salvation God does for mankind only what they cannot do for themselves. Man must do all he can for himself. The doctrine is that we are saved by

grace, "after all we can do" (2 Ne. 25:23). We recognize this principle both in the salvation of the living and in the work for the dead. We must do all we can do for ourselves. If Adam and Eve had been created mortal, they would have been denied one of the steps in the process that they were capable of performing themselves. As we read in the Book of Mormon, man "brought upon himself" his own Fall (Alma 42:12). Since the Fall was a necessary part of the plan of salvation, and since man was capable of bringing about the fallen condition himself, he was required—or rather it was his privilege—to take the necessary steps.

If God had created man mortal, then death, sin, and all the circumstances of mortality would be God's doing and would be eternal and permanent in their nature; whereas if man brings the Fall upon himself, he is the responsible moral agent and God is able to rescue and redeem him from his fallen state. Moreover, Adam and Eve's having brought about the Fall themselves made them subject to punishment or reward for their actions. A little reflection upon these matters leads one to conclude that the Fall was accomplished in the very best possible way. As Lehi said about the Fall and the Atonement, "all things have been done in the wisdom of him who knoweth all things" (2 Ne. 2:24). Furthermore, the Lord has explained to us that He does not create temporal or mortal conditions nor function on a mortal level (see D&C 29:34–35).[34]

What effects did the Fall have upon Adam and Eve?

The scriptures list a variety of things that happened to Adam and Eve after they partook of the forbidden fruit:

- They were "cut off from the presence of the Lord" and thereby suffered "spiritual death" (Alma 42:9; see also D&C 29:41).
- They "became subject to the will of the devil, because [they] yielded unto temptation" (D&C 29:40).
- They both experienced "sorrow" (Gen. 3:16–17).
- They had to work in order to survive (see Moses 4:25).

- They became subject to physical "death" (Moses 6:48).
- Their eyes were "opened" (Moses 5:10). They became like the "Gods, knowing good from evil," and they were "placed in a state to act according to their wills and pleasures, whether to do evil or to do good" (Alma 12:31).
- They were able to produce offspring. If Adam and Eve had not partaken of the forbidden fruit they "would have had no children" (2 Ne. 2:23). "Were it not for our transgression," said Eve, "we *never* should have had seed" (Moses 5:11, emphasis added). Indeed, it is stated in the book of 2 Nephi chapter 2 verse 25 that "Adam fell that men might be."
- They came to know "the joy of [their] redemption, and the eternal life which God giveth unto all the obedient" (Moses 5:11).
- Resurrection became a reality for them (see Moses 5:10).

Why did Adam and Eve need to be cast out of the Garden of Eden?

The Lord drove Adam and Eve out of their paradisiacal home and "placed at the east of the Garden of Eden, cherubim and a flaming sword, which turned every way to keep the way of the tree of life" (Moses 4:31). In the book of Alma it is stated that "if it had been possible for Adam to have partaken of the fruit of the tree of life at that time, there would have been no death, and the word [of the Lord] would have been void, making God a liar, for He said: 'If thou eat thou shalt surely die'. . . . [I]f it were possible that our first parents could have gone forth and partaken of the tree of life they would have been forever miserable, having no preparatory state; and thus *the plan of redemption would have been frustrated*, and the word of God would have been void, taking none effect" (Alma 12:23, 26, emphasis added; see also 42:5).[35]

THE ATONEMENT OF JESUS CHRIST

At some point after their expulsion from the Garden of Eden, Adam and Eve received a commandment from the Lord to "offer the firstlings of their flocks" unto Him (Moses 5:3–5). It was "many days" after they had begun to make these offerings that an angel of the Lord appeared unto Adam and asked him, "Why dost thou offer sacrifices unto the Lord?" Adam replied that he did not know the purpose behind this ceremony but that he acted out of obedience to the Lord's command (Moses 5:6). The angel then explained to Adam that his offering was "a similitude of the sacrifice of the Only Begotten of the Father, which is full of grace and truth. Wherefore," said the angel, "thou shalt do all that thou doest in the name of the Son, and thou shalt repent and call upon God in the name of the Son forevermore" (vv. 7–8).

The scriptural record relates that "in that day the Holy Ghost fell upon Adam," and he heard a voice saying, "I am the Only Begotten of the Father from the beginning, henceforth and forever, that as thou hast fallen thou mayest be redeemed, and all mankind, even as many as will" (Moses 5:9). This, according to Moses chapter 6 verse 62, is "the plan of salvation unto all men," which is brought to pass "through the blood of [the] Only Begotten" Son of God. Adam and Eve shared their knowledge of this plan with their children (see Moses 5:12) and the Lord, seeing that "it was expedient that m[e]n should know concerning the things whereof He had appointed unto them," sent angels down out of heaven to converse with them. And "God conversed with men, and made known unto them the plan of redemption, which had been prepared from the foundation of the world" (Alma 12:28–30).

"Nothing is more important in the entire divine plan of salvation," said President Howard W. Hunter, "than the atoning sacrifice of Jesus Christ. We believe that salvation comes because of the Atonement."[36] The scriptures testify that "redemption cometh in and through the Holy Messiah" and "there is no flesh that can dwell in the presence of God, save it be through the merits, and mercy, and grace of the Holy Messiah" (2 Ne. 2:6, 8). Since the Savior's Atonement has such a central importance in the eternal scheme of things, it is imperative that all of God's children learn about its nature and come to understand how it relates to them personally. The questions and answers that follow are designed to lay a foundation for the further study of this very important doctrine.

What does the word "atonement" mean?

Elder Russell M. Nelson notes that "in the English language, the components are *at-one-ment*, suggesting that a person is at one with another. Other languages [like Spanish, Portuguese, French, Italian, and German] employ words that connote either *expiation* or *reconciliation*. *Expiation* means 'to atone for.' *Reconciliation* comes from Latin roots *re*, meaning 'again'; *con*, meaning 'with'; and *sella*, meaning 'seat.' *Reconciliation*, therefore, literally means 'to sit again with'"[37] (cf. Matt. 8:11; Alma 5:24; 7:25; Hel. 3:28–30).

Dr. Hugh W. Nibley provides us with the insight that in the Hebrew language the word *kpr*, which translates as "to atone for," is cognate with the English word *cover*. "It's the same in Aramaic; it's 'to cover over your sins' . . . It means 'to arch over; to bend over; to cover; to pass over with the hand, especially the palm of the hand.' The word for *palm of the hand* in all Semitic languages is *kap*. It means 'to cover . . . to wipe over, hence to cleanse, to expiate, to forgive . . . [and also] to encircle.'"[38] In this light, one particular passage in the Book of Mormon takes on added meaning. In the book of 2 Nephi chapter 1 verse 15 we read, "the Lord hath *redeemed* my soul . . . I have beheld his glory, and *I am encircled about* eternally in the *arms* of his love" (emphasis added; see also Morm. 5:11).

How does the Atonement operate?

In order for people to begin to grasp how the Atonement works they must first understand something of how God's plan functions. Alma chapter 42 verse 22 provides us with an operational framework:

- A law is decreed; a punishment for violation is fixed; repentance is possible.
- The repentant are claimed by "mercy."
- The unrepentant are claimed by "justice" and the punishment is inflicted.

An understanding of the Atonement also requires a knowledge of the condition that all mortals are in. It is stated in Alma 42:13–14 that "all mankind [are] fallen, and they [are] in the grasp of justice" and "the justice of God . . . consign[s] them forever to be cut off from his presence." This situation cannot be circumvented because "the work of justice [cannot] be destroyed."

This dire set of circumstances can only be overcome in one way. "The Son [of God has] *power* to make intercession for the children of men." He stands "betw[een] them and justice; having . . . taken upon himself their iniquity and their transgressions, having redeemed them, and satisfied the demands of justice" (Mosiah 15:8–9, emphasis added). In other words, the Redeemer has "answered the ends of the law, and he claimeth all those who have faith in him." He can "claim of the Father his *rights* of mercy which he hath upon the children of men" (Moro. 7:27–28, emphasis added).

What does the word "redeemer" mean?

Gospel scholar Jennifer Clark Lane informs us that "a redeemer in an ancient Israelite setting was a close family member responsible for helping other family members who had lost their . . . liberty . . . by buying them out of their bondage." In the Old Testament the Hebrew word *ga'al* is primarily translated as "redeem." It incorporates the idea of "buying back" or "release by the payment of a price" (cf. 1 Tim. 2:6). This word also "refers to redemption made out of family obligation or responsibility." Sister Lane provides some insightful comments on what it means to be saved and redeemed:

> There is a common confusion in the use of the terms save and *redeem.* They may seem to be used interchangeably and sometimes are assumed to be synonyms. Although they both do convey the meaning of "deliver," redeem is a subclass of save. Saving refers to any kind of deliverance, and redeeming specifically refers to deliverance based upon a payment.

> The English word save is from the Latin *salvare,* "to save," and *salvus,* "safe." Its basic meaning is "to deliver or rescue from peril or hurt; to make safe, put in safety." There is no intrinsic indication of how this rescue is performed. With "redeem," on the other hand, the Latin root specifically means "to buy back," *re*(d) + *emere*. Accordingly, the basic meaning in English is "to buy back (a thing formerly possessed); to make payment for (a thing held or claimed by another)."[39]

In connection with this last concept it should be noted that the Lord has bought us "with a price" (1 Cor. 6:20; 7:23; 1 Pet. 2:1). The Savior through His mercy "has offered Atonement for sin," said Joseph Fielding Smith. "We belong to Jesus Christ who purchased us with His blood." The Redeemer "came into the world, offering Himself [as] a ransom to pay the price of transgression through the shedding of His blood that all men might be freed from death and have remission of their sins, on condition of their repentance."[40]

Why did Jesus Christ need to be the one to fulfill the role of the Redeemer?

"According to the great plan of the Eternal God," says Alma chapter 34 verse 9, "there must be an Atonement made, or else all mankind must unavoidably perish . . . [because] all are fallen and all are lost." But "there is not any man that can sacrifice his own blood which will atone for the sins of another" (v. 11).[41] Therefore, the atoning "sacrifice" had to be made by "the Son of God" (v. 14). Brother Robert J. Matthews provides a number of insights into why this was so. He points out that all mankind are dominated by the effects of the Fall; they are subject to death (see 1 Cor. 15:22) and to sin (see 1 Jn. 1:8). Brother Matthews also asserts that Jesus Christ was not dominated by the effects of the Fall; He was not subject to death (see John 10:17–18) and not subject to sin (see 2 Cor. 5:21).

The Savior was the only person who ever lived in the mortal sphere who was capable of conquering both physical and spiritual death because they held no dominion over Him. The sacrifice that He made was not that of a man. Instead, it was of the highest order possible; it was the sacrifice of a "God" who voluntarily "*gave* His own life" to pay the debt of the law that was broken in the Garden of Eden (D&C 34:1, 3, emphasis added).[42]

Why did the Savior's blood need to be shed?

In the book of Leviticus chapter 17 verses 11 and 14, the Lord says that "blood" represents the "life" of the mortal body and is the agent that makes "atonement" for mortal beings. Hebrews chapter 9 verse 22 states that blood has the power to purge or cleanse; further-more, "without [the] shedding of blood [there] is no remission" of sins (cf. Matt. 26:28). President Joseph Fielding Smith draws attention to the fact that "it was by the creation of blood that mortality came [and] it is by the sacrifice of blood that the redemption from death was accomplished."[43]

It is by "*the virtue of the blood*" that Jesus Christ has shed that He is able to plead before the Father, in His own name, for those who believe in Him (D&C 38:4, emphasis added). As the Savior petitions His Creator and King He may speak words similar to those found in Doctrine and Covenants section 45 verses 3 through 5. "Father, behold the sufferings and death of him who did no sin, in whom thou wast well pleased; behold the blood of thy Son which was shed, the blood of him whom thou gavest that thyself might be glorified. Wherefore, Father, spare these my brethren that believe on my name, that they may come unto me and have everlasting life."

How is the Atonement of Jesus Christ applied to those who commit sin?

In order to answer this question it is first necessary to understand what the scriptures say about human nature and salvation. They relate that a person who "persists in his own carnal nature, and goes on in the ways of sin and rebellion against God, remaineth in his fallen state and the devil hath all power over him. Therefore he is as though there was no redemption made" (Mosiah 16:5). Since "the Lord cannot look upon sin with the least degree of allowance" (D&C 1:31), "all men, everywhere, must repent, or they can in nowise inherit the kingdom of God, for no unclean thing can dwell there" (Moses 6:57).[44]

Jesus Christ endured the intense agony of the Atonement "for all, that they might not suffer if they would repent. But if they [will] not repent," says the Lord, "they must suffer even as I; which suffering caused myself, even God, the greatest of all, to tremble because of pain, and to bleed at every pore, and to suffer both body and spirit" (D&C 19:15–18). All of the Father's children are *commanded* to repent and obey His holy laws so that they might avoid this fearful pain.

Gospel scholar Gary P. Gillum provides a noteworthy insight on repentance. He points out that one of the Hebrew words translated in the Old Testament as "repentance" (*teshuvah*) means "'recover,' 'refresh,' 'restore,' 'convert,' 'return,' 'reverse,' or 'turn again.' It indicates a return to God and the right path."[45] When someone sincerely repents and turns again to God, the atoning blood of Jesus Christ is able to cleanse them from their sins (see 1 Jn. 1:7). The scriptural imagery is that of "garments" being "washed white through the blood of the Lamb" (Alma 13:11–12; see also 5:21). The Redeemer Himself has declared that "no unclean thing can enter into [the Father's] kingdom; therefore nothing entereth into His rest save it be those who have washed their garments in my blood, because of their faith, and the repentance of *all* their sins, and their faithfulness unto the end" (3 Ne. 27:19, emphasis added).

The Lord has provided several keys to seeking forgiveness at His hand. In latter-day revelations He says, "I, the Lord, forgive sins unto those who confess their sins before me and ask forgiveness" (D&C 64:7). "I, the Lord, forgive sins, and am merciful unto those who confess their sins with humble hearts" (D&C 61:2; cf. 58:43). "He that repents and does the commandments of the Lord shall be forgiven" (D&C 1:32). Through sincere repentance and obedience it is possible to "take full advantage of [the Lord's] redemption," said President Howard W. Hunter. "The offer is always there; the way is always open. We can always, even in our darkest hour and most disastrous errors, look to the Son of God and live."[46] Elder Boyd K. Packer confirms this teaching with these reassuring words:

> The gospel teaches us that relief from torment and guilt can be earned through repentance. Save for those few who defect to perdition after having known a fullness, there is no habit, no addiction, no rebellion, no transgression, no offense exempted from the promise of complete forgiveness. "Come now, and let us reason together, saith the Lord: though your sins be as scarlet, they shall be as white as snow; though they be red like crimson, they shall be as wool." That is, Isaiah continued, "if ye be willing and obedient" [Isa. 1:18–19]. . . . I repeat, save for the exception of the very few who defect to perdition, there is no habit, no addiction, no rebellion, no transgression, no apostasy, no crime exempted from the promise of complete forgiveness. That is the promise of the Atonement of Christ.[47]

As a special witness of the Lord Jesus Christ, Elder Marion G. Romney testified that the Redeemer "paid the debt . . . for the personal sins of every living soul that ever dwelt upon the earth or that ever will dwell in mortality upon the earth. But," said Elder Romney, "this He did conditionally. The benefits of this suffering for our individual transgressions will not come to us unconditionally in the same sense that the Resurrection will come regardless of what we do. If we partake of the blessings of the Atonement as far as our individual transgressions are concerned, we must obey the law [of the Lord]."[48] But the recompense is sweet for those who comply with the order of heaven. To them the assurance of a merciful God is given: "Behold, he who has repented of his sins, the same is forgiven, and I, the Lord, remember them no more" (D&C 58:42; see also Isa. 43:25).

NOTES: CHAPTER 3

1.   Bruce R. McConkie, *A New Witness for the Articles of Faith* (Salt Lake City: Deseret Book, 1985), 81–82, hereafter cited as *NWAF*.

2.   George D. Watt, comp., *Journal of Discourses* (London, England: F. D. and S. W. Richards and Sons, 1854–1886), 1:51, hereafter cited as *JD*.

3.   Ibid., 3:319.

4.   Andrew F. Ehat and Lyndon W. Cook, eds., *The Words of Joseph Smith: The Contemporary Accounts of the Nauvoo Discourses of the Prophet Joseph* (Orem, Utah: Grandin Book, 1991), 60, hereafter cited as *WJS*.

5.   Ibid., 359.

6.   Elder Bruce R. McConkie notes that "our knowledge about the creation is limited. We do not know the how and why and when of all things. Our finite limitations are such that we could not comprehend them if they were revealed to us in all their glory, fullness, and perfection. What has been revealed is that portion of the Lord's eternal word which we must believe and understand if we are to envision the truth about the Fall and the Atonement and thus become heirs of salvation" (*Ensign*, June 1982, 10).

7.   Bruce R. McConkie, *The Promised Messiah* (Salt Lake City: Deseret Book,

1981), 62.

8. Bruce R. McConkie, *Doctrinal New Testament Commentary* (Salt Lake City: Bookcraft, 1965), 1:95, hereafter cited as *DNTC*.

9. Bruce R. McConkie, "Eve and the Fall," in *Woman* (Salt Lake City: Deseret Book, 1979), 60–61.

10. *Deseret Evening News*, 27 December 1913, section III, 7.

11. *JD*, 11:122. President Young provides a possible answer to the question of how celestial Parents could produce terrestrial children. "The Father actually begat the spirits, and they were brought forth and lived with Him. Then He commenced the work of creating earthly tabernacles . . . by partaking of the coarse material that was organized and composed this [paradisiacal or terrestrial] earth, until His system was charged with it. Consequently, the tabernacles of His children were organized from the coarse materials of this [terrestrial] earth" (ibid., 4:218).

12. *Ensign*, March 1976, 71, emphasis added. Elder Bruce R. McConkie writes that Eve "was placed on earth in the same manner as was Adam, the Mosaic account of the Lord creating her from Adam's rib being merely figurative" (Bruce R. McConkie, *Mormon Doctrine*, 2d ed. [Salt Lake City: Bookcraft, 1966], 242, hereafter cited as *MD*). An entry in the *Encyclopedia of Mormonism* states that Eve "was created spiritually and physically in the same manner as was Adam" (Daniel H. Ludlow, ed., *Encyclopedia of Mormonism* [New York: Macmillan, 1992], 2:475).

13. Parley P. Pratt, *Key to the Science of Theology* (Salt Lake City: Deseret Book, 1978), 30. It might be argued by some that if Adam was procreated by the Father then Jesus Christ could not be the Only Begotten Son of the Father. Gospel scholar Robert J. Matthews offers the following remarks on this topic. "I am in no position to speak for the Church or for the Brethren, but I want to express my personal belief on the subject of the creation of Adam. I believe that Adam's physical body was the offspring of God, literally (Moses 6:22); that he was begotten as a baby with a physical body not subject to death, in a world without sin or blood; and that he grew to manhood in that condition and then became mortal through his own actions. I believe that Adam's physical body was begotten by our immortal celestial Father and an immortal celestial Mother, and thus not into a condition of mortality, a condition which would have precluded Jesus from being the Only Begotten of the Father in the flesh (D&C 93:11)—*flesh* meaning *mortality*. Jesus' physical body was also begotten

of the same celestial Father but through a mortal woman and hence into mortality. Commenting on Luke 3:38 ('Adam, which was the son of God'), Elder Bruce R. McConkie wrote: 'This statement, found also in Moses 6:22, has a deep and profound significance and also means what it says. Father Adam came, as indicated, to this sphere, gaining an immortal body, because death had not yet entered the world (2 Ne. 2:22). Jesus, on the other hand, was the Only Begotten in the flesh, meaning into a world of mortality where death already reigned' [*DNTC*, 1:95]" (Robert J. Matthews, *A Bible! A Bible!* [Salt Lake City: Bookcraft, 1990], 188, emphasis in original).

14. Joseph Fielding Smith, *Answers to Gospel Questions* (Salt Lake City: Deseret Book, 1998), 3:100, hereafter cited as *AGQ*. The same author makes this claim in an official Church publication. See Joseph Fielding Smith, *Church History and Modern Revelation* (Salt Lake City: The Church of Jesus Christ of Latter-day Saints, 1947), 2:5–6; see also Jeffrey R. Holland, *Christ and the New Covenant: The Messianic Message of the Book of Mormon* (Salt Lake City: Deseret Book, 1997), 205–206.

15. *JD*, 21:289. The truth that Adam and Eve were created as the immortal offspring of God the Father precludes the possibility that they evolved from lower life forms. For reading on the theory of evolution and its relationship to scriptural teachings see Boyd K. Packer, "The Law and the Light," in Monte S. Nyman and Charles D. Tate, Jr., eds., *The Book of Mormon: Jacob through Words of Mormon* (Provo, Utah: BYU Religious Studies Center, 1990), 1–31; Matthews, *A Bible! A Bible!*, 188–90; Joseph Fielding Smith, *Doctrines of Salvation* (Salt Lake City: Bookcraft, 1999), 1:139–44.

16. Genesis 2:8 and Moses 3:8 suggest that Adam was created at some location outside of the Garden of Eden. Gospel scholar Daniel H. Ludlow writes: "After Adam became a living soul on the earth, a female helpmate was given to him, and he called her Eve. God then placed Adam and Eve in the garden He had prepared for them" (Daniel H. Ludlow, *Gospel Scholars Series: Selected Writings of Daniel H. Ludlow* [Salt Lake City: Deseret Book, 2000], 323–24).

17. *Lectures on Faith* (Salt Lake City: Deseret Book, 1985), 12.

18. Brigham Young taught that "when [God] sent Adam [to] this earth He decreed . . . that he might forget all about his former estate" (*BYU Studies*, vol. 18, no. 2, Winter 1978, 178). President Young also asked, "Which would produce the greatest good to man, to give him his agency, and draw a veil over him, or, to give him certain blessings and privileges, let him live in a certain

degree of light, and enjoy a certain glory, and take his agency from him, compelling him to remain in that position, without any possible chance of progress? I say, the greatest good that could be produced by the all wise Conductor of the universe to His creature, man, was to do just as He has done—bring him forth on the face of the earth, drawing a veil before his eyes. He has caused us to forget everything we once knew before our spirits entered within this veil of flesh" (*JD*, 1:351). Bishop Orson F. Whitney reminds us that "we are placed in this world measurably in the dark. We no longer see our Father face to face. While it is true that we once did; that we once stood in His presence, seeing as we are seen, knowing, according to our intelligence, as we are known. The curtain has dropped, we have changed our abode, we have taken upon ourselves flesh; the veil of forgetfulness intervenes between this life and that, and we are left, as Paul expresses it, to 'see through a glass darkly,' to 'know in part and to prophesy in part;' to see only to a limited extent, the end from the beginning. We do not comprehend things in their fullness. But we have the promise, if we will receive and live by every word that proceeds from the mouth of God, wisely using the intelligence, the opportunities, the advantages, and the possessions which He continually bestows upon us—the time will come, in the eternal course of events, when our minds will be cleared from every cloud, the past will recur to memory, the future will be an open vision, and we will behold things as they are, and the past, present and future will be one eternal day" (*JD*, 26:195–96).

19. *AGQ*, 4:81.

20. Victor L. Ludlow, *Principles and Practices of the Restored Gospel* (Salt Lake City: Deseret Book, 1992), 184.

21. Conference Report, April 1967, 122, hereafter cited as CR. The Prophet Joseph Smith noted that "to Adam the Lord said, 'In the *day* thou shalt eat thereof thou shalt surely die.' Now the *day* the Lord has reference to is spoken of by Peter; a thousand of our years is with the Lord as one *day* [see 2 Pet. 3:8]. At the time the Lord said this to Adam there was no mode of counting time by man, as man now counts time [see Abr. 5:12–13]" (*WJS*, 64–65, emphasis added). And indeed, after Adam partook of the forbidden fruit he lived 930 years—he died within the *day* of the Lord (see Gen. 5:3–5).

22. B. H. Roberts, ed., *History of the Church*, rev. ed. (Salt Lake City: The Church of Jesus Christ of Latter-day Saints, 1932–1951), 4:597. The Prophet, using a more specific term, said that God "*foreordained* the Fall of man; but all

merciful as He is He foreordained, at the same time, a plan [of] redemption for all mankind. . . . [I]t was foreordained [that man] should fall, and be redeemed" (*WJS*, 33, emphasis added).

23. James E. Talmage, *Articles of Faith* (Salt Lake City: Deseret Book, 1984), 63.

24. Orson F. Whitney, *Saturday Night Thoughts* (Salt Lake City: Deseret News Press, 1921), 91.

25. *NWAF*, 86, emphasis added.

26. *WJS*, 63.

27. *MD*, 735, emphasis in original.

28. *Ensign*, November 1993, 73.

29. Ludlow, *Gospel Scholars Series: Selected Writings of Daniel H. Ludlow*, 314.

30. CR, April 1908, 90, emphasis added.

31. Talmage, *Articles of Faith*, 62–63. Elder John A. Widtsoe likewise states that "Adam and Eve were eternal beings, not under the ban of mortal death. Subject to death they must become, however, if their posterity should inherit corruptible bodies. The Fall, then, was a deliberate use of a law, by which Adam and Eve became mortal, and could beget mortal children" (John A. Widtsoe, *A Rational Theology* [Salt Lake City: Deseret Book, 1965], 51).

32. *JD*, 2:302. President Brigham Young spoke of the connection between the veil of forgetfulness and the concept of descending below all things. "The spirit from the eternal worlds enters the tabernacle at the time of what is termed quickening, and forgets all it formerly knew. It descends below all things, as Jesus did. All beings, to be crowned with crowns of glory and eternal lives, must in their infantile weakness begin, with regard to their trials, the day of their probation: they must descend below all things, in order to ascend above all things" (ibid., 6:333).

33. These points are listed in Gerald N. Lund's, "The Fall of Man and His Redemption," in Monte S. Nyman and Charles D. Tate, Jr., eds., *The Book of Mormon: Second Nephi, The Doctrinal Structure* (Provo, Utah: BYU Religious Studies Center, 1989), 102. For an informative discussion on fourteen false doctrines or heresies that are related to the Fall see *NWAF*, 98–104.

34. Robert J. Matthews, *Gospel Scholars Series: Selected Writings of Robert J. Matthews* (Salt Lake City: Deseret Book, 1999), 479–80.

35. It might be argued that the Lord could have left Adam and Eve inside the garden and simply restricted their access to the tree of life. President George Q. Cannon, however, provides a conceptual framework for why this was not done. In speaking of access to the tree of knowledge President Cannon said that God "might have put it out of [Adam's] power to touch or taste it. But not so; He gave [Adam] the opportunity of exercising his agency. . . . There was no attempt on the part of our Father to interfere with the agency of Adam in this respect. He left him perfectly free and in the exercise of that freedom Adam did partake of the tree of knowledge of good and evil. . . . Now, it may be said, 'Why did not God prevent man and woman from taking this course?' Because, as I have before said, it was right that they should exercise their agency. God—shall I say could not? Do I detract from His majesty and His glory by placing a limit on His power? I will say that God would not, because it would be in violation of His own laws; it would be in violation of those eternal laws which our God Himself recognizes, for Him to have interfered and deprived man and woman of their agency" (*JD*, 26:189–90). From the foregoing it could be postulated that in order to maintain the law of agency, make certain that the plan of salvation went forward, and ensure the sanctity of His own words, God drove Adam and Eve from the garden.

36. CR, October 1968, 139.

37. Russell M. Nelson, *Perfection Pending, and Other Favorite Discourses* (Salt Lake City: Deseret Book, 1998), 165–66, emphasis in original.

38. Hugh W. Nibley, *Teachings of the Book of Mormon, Semester 1: Transcripts of Lectures Presented to an Honors Book of Mormon Class at Brigham Young University, 1988–1990* (Provo, Utah: Foundation for Ancient Research and Mormon Studies, 1993), 250, emphasis in original.

39. Jennifer Clark Lane, "The Lord Will Redeem His People: Adoptive Covenant and Redemption in the Old Testament and Book of Mormon," *Journal of Book of Mormon Studies*, vol. 2, no. 2, Fall 1993, 39–41, emphasis in original.

40. Joseph Fielding Smith, *Church History and Modern Revelation* (Salt Lake City: The Church of Jesus Christ of Latter-day Saints, 1946), 1:130–31.

41. President Marion G. Romney of the First Presidency says in this regard: "All have sinned. Each person is therefore unclean to the extent to which he has sinned, and because of that uncleanness is banished from the presence of the Lord so long as the effect of his own wrongdoing is upon him. Since we suffer this spiritual death as a result of our own transgressions, we cannot claim deliv-

erance therefrom as a matter of justice. Neither has any man the power within himself alone to make restitution so complete that he can be wholly cleansed from the effect of his own wrongdoing. If men are to be freed from the results of their own transgressions and brought back into the presence of God, they must be the beneficiaries of some expedient beyond themselves which will free them from the effects of their own sins. For this purpose was the Atonement of Jesus Christ conceived and executed" (CR, April 1982, 9).

42. These insights (which are summarized in this section) have been gathered from the following sources: Robert J. Matthews, "The Doctrine of the Atonement: The Revelation of the Gospel to Adam," in Robert L. Millet and Kent P. Jackson, eds., *Studies in Scripture: Volume 2, The Pearl of Great Price* (Salt Lake City: Randall Book, 1985), 125; Robert J. Matthews, *Behold the Messiah* [Salt Lake City: Bookcraft, 1994], 101; Matthews, *A Bible! A Bible!*, 191–92; Matthews, *Gospel Scholars Series: Selected Writings of Robert J. Matthews*, 521–22. Elder Bruce R. McConkie had the following to say in regard to Jesus Christ not being subject to death. "God, an immortal man, was His Father; and Mary, a mortal woman, was His mother. He was begotten; He was conceived; He was born. From His immortal Father He inherited the power of immortality, which is the power to live; from His mortal mother He inherited the power of mortality, which is the power to die; and being thus dual in nature, being able to choose life or death, according to the will of the Father, He was able to work out the infinite and eternal Atonement. Having chosen to die, as He did because He had the power of mortality, He could choose to live again because He had the power of immortality. . . . It took our Lord's mortal and His immortal powers to work out the Atonement, for that supreme sacrifice required both death and resurrection. There is no salvation without death, even as there is no salvation without resurrection" (*NWAF*, 111).

43. *AGQ*, 3:103.

44. President Joseph Fielding Smith spoke of the necessity of repentance before entrance into the kingdom of God is granted. In referring specifically to "all those who are married in the temple for time and all eternity," he said that "if it so happens that they do sin and break their covenants, but have not sinned unto death, they will have to repent completely and faithfully of all their sins or they will never enter the celestial glory. *No unrepentant person who remains in his sins will ever enter into the glories of the celestial kingdom*" (ibid., 1:73, emphasis in original).

45. Gary P. Gillum, "Repentance Also Means Rethinking," in John M. Lundquist and Stephen D. Ricks, eds., *By Study and Also by Faith* (Salt Lake City: Deseret Book and The Foundation for Ancient Research and Mormon Studies, 1990), 2:409. Elder Derek A. Cuthbert notes that "service . . . helps to recompense for sin. . . . We can express regret and feel remorse for things done wrong, but *full* repentance should include recompense, such as service gives" (*Ensign*, May 1990, 12, emphasis in original).

46. Clyde J. Williams, ed., *The Teachings of Howard W. Hunter* (Salt Lake City: Bookcraft, 1997), 34.

47. *Ensign*, November 1995, 19–20. On page 21 of this same article, note #15, Elder Packer says, "Forgiveness will come eventually to all repentant souls who have not committed the unpardonable sin (see Matt. 12:31). Forgiveness does not, however, necessarily assure exaltation, as is the case with David" (see D&C 132:38–39; see also Ps. 16:10; Acts 2:25–27; *TPJS*, 339). Elder Bruce R. McConkie clarifies that "there is a difference between gaining forgiveness of sins and gaining salvation in the celestial kingdom. All men who do not commit the unpardonable sin will gain eventual pardon; that is, they will be forgiven of their sins; but those so forgiven, having been judged according to their works, will then be sent either to a telestial, terrestrial, or celestial kingdom, as the case may be. As a matter of fact, those destined to inherit kingdoms of glory will not be resurrected until they have repented and gained forgiveness of their sins. The telestial kingdom will be inhabited by those who have been tormented and buffeted in hell until they have gained forgiveness and become worthy to attain a resurrection" (*DNTC*, 1:274–75). Elder McConkie said in another of his publications that "particular note should be taken . . . of the fact that *forgiveness of sins does not thereby confer celestial salvation upon a person*. 'All will suffer until they obey Christ Himself,' the Prophet [Joseph Smith] said (*TPJS*, 357). The wicked and ungodly will suffer the vengeance of eternal fire in hell until they finally obey Christ, repent of their sins, and gain forgiveness therefrom. Then they shall obtain the Resurrection and an inheritance in the telestial and not the celestial kingdom (D&C 76:81–107)" (*MD*, 816, emphasis in original).

48. CR, October 1953, 35. In the writings of Joseph Fielding Smith we find the following question and answer. "*Question*: 'In our discussion of doctrinal subjects the question arose whether or not the Savior by virtue of His Atonement paid for the sins of all the human family of Adam, or was He

suffering for [the] sins of Adam and those who obey the gospel only?'. . . *Answer*: The question of salvation to mankind was clearly answered by the Redeemer in many discourses while He was with the Jews in His ministry. He offered peace and rest in His Father's kingdom to all who would repent and accept the *ordinances* and teachings of His gospel. He clearly stated that those who reject the plan of salvation are not cleansed from their sins" (*AGQ*, 5:5, emphasis added). Apostle Franklin D. Richards and James A. Little state that "only by being buried with Christ in water, by baptism, is the shedding of His blood available to man for the remission of sins" (Franklin D. Richards and James A. Little, *Compendium of the Doctrines of the Gospel* [Salt Lake City: Bookcraft, 1882], 37). Gospel scholar Roy W. Doxey concurs with this position. He writes that "the Atonement of Christ remits sins only if the person repents and accepts the Savior by baptism" (Roy W. Doxey, *The Doctrine and Covenants Speaks* [Salt Lake City: Deseret Book, 1970], 2:168).

CHAPTER 4

THE PURPOSE OF MORTALITY

The purpose of mortality is a perplexing mystery to a great many citizens of the earth. The Book of Mormon solves this puzzle easily enough when it says that "men are, that they might have joy" (2 Ne. 2:25), but Joseph F. Smith takes this even further. He declares that "the object of our earthly existence is that we might have a fullness of joy, and that we may become the sons and daughters of God, in the fullest sense of the word, being heirs of God and joint-heirs with Jesus Christ, to be kings and priests unto God, to inherit glory, dominion, exaltation, thrones, and every power and attribute developed and possessed by our Heavenly Father. This is the object of our being on this earth."[1] Such a statement is in complete accord with Joseph Smith's proclamation that "the design of the Almighty in making man . . . was to exalt him to be as God."[2] It is, in fact, a divine commandment for mortals to strive to become like God the Father and His Son Jesus Christ (see Matt. 5:48; 3 Ne. 12:48). And surely, as it is explained by the prophet Nephi, "the Lord God giveth no commandments unto the children of men, save he shall prepare a way for them that they may accomplish the thing which he commandeth them" (1 Ne. 3:7).

The pattern for achieving a fullness of joy in the world to come can be seen in the life of the Son of God. The Redeemer of all mankind rose to the heights of exaltation and glory by doing three essential things. First, He obtained a physical body (see Luke 2:6–7). Second, He developed divine or godly attributes (see Luke 2:40; Heb. 5:8). And third, He overcame the trials of the fallen, mortal sphere in which He was placed (see Matt. 4:1–11; Heb. 2:16–18). Let us now discuss these points in their turn and focus on how they relate to each individual.

OBTAINING A BODY

President Marion G. Romney reminds us that because we are all the literal offspring of God "we inherit the capability of reaching, in full maturity, the status of our Heavenly Parents just as we inherit from our mortal parents the capability to attain to their mortal status." He also points out that "since God has a body of flesh and bones, it was necessary and perfectly natural for us, His spirit offspring, to obtain such bodies in order that we might be like Him."[3] Our mortal bodies are "all important to us," said President Brigham Young, and "we are in this state of being for the express purpose of obtaining habitations for our spirits to dwell in, that they may become personages of tabernacle."[4]

It must not be forgotten, however, that there is an hierarchical relationship between the body and the spirit. Elder Erastus Snow provides us with the following perspective on this affiliation:

> [T]he spirit, being first created, [is] of paramount importance, and consequently the body is secondary. The body was not first created and afterward the spirit formed in the tabernacle, but we are informed in the revelations that God has given, that we were created and organized in the spirit world, in the image and likeness of our Father in heaven, and consequently our physical tabernacles were formed for the benefit and in behalf of the spirit, and adapted to the use of the spirit prepared for its habitation and dwelling place; not to be the master and controller of the spirit, to govern and dictate it, but, on the contrary, to be for the spirit, to be subject to it, under its control, dictation, and guidance in every sense of the word. And it is with this view and for this purpose that the Lord has revealed unto us that those spirits will be held accountable for the acts of the mortal tabernacle; for it is understood that the deeds

done in and by the tabernacle are done by and with the consent of the spirit.[5]

With this being said, we now turn to a revelation in section 45 of the Doctrine and Covenants and learn that when the spirits of men and women are separated from their physical bodies they view their situation as a form of bondage (v. 17). This is true because the "spirit" of a righteous person must be "inseparably connected" to the "elements" of a resurrected body before it can "receive a fullness of joy" (D&C 93:33–34). The Apostle Paul relates that in the day of redemption from the grave "the Lord Jesus Christ . . . shall change our vile [Greek *tapeinosis*—lowly, humble] body, that it may be fashioned like unto His glorious body" (Philip. 3:20–21), and that will bring a fullness of joy indeed.

John Taylor writes that "the object of man's taking a body is, that through the redemption of Jesus Christ, both soul [i.e., spirit] and body may be exalted in the eternal world, when the earth shall be celestial, and to obtain a higher exaltation than he would be capable of doing without a body. For when man was first made, he was made 'a little lower than the angels' (Heb. 2:7); but through the Atonement and Resurrection of Jesus Christ, he is placed in a position to obtain an exaltation higher than that of angels. Says the Apostle, 'know ye not that we shall judge angels?' (1 Cor. 6:3)."[6] Even those people who do not receive a resurrected body of the highest order will still have a great advantage given to them. The Prophet Joseph Smith says that when "spirits have come into this [world and] risen and received glorified bodies they will have an ascendancy over spirits who have no bodies or kept not their first estate, like the devil."[7]

Elder Taylor states that "another object that we came here for, and took bodies, was to propagate our species. For if it is for our benefit to come here, it is also for the benefit of others. Hence the first commandment given to man was, 'Be fruitful and multiply, and replenish the earth, and subdue it' (Gen. 1:28). And as man is an eternal being, and all his actions have a relevancy to eternity, it is necessary that he understand his position well, and thus fulfill the measure of his creation."[8]

When the devil and his followers were cast out of heaven in premortal times they lost the opportunity to receive a physical body.

"Lucifer and his legions rebelled over the choice of the Christ, and were cast down," said Orson F. Whitney. "Failing to keep their first estate, they could not be 'added upon.' This was their punishment— that they should not have bodies, by means of which spirits become souls [see D&C 88:15], capable of eternal progression. All the rest— two-thirds of the population of the spirit world—were given bodies as a reward for keeping their first estate, and were promised a glorious resurrection after death, as a further reward, if they succeeded in keeping their second estate."[9] Elder Orson Pratt made an interesting observation about the fallen spirits. He said, "The devil and his angels having forfeited, in their first estate, all right to enter a second with bodies of flesh and bones, and having lost the privilege of marrying and propagating their species, feel maliciously wicked and envious against the sons of men who kept their first estate and are now in the enjoyment of the second, marrying and increasing their families or kingdoms. These arch seducers," said Elder Pratt, "know full well the blessings which they have lost, and which they see mankind in posses-sion of, namely, the blessings of wives and children. Could they seduce mankind and forbid them to marry, it would greatly gratify their hellish revenge; for they know that all such would lose their promised glory, being left wifeless and childless like themselves, without any possible means of reigning over an endless increase of posterity."[10]

Since the human body plays such a vital role in the plan of salva-tion, the adversary attempts to use it as a weapon against the unwary. "The body or flesh is what the devil has power over," said Brigham Young. "God gave Lucifer power, influence, mastery, and rule—to a certain extent—to control the life pertaining to the elements composing the body."[11] Elder Melvin J. Ballard expounds upon this concept. He says that "all the assaults that the enemy of our souls will make to capture us will be through the flesh, because it is made up of the unredeemed earth [see Gen. 3:17, 19], and he has power over the elements of the earth [see Eph. 2:2; D&C 61:18–19; Rev. 16:14]. The approach he makes to us will be through the lusts, the appetites, the ambitions of the flesh. All the help that comes to us from the Lord to aid us in this struggle will come to us through the spirit that dwells within this mortal body. So these two mighty forces are oper-ating upon us through these two channels."[12]

DEVELOPING DIVINE ATTRIBUTES

An important statement on salvation is found in a series of early Church sermons called the *Lectures on Faith*. In this statement it is pointed out that the "teachings of the Savior most clearly show unto us the nature of salvation, and what He proposed unto the human family when He proposed to save them—that He proposed to make them like unto Himself, and He was like the Father, the great prototype of all saved beings; and for any portion of the human family to be assimilated into their likeness is to be saved."[13] In light of the foregoing it is logical to ask, How do mortals become assimilated into the likeness of the Father and the Son? An article that was published in the *Times and Seasons* in the year 1842 provides the answer to this question. This article submits that "in order for [anyone] to be assimilated [i]nto the likeness of God in the least degree, and be perfect as He is" they must not only obey the first principles and ordinances of the gospel but they must also do three other things. They must 1) increase in their knowledge, 2) order their conduct so that it exemplifies righteousness, and 3)avail themselves of all spiritual blessings.[14]

Knowledge

Joseph Smith spoke often about the acquisition of knowledge and the role that it plays in the plan of salvation. "In knowledge there is power," said the Prophet. "God has more power than all other beings because He has greater knowledge, and hence He knows how to subject all other beings to Him."[15] In the mortal sphere "knowledge is the power of God unto salvation."[16] Indeed, "a man is saved no faster than he gets knowledge [and] if he does not get knowledge he will be brought into captivity by some evil power in the other world as evil spirits will have more knowledge and consequently more power than many men who are on the earth. Hence, [we need] revelation to assist us and give us knowledge of the things of God."[17] This knowledge comes through "prophets, apostles, angels, revelation . . . and visions." It is the "grand key that unlocks the glories and mysteries of the kingdom of heaven."[18]

President Spencer W. Kimball reminds us that "secular knowledge, important as it may be, can never save a soul nor open the celestial kingdom nor create a world nor make a man a god, but it can be most helpful to that man who, placing first things first, has found the way to eternal life and who can now bring into play all knowledge to be his tool and servant."[19] President Brigham Young was one prophet who advocated the acquisition of knowledge in secular fields. He said that the religion of Jesus Christ "holds out every encouragement and inducement possible for [people] to increase in knowledge and intelligence, in every branch of mechani[cs], or in the arts and sciences, for all wisdom and all the arts and sciences in the world are from God and are designed for the good of His people."[20] We should be diligent, said President Young, to learn and "store up the knowledge of heaven and of earth. . . . Read good books [cf. D&C 88:118], and extract from them wisdom and understanding as much as you possibly can, aided by the Spirit of God."[21] The First Presidency of the Church, under the administration of Brother Brigham, encouraged the Saints to "strive to know what God knows, and use that knowledge as God uses it, and then you will be like Him."[22]

Character

President David O. McKay once asked, "What is the crowning glory of man in this earth so far as his individual achievement is concerned?" His answer was simple. "It is character—character developed through obedience to the laws of life as revealed through the gospel of Jesus Christ, who came that we might have life and have it more abundantly [see John 10:10]. Man's chief concern in life should not be the acquiring of gold nor fame nor material possessions. It should not be the development of physical prowess nor of intellectual strength, but his aim, the highest in life, should be the development of a Christlike character."[23]

Jesus Christ asked His New World disciples, "What manner of men ought ye to be?" He answered by saying, "Verily I say unto you, even as I am" (3 Ne. 27:27). In the form of a commandment He has said, "Follow me, and do the things which ye have seen me do" (2 Ne. 31:12). President Howard W. Hunter explained that "to follow an individual means to watch him or listen to him closely; to accept his authority, to take him as a leader, and to obey him; to support and advocate his ideas; and to take him as a model. . . . Just as teachings that do not conform to Christ's doctrine are false, so a life that does not conform to Christ's example is misdirected, and may not achieve its high potential destiny."[24] President Hunter also taught that those who desire to rise above their worldly nature must "think more of holy things and act more like the Savior would expect His disciples to act. We should at every opportunity ask ourselves, 'What would Jesus do?' and then act more courageously upon the answer."[25]

Those who seek to become like the Lord must willfully separate themselves from unholy things. In the Joseph Smith Translation of the book of Matthew, the Savior is reported to have said, "If any man will come after me, let him deny himself . . . of all ungodliness, and every worldly lust, and keep my commandments" (JST, Matt. 16:25–26). In connection with this, Elder Robert E. Wells of the First Quorum of the Seventy teaches:

> [W]e should not do as the world would have us do, if it is at variance with what Christ did and what He wants us to do. Part of the inspiration of the [Sermon on the Mount] is that it teaches us to lay aside those things which do not contribute to our progress toward eternal life and exaltation. Instead, we are encouraged to sacrifice, to deny ourselves, and to render service to others. We must do His will rather than our own. Self-control will lead to Christ, but that means giving up the things of the world and changing our thoughts, our words, our actions, our habits, our very heart and character in order to become like Him and to think like Him.[26]

Spirituality

Lorenzo Snow reminds us that "we possess in our spiritual organizations the same capabilities, powers and faculties that our Father possesses, although in an infantile state, requiring [us] to pass through a certain course or ordeal by which they will be developed and improved according to the heed we give to the principles we have received."[27] The process of spiritual growth can take an appreciable amount of time. "Newly baptized persons," explained Elder Bruce R. McConkie, "are newborn babes in spiritual things. Growth and strength come gradually. The most stable Saints and powerful prophets did not attain their high states of spiritual maturity all at once. Even the Lord Jesus 'increased in wisdom and stature, and in favor with God and man' (Luke 2:52). Deity gives His truths to the obedient line upon line and precept upon precept. A student cannot learn calculus until he first knows the basic principles of mathematics."[28]

Spiritual growth requires more than just the passage of years, however. A certain amount of exertion is also necessary on the part of the individual. President Howard W. Hunter observed that "developing spirituality and attuning ourselves to the highest influences of godliness is not an easy matter. It takes time and frequently involves a struggle. It will not happen by chance, but is accomplished only through deliberate effort and by calling upon God and keeping His commandments."[29] President Hunter also said that "we must take time to prepare our minds for spiritual things. The development of spiritual capacity does not come with the conferral of authority. There must be desire, effort, and personal preparation. This requires . . . fasting, prayer, searching the scriptures, experience, meditation, and a hungering and thirsting after the righteous life."[30]

President Thomas S. Monson offered a few simple suggestions to those who wish to increase their spiritual capacity. He said that spirituality comes from focusing on Christ every day of one's life. He listed three things that should be done in order to draw nearer to the Savior and to grow in spirituality.

1. "Fill our minds with thoughts of Christ and the kind of thoughts He wants us to have.
2. Fill our hearts with love of Christ, gratitude for His atoning sacrifice, and love for all mankind as He wants us to do.
3. Fill our lives with service to Christ and to everyone about us; serve as He wants us to serve."[31]

TESTS AND TRIALS

Mortality is designed as a testing ground for the children of God. It is "a probationary state; a time to prepare to meet God; a time to prepare for that endless state which . . . is after the resurrection of the dead" (Alma 12:24). In other words, "this day of life . . . is given us to prepare for eternity" (Alma 34:33). An article in the *Encyclopedia of Mormonism* indicates that "God loves all mankind and works to bring His children back to dwell with Him. No one can endure God's presence who has not been purified to become like Him. For this reason, Latter-day Saints view life on this earth as a period of testing and training, a time to instruct, refine, and purify the individual, making the child of God more like the Father."[32]

Part of the test of mortality is to determine whether God's progeny will be obedient to His divine will. In the premortal world the Lord said, "we will *prove* [the children of men] . . . to see if they will do all things whatsoever the Lord their God shall command them" (Abr. 3:25, emphasis added). And to the inhabitants of the earth the Lord said, "I give unto you a commandment, that ye shall *forsake all evil and cleave unto all good*, that ye shall *live by every word which proceedeth forth out of the mouth of God*. For he will give unto the faithful line upon line, precept upon precept; and *I will try you and prove you herewith*" (D&C 98:11–12, emphasis added).

Another part of mortality's test is to see if men and women will be willing to rise above their fallen nature. Elder Bruce R. McConkie of the Quorum of the Twelve Apostles informs us that "God has deliberately and advisedly placed us in the circumstances in which we now find ourselves, with enticements and lusts of every sort around us, for the very purpose of determining whether we will overcome the world, whether we will turn to spiritual things rather than be engulfed in carnal things."[33] This same Church leader has also stated that "those of us who arrive at the years of accountability are here to develop and to be tried and tested, to see if we can so live as to *regain the state of innocence and purity which we enjoyed as children*, and thereby be qualified to go where God and Christ are."[34]

Candidates for the highest degree of the heavenly world can expect that they will be tested in a most thorough manner. "If any man or woman expects to enter into the celestial kingdom of our God without making sacrifices and without being tested to the very utmost," said President George Q. Cannon, "they have not understood the gospel. If there is a weak spot in our nature, or if there is a fiber that can be made to quiver or to shrink, we may rest assured that it will be tested. Our own weaknesses will be brought fully to light, and in seeking for help the strength of our God will also be made manifest to us."[35]

The Furnace of Affliction

Not only are the Lord's earthly offspring expected to demonstrate their willingness to obey Him, but they are also expected to overcome a host of tribulations and afflictions. The trials of life have at least four discernable purposes: (1) to give mortals experience, (2) to determine their level of devotion, (3) to develop their faith, and (4) to purify their hearts so that they will be qualified to stand in the presence of holy beings.

Give Experience: The Lord once said to the Prophet Joseph Smith: "If the very jaws of hell shall gape open the mouth wide after thee, know thou . . . that all these things shall give thee experience, and shall be for thy good" (D&C 122:7). In the Joseph Smith Translation of the book of Hebrews it is made known that "without sufferings [we] could not be made perfect" (JST, Heb. 11:40). Why is this so? According to Lorenzo Snow, "we are here that we may be educated in a school of suffering and of fiery trials, which school was necessary for Jesus, our elder brother, who, the scriptures tell us, was made perfect through suffering [see Heb. 2:10]. It is necessary [that] we suffer in all things, that we may be qualified and worthy to rule and govern all things, even as our Father in heaven and His eldest Son Jesus."[36] John Taylor taught that "it is necessary . . . that we pass through the school of suffering, trial, affliction, and privation [in order] to know ourselves, to know others, and to know our God."[37]

Determine Devotion: The Prophet Joseph Smith reportedly told the Twelve Apostles, "You will have all kinds of trials to pass through. And it is quite as necessary for you to be tried as it was for Abraham and other men of God. . . . God will feel after you, and He will take hold of you and wrench your very heart strings, and if you cannot stand it you will not be fit for an inheritance in the celestial kingdom of God."[38] This statement is in perfect accord with the Lord's own pronouncement found in Doctrine and Covenants section 98 verses 14 and 15. This passage reads: "I will prove you in all things, whether you will abide in my covenant, even unto death, that you may be found worthy. For if ye will not abide in my covenant ye are not worthy of me."

Develop Faith: "I will try the faith of my people," declared the Lord God of Israel (3 Ne. 26:11). And surely, the Saints can expect the Lord to be true to His word. James E. Faust explained that faith can be strengthened during the tribulations of mortality. "In the pain, the agony, and the heroic endeavors of life, we pass through the refiner's fire, and the insignificant and the unimportant in our lives can melt away like dross and make our faith bright, intact, and strong. In this way the divine image can be mirrored from the soul. It is part of the purging toll exacted of some to become acquainted with God. In the agonies of life, we seem to listen better to the faint, godly whisperings of the Divine Shepherd."[39]

Celestial Preparation: In one latter-day revelation the Lord reminds the Saints that for the present time they cannot behold "the glory which shall follow after much tribulation." Nevertheless, He assures His followers that "he that is faithful in tribulation, the reward of the same is greater in the kingdom of heaven" (D&C 58:2–3). In another revelation the Lord is more specific regarding this glorious prize. He says, "My people must be tried in all things, that they may be prepared to receive the glory that I have for them, even the glory of Zion" (D&C 136:31). And what is the glory of Zion? It is the glory of the celestial kingdom (see D&C 76:66, 70).

The Lord is working with us, said George Q. Cannon. "He is trying us . . . that He may approve of us in every respect. If we have set out to obtain celestial glory, the precious and inestimable gift of eternal lives, there [isn't any] trial necessary for our purification and perfection as Saints of God that we will not have to meet, contend with and overcome." Such trials, said Elder Cannon, "will come in various shapes, on the right hand and on the left, whether they be in having everything move on prosperously, or in adversity, hardship and the laying down of our lives for the truth." These trials will continue "until the design [of the Lord] is fully accomplished and the dross of our natures is purified and these earthly tabernacles are redeemed from everything that is groveling and low and brought into entire subjection to the mind and will of God."[40]

During the various tribulations of mortal life it must never be forgotten that "no pain that we suffer, no trial that we experience is wasted." Indeed, said Elder Orson F. Whitney, "it ministers to our education, to the development of such qualities as patience, faith, fortitude, and humility. All that we suffer builds up our characters, purifies our hearts, expands our souls, and makes us more tender and charitable, more worthy to be called the children of God. . . . [I]t is through sorrow and suffering, toil and tribulation, that we gain the education that we come here to acquire and which will make us more like our Father and Mother in heaven."[41]

NOTES: CHAPTER 4

1. George D. Watt, comp., *Journal of Discourses* (London, England: F. D. and S. W. Richards and Sons, 1854–1886), 19:259–60, hereafter cited as *JD*. The great objectives of the plan of salvation, said the Prophet Joseph Smith, are for the "King of heaven" to bring His children back into His presence "in the celestial glory" and crown them as "heirs with the Son" (B. H. Roberts, ed., *History of the Church*, rev. ed. [Salt Lake City: The Church of Jesus Christ of Latter-day Saints, 1932–1951], 2:5).

2. Andrew F. Ehat and Lyndon W. Cook, eds., *The Words of Joseph Smith: The Contemporary Accounts of the Nauvoo Discourses of the Prophet Joseph* (Orem, Utah: Grandin Book, 1991), 247, hereafter cited as *WJS*. Brigham Young echoed the Prophet's teaching. He said, "The Lord created you and me for the purpose of becoming gods like Himself—when we have been proved in our present capacity, and been faithful with all things [that] He puts into our possession. We are created, we are born for the express purpose of growing up from the low estate of manhood, to become gods like unto our Father in heaven. That is the truth about it, just as it is. The Lord has organized mankind for the express purpose of increasing in that intelligence and truth which is with God, until he is capable of creating worlds on worlds, and becoming gods, even the sons of God. How many will become thus privileged? Those who honor the Father and the Son; those who receive the Holy Ghost, and magnify their calling, and are found pure and holy; they shall be crowned in the presence of the Father and the Son" (*JD*, 3:93).

3. Conference Report, April 1976, 118, hereafter cited as CR. President George Albert Smith tells us that our "body has been given to us as a reward for faithfulness in the spirit world before we came here" (Robert McIntosh and Susan McIntosh, eds., *The Teachings of George Albert Smith* [Salt Lake City: Bookcraft, 1996], 16). Along with this marvelous gift comes a high expectation. "We came to this earth," said the Prophet Joseph Smith, "that we might have a body and present it pure before God in the celestial kingdom" (*WJS*, 60).

4. *JD*, 9:286.

5. Ibid., 8:217.

6. John Taylor, *The Government of God* (Liverpool, England: S. W. Richards, 1852), 33–34.

7. *WJS*, 205. The Prophet made the following comments about the devil and physical bodies. "The mortification of Satan consists in his not being permitted to take a body. He sometimes gets possession of a body but when the proven authorities turn him out-of-doors he finds it was not his but a stolen one" (ibid., 208). "The devil has no body, and herein is his punishment. He is pleased when he can obtain the tabernacle of man and when cast out by the Savior he asked to go into the herd of swine showing that he would prefer a swine's body to having none" (ibid., 60).

8. Taylor, *The Government of God*, 34–35. President Taylor made some similar remarks that bear repeating. "Man was created in the image of God, and he was the offspring of Deity Himself, and consequently made in His likeness; and being made in that likeness, he was a son of God, and the very object of his being planted upon the earth was that he might multiply. Why? That the spirits which had existed with their Heavenly Father might have tabernacles to inhabit and become mortal, and, through the possession of these tabernacles and the plan of salvation, that they might be raised to greater dignity, glory and exaltation than it would be possible for them to enjoy without these. . . . God had a purpose, therefore, in the organization of this earth, and in the placing of man upon it, and He has never deviated one hair to the right or to the left in regard to man and his destiny from that time until the present" (*JD*, 17:370).

9. Orson F. Whitney, *Gospel Themes* (Salt Lake City: The Church of Jesus Christ of Latter-day Saints, 1914), 145.

10. *The Seer*, vol. 1, no. 5, May 1853, 79.

11. *JD*, 3:277. President Young also taught that "the spirit is pure, and under the special control and influence of the Lord, but the body is of the earth, and is subject to the power of the devil, and is under the mighty influence of that fallen nature that is of the earth. If the spirit yields to the body, the devil then has power to overcome both the body and [the] spirit" (ibid., 2:256).

12. *New Era*, March 1984, 35.

13. *Lectures on Faith* (Salt Lake City: Deseret Book, 1985), 79.

14. *Times and Seasons*, vol. 3, no. 6, 15 January 1842, 656–57. An interesting statement on perfection is found in this same source. It reads: "*Perfection*, in the extended import of the word, is that which is beyond improvement. Christ commanded His people, saying: 'Be ye therefore perfect, even as your Father who is in heaven is perfect.' We do not understand from this, that mankind while in a state of probation on earth, are to become perfect in all things, as the Lord is, or to that degree that He is; but that we have appointed unto us a certain sphere to act in, and that we can be perfect in it; and that we have certain laws to comply with, and we can harmoniously do it. . . . It is not to be expected that mankind are required to be perfect in all things, while in a state of mortality, as God is. His power is unlimited; but we have a certain sphere to act in; therefore our intelligence is limited; but as we have before stated, we can be perfect in this sphere; or in other words we can obey the law of the Lord, walk circumspectly, orderly, and harmoniously before Him" (ibid., 655, emphasis in original).

15. *WJS*, 183. "The reason why God is greater than all others is He knows how to subject all things to Himself. Knowledge is power" (ibid., 189–90).

16. Ibid., 207.

17. Ibid., 113–14.

18. Ibid., 201–202.

19. Edward L. Kimball, ed., *The Teachings of Spencer W. Kimball* (Salt Lake City: Bookcraft, 1982), 390–91.

20. *JD*, 13:147.

21. Ibid., 12:124.

22. *Millennial Star*, vol. 14, no. 2, 15 January 1852, 22, hereafter cited as *MS*. Brigham Young said that "there are a great many branches of education: some go to college to learn languages, some to study law, some to study [medicine], and some to study

astronomy, and various other branches of science. . . . But our favorite study is that branch which particularly belongs to the Elders of Israel—namely, theology. Every Elder should become a profound theologian—should understand this branch better than all the world" (*JD*, 6:317; cf. D&C 97:12–14).

23. *Instructor*, August 1965, 301.

24. *Ensign*, September 1994, 2.

25. *Ensign*, November 1994, 87.

26. Robert E. Wells, *The Mount and the Master* (Salt Lake City: Deseret Book, 1991), xiii.

27. *JD*, 14:300.

28. Bruce R. McConkie, *Doctrinal New Testament Commentary* (Salt Lake City: Bookcraft, 1973), 3:290.

29. *Ensign*, May 1979, 25–26.

30. Clyde J. Williams, ed., *The Teachings of Howard W. Hunter* (Salt Lake City: Bookcraft, 1997), 36.

31. Quoted in Wells, *The Mount and the Master,* 210.

32. Daniel H. Ludlow, ed., *Encyclopedia of Mormonism* (New York: Macmillan, 1992), 1:264–65. Joseph Smith said, "If you wish to go where God is you must be like God or possess the principles which God possesses. For if we are not drawing towards God in principle we are going [away] from Him and drawing towards the devil. . . . Search your hearts and see if you are like God; I have searched mine and feel to repent of all my sins" (*WJS*, 113).

33. CR, April 1958, 70.

34. *Ensign*, April 1977, 4, emphasis added.

35. Jerreld L. Newquist, ed., *Gospel Truth: Discourses and Writings of President George Q. Cannon* (Salt Lake City: Deseret Book, 1987), 304.

36. *MS*, vol. 13, no. 23, 1 December 1851, 363.

37. *JD*, 1:148.

38. Ibid., 24:197.

39. *Ensign*, May 1979, 53. President George Q. Cannon said that "God will have a tried people. He will bring us through the furnace of affliction, and if we endure the fiery trial, the dross of our natures will be burned out and the gold will appear the brighter and the purer" (*Juvenile Instructor*, vol. 22, no. 1,

1 January 1887, 8). This is similar to a statement made by John Taylor. He said that suffering and trials are "for the purpose of purifying the Saints of God, that they may be, as the scriptures say, as gold that has been seven times purified by the fire" (*JD*, 23:336).

40. *JD*, 10:347.

41. *Improvement Era*, March 1966, 211.

CHAPTER 5

ORDINANCES OF SALVATION

The English word *ordinance* is derived from the Latin word *ordinare*, "which means to put in order or sequence."[1] The Lord has declared that His house is "a house of order" and "not a house of confusion" (D&C 132:8; cf. 88:119). Furthermore, says the Savior, "none shall be exempted from the . . . laws of God, that all things may be done in order" (D&C 107:84).

The Prophet Joseph Smith revealed that "the order and ordinances of the kingdom were instituted by the Priesthood in the Council of heaven before the world was" formed.[2] "All these ordinances and ceremonies instituted by the Almighty and comprehended in that which is called the gospel are necessary," said Charles W. Penrose. "There is no such thing as non-essential ordinances; every one of them is essential. Exaltation cannot be arrived at without them."[3] Those people who deliberately choose not to comply with these divinely established rites will face dire consequences. Joseph Smith tells us that those people who "have not taken upon themselves those ordinances and signs which God ordained for man to receive in order to receive a celestial glory" will seek to enter that realm "in vain for God will not receive them." The Father has "decreed that all who will not obey His voice shall not escape the damnation of hell. What is the damnation of hell? To go with that society who have not obeyed [God's] commands."[4]

In conjunction with the order of heaven, the Lord demands that ordinances be performed only by His duly authorized representatives.

According to the Prophet Joseph Smith "a man must be called of God, by prophecy, and by the laying on of hands by those who are in authority" before he can "administer in the ordinances" (A of F #5). Without the authority of the Priesthood, said the Prophet, "the ordinances could not be administered in righteousness."[5] Elder John A. Widtsoe points out that since "The Church of Jesus Christ of Latter-day Saints is in possession of the Priesthood [it] is sufficient to make any and every ordinance administered by due authority within the Church an event of supreme importance. In performing any such ordinance the one who officiates speaks and acts, not of himself and of his personal authority, but by virtue of his ordination and appointment as a representative of the powers of heaven."[6] Without Priesthood "authority," says a modern-day revelation, "the power of godliness" cannot be "manifest unto men in the flesh" through the "ordinances" (D&C 84:19–21).

The ordinances of the gospel of Jesus Christ are designed to bring about a new birth and transform a person from an earthly being to a heavenly being. Joseph Smith indicates that "being born again comes by the Spirit of God through ordinances."[7] An article in one of the Church's early publications speaks of the transformation that is accomplished through the reception of these rites. It says, "The baptism of water in the likeness of a new birth, and of the Spirit through the laying on of hands, the washings and anointings, and the holy ordinances of the House of God are all designed for the purification and sanctification of the spirit and of the body of man. The earthly tabernacle that has thus been purified, sanctified, and cleansed is fitted to receive a resurrection in the celestial glory; to come forth from the grave a glorious, resplendent, effulgent form surpassing in its lustrous splendor the brilliancy of the sun at noonday. It is with such a tabernacle as this that the spirits of Saints, elected to a celestial glory, will be clothed."[8]

With all of these concepts firmly fixed in our minds let us now examine the ordinances of salvation and exaltation and learn something of their form, nature, and meaning.

BAPTISM BY IMMERSION

Shortly after the Savior had risen from the tomb, He commanded His apostles in the Old World to baptize all of those who heard the gospel and believed in Him (see Matt. 28:16–20). "He that believeth and is baptized shall be *saved*," said the Lord, "but he that believeth not shall be *damned*" (Mark 16:15–16, emphasis added). Since baptism is classified as "the counsel of God" (Luke 7:29–30) the Savior said that those who will not receive it "cannot enter into the kingdom of God" (John 3:1–5; cf. 1 Pet. 3:21; Titus 3:5). In the latter days the Lord has made this undeviating declaration: "Verily, verily, I say unto you, they who . . . are not baptized in water in my name, for the remission of their sins, that they may receive the Holy Ghost, shall be damned, and shall not come into my Father's kingdom where my Father and I am" (D&C 84:74).

The Age of Accountability

Latter-day scriptures teach that "little children are redeemed from the foundation of the world through [the] Only Begotten. Wherefore, they cannot sin, for power is not given unto Satan to tempt little children until they begin to become accountable" before God (D&C 29:46–47). The scriptures specify that "children are not accountable before [God] until they are eight years old" (JST, Gen. 17:11) and "no one can be received into the Church of Christ unless he has arrived unto the years of accountability before God, and is capable of repentance" (D&C 20:71; cf. 18:41–42).

Baptism is taken very seriously by the Lord. A divine "law" decreed for parents in the Church necessitates that they "teach their children to pray, and to walk uprightly before the Lord" and also "teach them . . . to understand the doctrine of repentance, faith in Christ the Son of the living God, and of baptism and the gift of the Holy Ghost by the laying on of the hands, when eight years old." Failure to comply with this law will bring the condemnation and accountability of "sin . . . upon the heads of the parents" (D&C 68:25–28).

The Lord recognizes that some mortals will never arrive at a state of "knowledge" or "understanding" because of various mental handicaps (D&C 29:49–50). Such persons are "without the law" in the Lord's estimation and since they are "under no condemnation [they] cannot repent; and unto such baptism availeth nothing." In the infinite mercy of Jesus Christ "the power of redemption cometh on all them that have no law" (Moro. 8:22–24).[9]

Immersion Is the Only Legitimate Method

Elder Delbert L. Stapley of the Quorum of the Twelve Apostles said that "man must unlearn the idea that any and all baptisms are acceptable unto God. There is only one true mode of baptism, and that is immersion."[10] In support of this statement we turn to the writings of Elder James E. Talmage, who points out that the verb "baptize," as found in the New Testament, comes from the Greek word *bapto* or *baptizo* and literally means "to dip or to immerse."[11]

Baptism by immersion is as old as Adam. We are informed in the Pearl of Great Price that the first man "was carried down into the water, and was laid under the water, and was brought forth out of the water. And thus he was baptized" (Moses 6:64–65). When John the Baptist restored the authority to baptize to Joseph Smith and Oliver Cowdery in 1829, he indicated that this power was to be used for "baptism by immersion" (D&C 13:1). When Joseph Smith and Oliver Cowdery authored the "Articles and Covenants of the Church of Christ" (D&C 20) they included instructions on the baptismal rite. Those instructions were recorded as follows:

> Baptism is to be administered in the following manner unto all those who repent—
>
> The person who is called of God and has authority from Jesus Christ to baptize, shall go down into the water with the person who has presented himself or herself for baptism, and shall say, calling him or her by name: "Having been commissioned of Jesus Christ, I baptize you in the name of the Father, and of the Son, and of the Holy Ghost. Amen."
>
> Then shall he *immerse* him or her in the water, and come forth again out of the water (D&C 20:72–74, emphasis added).

President Joseph F. Smith made it clear that unless a baptism is performed "in the manner prescribed," and by one who is duly commissioned by divine authority, it is not valid but is "illegal and will not be accepted by [God], nor will it effect a remission of sins, the object for which it is designed."[12]

Symbolism in the Baptismal Ordinance

There are several layers of symbolism associated with the baptismal ordinance. We will briefly examine a few of them on the pages that follow.

Immersion: Baptism reflects the death and Resurrection of the Lord Jesus Christ. In Romans chapter 6 verses 2 through 6 the Apostle Paul teaches that when the disciples of the Savior are immersed in water it symbolizes that their "old" self has become "dead to sin;" they are therefore symbolically buried in a grave. After these believers have been "buried with [Christ] . . . in the likeness of his death" they are brought forth out of the water "in the likeness of his Resurrection;" they therefore arise to a "newness of life" without sin.

Baptismal fonts are typically designed so as to allow the person being baptized to be physically laid below the level of the ground. "The ordinance of baptism by water, to be immersed therein . . . and come forth out of the water is in the likeness of the resurrection of the dead in coming forth out of their graves," said Joseph Smith. The Nauvoo Temple's "baptismal font was instituted as a similitude of the grave, and was [thus] commanded to be [located] in a place *underneath* where the living are [accustomed] to assemble" (D&C 128:12–13, emphasis added).

Water: In December of 1830 the Savior said to His Saints, "I give unto thee a *commandment*, that thou shalt *baptize by water*" (D&C 35:6, emphasis added). The water's symbolic function is identified by the Lord in Doctrine and Covenants section 39 verse 10 where He says, "Arise and be baptized, and *wash away your sins*" (emphasis added). The same imagery can be found in the seventh chapter and fourteenth verse of the book of Alma which says, "come and be baptized unto repentance, that ye may be *washed from your sins*" (emphasis added; see also D&C 76:51–52; Acts 22:16).

White Clothing: Several scriptural passages present the startling imagery of garments being washed white through the atoning blood of Jesus Christ. The Savior employed this symbolism when He said that "no unclean thing can enter into [the Father's] kingdom" and nobody can enter into His rest "save it be those who have washed their garments in my blood" (3 Ne. 27:19). And again, in the book of Alma it is stated, "for there can no man be saved except his garments are washed white; yea, his garments must be purified until they are cleansed from all stain, through the blood of him . . . who should come to redeem his people from their sins" (Alma 5:21; see also 13:11; Rev. 1:5; 7:14; Ether 13:10–11).

Right Arm to the Square: In the scriptural accounts of the baptismal ordinance there is no mention of the officiator raising his right arm to the square, as is the custom among contemporary Latter-day Saints (see D&C 20:72–74; Matt. 3:13–17; Mosiah 18:12–16). In a 1951 issue of a Church periodical called the *Improvement Era*, the Presiding Bishopric published instructions for performing the baptismal rite and therein stated that the person who officiates in the ordinance should have their "right hand and arm raised to a square behind the candidate."[13] This procedure is mentioned as early as 1938 by Elder Rulon S. Wells of the Quorum of the Seventy. He said that "when we enter into the waters of baptism, we go in company with a servant of the Lord who has been commissioned of Jesus Christ to perform that sacred ordinance. In performing this ceremony the duly authorized servant of God will take the candidate's hands into his left hand, and raise his right hand to the square, saying this: 'Having been commissioned of Jesus Christ I baptize you in the name of the Father, and of the Son, and of the Holy Ghost. Amen.'" Elder Wells then explained that "this is the formality of entering into the covenant with God. And those who do thus enter into that covenant do so with a full understanding that they are to keep His holy commandments."[14]

In an earlier era of Church history it was the baptismal candidates themselves who made the covenant by raising their own right arm to the square (cf. Gen. 14:22; Deut. 32:40; Rev. 10:5–6). Elder George F. Richards of the Quorum of the Twelve Apostles relates the following:

> The greatest and most important blessings our Heavenly
> Father has for His faithful sons and daughters are received

by covenant. One of the greatest blessings He has to bestow is membership in His Church and kingdom. This is received by solemn covenant.

When I was baptized, and confirmed a member of The Church of Jesus Christ of Latter-day Saints [in 1873], I was required to raise my right arm to the square, and covenant before God, angels, and witnesses present, that I would henceforth keep the commandments of God, as fast as they should be made known unto me. This represents the nature of the covenant entered into, by every person who is baptized and confirmed a member of The Church of Jesus Christ of Latter-day Saints. It is frequently spoken of as the covenant made in the waters of baptism.[15]

Baptism Is for the Celestial Kingdom

President Joseph Fielding Smith asked, "Will those who enter the terrestrial and telestial kingdoms have to have the ordinance of baptism?" He answered with an emphatic "No! Baptism is the door into the celestial kingdom. The Lord made this clear to Nicodemus [see John 3:1–5]. We are not preaching a salvation for the inhabitants of the terrestrial or the telestial kingdoms. *All of the ordinances of the gospel pertain to the celestial kingdom, and what the Lord will require by way of ordinances, if any, in the other kingdoms He has not revealed.*"[16] A statement made by the First Presidency of The Church of Jesus Christ of Latter-day Saints confirms this view. These presiding authorities say, "We know of no ordinances pertaining to the terrestrial or the telestial kingdom. All of the ordinances of the gospel are given for the salvation of men in the celestial kingdom and pertain unto that kingdom."[17] As put so succinctly by Elder Bruce R. McConkie, "Baptism pertains to the celestial kingdom and to no other."[18]

CONFIRMATION AND GIFT OF THE HOLY GHOST

After baptism has been administered to a disciple of Jesus Christ, confirmation—which is a two-fold ceremony—takes place. The Lord has directed by revelation that the newly baptized are to be "confirmed" in His Church "by the laying on of the hands of the *elders*," meaning those who hold the Melchizedek Priesthood (D&C 20:68, emphasis added; see also 33:15). During this rite the officiator, who usually stands at the head of a circle of Priesthood bearers, speaks the following phrase after calling the person by their full name: "We confirm you a member of The Church of Jesus Christ of Latter-day Saints, and say unto you, receive the Holy Ghost."[19]

At the most basic level, confirmation is defined as "a Church rite supplementing baptism, which admits the person to membership and to the privileges of the Church."[20] Joseph Fielding Smith mentions in his writings that "those who are not literal descendants of Abraham and Israel must *become* such, and *when they are baptized and confirmed they are grafted into the tree and are entitled to all the rights and privileges as heirs*"[21] (see Rom. 11:17–24; Jacob 5:1–77; 2 Ne. 30:2; 1 Ne. 15:16). He further states that "all souls coming into the Church become the seed of Abraham according to the promise, and there is a literal change which comes over them by which they are grafted into the House of Israel even if they are not literally of his lineage."[22] The Prophet Joseph Smith said that this change is brought about by the Holy Ghost.[23]

Dr. George H. Brimhall, Professor N. L. Nelson, and Professor J. B. Keeler expressed the idea that "in its widest sense, confirmation is evidently the witness of the Holy Ghost that the ordinance of baptism just performed is counted valid by God, (1) as a token of the remission of the subject's sins, and (2) as a testimony of his acceptance in the kingdom of God. In other words, just as baptism is the witness from the earth-side of life that a covenant has been made, so confirmation is the witness of the heaven-side. Entrance into the kingdom requires both witnesses." These educators point out that "no sooner was Christ baptized than the covenant He had made was confirmed by His receiving the Holy Ghost. Wherefore Christ says: 'Except a man be born of the water *and of the Spirit*, he cannot enter the kingdom of God.' There are thus two doors, it seems—an outer and an inner. Baptism admits through the first, and confirmation through the second." It might therefore be said that "the Holy Ghost confirms the ordinance of baptism."[24]

Adam was the first person to receive "the gift of the Holy Ghost"

(Moses 6:52). After he had been baptized by immersion "the Spirit of God descended upon him, and thus he was born of the Spirit, and became quickened in the inner man. And he heard a voice out of heaven saying: 'Thou art baptized with fire, and with the Holy Ghost'" (Moses 6:65–66).[25] All of the Father's children are to follow Adam's example in receiving this divine gift.

Symbolism of the Ordinance

The Lord has issued a commandment to the leaders of His restored Church in regard to the bestowal of the Holy Ghost. He says, "It shall come to pass that on as many as ye shall baptize with water, ye shall lay your hands, and they shall receive the gift of the Holy Ghost" (D&C 39:23). The laying on of hands, according to Brother Richard O. Cowan, "is a tangible representation of the link necessary to transmit a blessing, gift, or Priesthood authority from one person to another."[26] It is apparent from Doctrine and Covenants section 36 verse 2 that the person who takes this action in the confirmation rite stands as a proxy for the Lord Jesus Christ. In this passage the Lord states, "*I will lay my hand upon you by the hand of my servant* . . . and you shall receive my Spirit, the Holy Ghost, even the Comforter, which shall teach you the peaceable things of the kingdom" (emphasis added).

Purpose of the Ordinance

Men such as Wilford Woodruff, Heber J. Grant, and George Q. Cannon have all taught that the gift of the Holy Ghost is sealed upon a person when the officiator's hands are laid upon their head.[27] The command that is given by the Lord's proxy on this occasion is "Receive the Holy Ghost" (cf. John 20:22). President Charles W. Penrose points out that "the gift is ours whether we act upon it or receive it or not."[28] Spencer W. Kimball informed a gathering of Latter-day Saints that the enjoyment of this gift depended on them. He said, "When you received your confirmation, *you* were commanded to receive the Holy Ghost. *He* was not obligated to seek you out. The Lord says, 'I will visit thy brethren according to their diligence in keeping my commandments' (Enos 1:10). If our lives are responsive and clean, if we are reaching and cultivating, the Holy

Ghost will come, and we may retain Him and have the peace His presence thus affords."[29]

President Charles W. Penrose explains the nature of this extraordinary and precious gift:

> It is a greater and higher endowment of the same Spirit which enlightens every man that comes into the world; a greater power given unto us as an abiding witness, to be a light to our feet and a lamp to our path; as a restraint against sin, to guide us into all truth, to open up the vision of the mind, to bring things past to our remembrance, and to make manifest things to come. It is the Spirit of truth that reveals the things of the Father and the Son, proceeding from the presence of the Almighty and the very glory in which He is enrobed, which makes Him like unto a consuming fire.
>
> If we receive that heavenly gift [we] all are brought into communion with Him; we can understand something concerning Him, that we may pattern after Him until we become like Him; for if we are continually guided by that Spirit, eventually we will come back to His presence and be able to enjoy the fullness of His glory. And while we remain in the flesh He will not be a stranger to us; we will not walk in the dark like the majority of mankind, but we will be the children of light, comprehending the truth as it is in Him, and seeing the path in which we should walk.[30]

The gift of the Holy Ghost is essential to every individual's salvation. Those who receive this gift have the opportunity to be "cleansed" and "sanctified" by the power of the third member of the Godhead (Moro. 6:4; 3 Ne. 27:20). The prophet Nephi made it known that after "baptism by water . . . *then* cometh a remission of your sins *by fire and by the Holy Ghost*" (2 Ne. 31:17, emphasis added). Elder Bruce R. McConkie expounds upon this particular point of doctrine:

> Sins are remitted not in the waters of baptism, as we say in speaking figuratively, but when we receive the Holy Ghost.

It is the Holy Spirit of God that erases carnality and brings us into a state of righteousness. We become clean when we actually receive the fellowship and companionship of the Holy Ghost. It is then that sin and dross and evil are burned out of our souls as though by fire. The baptism of the Holy Ghost is the baptism of fire. There have been miraculous occasions when visible flames enveloped penitent persons, but ordinarily the cleansing power of the Spirit simply dwells, unseen and unheralded, in the hearts of those who have made the Lord their friend.[31]

THE SACRAMENT

When Jesus Christ instituted the sacrament[32] of bread and wine[33] among His Old World Apostles He taught them that the bread represented His body and the wine represented His blood which was about to be shed "for the remission of sins" (Matt. 26:26–29; see also Mark 14:22–25; Luke 22:19–20). The Lord instructed His disciples to partake of these emblems "in remembrance" of His sacrifice (1 Cor. 11:24–26). When the Lord instituted the sacrament among the Nephites in the New World He assured them that if they would partake of these emblems as "a testimony unto the Father" that they did "always remember" Him they would have His Spirit to be with them (3 Ne. 18:1–11; cf. Moro. 4:1–3; 5:1–2; D&C 20:75–79).

The sacrament provides a weekly opportunity for individuals to "examine" their lives (1 Cor. 11:28) and renew their commitment to keep themselves "unspotted from the world" (D&C 59:9). President David O. McKay draws attention to the fact that the sacrament is associated with "principles fundamental in character building and essential to man's advancement and exaltation in the kingdom of God." In this way it is a ritual of "deep spiritual significance."[34] The Savior's disciples partake of the sacramental emblems in order to "renew spiritual life, and thus keep [their] fellowship with God, that the blood of Christ may cleanse [them] from all sin."[35] The prayers that are said over "the symbols of our salvation," said Elder B. H. Roberts, "evoke in the soul a spiritual power that is as palpably food to the spirit of man as is the material food that he partakes of to strengthen his body from day to day."[36]

Personal Worthiness

Those who might partake of the sanctified sacramental emblems unworthily are warned of the dire consequences for such an action. Both the Lord Jesus Christ and the Apostle Paul have said that persons who do such a thing will reap damnation (3 Ne. 18:29; 1 Cor. 11:29). "The Lord has said that we should not permit anyone to partake of the sacrament unworthily," said President Joseph Fielding Smith. "This means, as I understand it, anyone in the Church who has been in transgression of some kind and who has not repented."[37] Apostle Francis M. Lyman expounded upon this concept:

> It is not pleasing in the sight of the Lord, for us to partake of the sacrament if there be hard feelings in our hearts, if there be jealous[y], if there be enmity or strife, if we are not in fellowship with one another, if we are not in fellowship with the Church, if we are not keeping the commandments of the Lord, if we are not living in peace, if we are not obedient to the counsels of heaven; I say that it is not pleasing in the sight of the Lord to partake of the sacrament under such circumstances. This is an ordinance that should be partaken of properly, understandingly, thoughtfully, and with faith that we will receive an increased portion of the Holy Spirit.[38]

Elder John H. Groberg of the Quorum of the Seventy also had a few words to say in regard to the circumstances under which one partakes of the sacrament. Since no mortal functions in a state of absolute perfection, Elder Groberg confirmed the following:

> If we desire to improve (which is to repent) and are not under Priesthood restriction, then, in my opinion, we are worthy. If, however, we have no desire to improve, if we have no intention of following the guidance of the Spirit, we must ask: Are we worthy to partake, or are we making a mockery of the very purpose of the sacrament, which is to

act as a catalyst for personal repentance and improvement? If we remember the Savior and all He has done and will do for us, we will improve our actions and thus come closer to Him, which keeps us on the road to eternal life. If, however, we refuse to repent and improve, if we do not remember Him and keep His commandments, then we have stopped our growth, and that is damnation to our souls. The sacrament is an intensely personal experience, and we are the ones who knowingly are worthy or otherwise.[39]

Sacrament Prayers

It is commonly said among Latter-day Saints that when they partake of the sacrament they are renewing their baptismal covenant. Marion G. Romney points out why this is so. He says that the elements listed in the sacrament prayers amount to "a virtual renewal of the covenant of baptism."[40] Indeed, a comparison between the sacrament prayers and a passage in the Book of Mormon demonstrates that they have a close relationship. Mosiah chapter 18 verse 10 states that when people are baptized in the name of the Lord they "witness before Him that [they] have entered into a covenant with Him, that [they] will serve Him and keep His commandments, that He may pour out His Spirit more abundantly upon [them]."

An interesting thing about the sacrament prayers is that the blessings on the bread and water have several thematic similarities (see D&C 20:77, 79). First, they both "bless and sanctify" emblems that are to be distributed among the Saints. Second, they both are centered on a remembrance of the Son of God. Third, they both have to do with offering a witness or testimony unto the Father. And fourth, they both are concerned with an individual's retention of the Spirit.

There is a subtle variation in the wording of the two sacramental prayers that calls for a bit of commentary. The blessing on the bread states that those who partake of it are "willing" to do certain things, while the blessing on the water witnesses that those who partake of it actually "do" certain things. In regard to the blessing on the bread Elder Dallin H. Oaks explains this important distinction:

[W]hat we witness is not that we *take* upon us [Christ's] name but that we are *willing* to do so. In this sense, our witness relates to some future event or status whose attainment is not self-assumed, but depends on the authority or initiative of the Savior Himself.

Scriptural references to the name of Jesus Christ often signify the authority of Jesus Christ. In that sense, our willingness to take upon us His name signifies our willingness to take upon us the authority of Jesus Christ in the sacred ordinances of the temple, and to receive the *highest blessings available* through His authority when He chooses to confer them upon us.[41]

The Right Hand

In biblical texts the right hand is symbolically associated with divine favor (see Matt. 25:31–34, 41). It is also the hand used in ancient oath and covenant ceremonies (see Gen. 14:22; Isa. 62:8). According to Elder Russell M. Nelson "the word *sacrament* comes from two Latin stems: *sacr* meaning 'sacred,' and *ment* meaning 'mind.' It implies sacred thoughts of the mind. Even more compelling," says Elder Nelson, "is the Latin word *sacramentum*, which literally means 'oath or solemn obligation.' Partaking of the sacrament might therefore be thought of as a renewal *by oath* of the covenant previously made in the waters of baptism. It is a sacred mental moment, including (1) a silent oath manifested by the use of one's hand, symbolic of the individual's covenant, and (2) the use of bread and water, symbolic of the great atoning sacrifice of the Savior of the world."

Elder Nelson goes on to say that "the hand used in partaking of the sacrament would logically be the same hand used in making any other sacred oath. For most of us, that would be the right hand. However, sacramental covenants—and other eternal covenants as well—can be and are made by those who have lost the use of the right hand."[42]

Forgiveness of Sins

Since baptismal covenants are renewed each time the sacrament is taken, it is not uncommon for some people to view the sacramental rite as a sort of weekly rebaptism. However, several leaders of the LDS

Church have indicated that this is a mistaken idea. President Anthon H. Lund, former First Counselor in the First Presidency, said to the Saints, "We do not partake of the sacrament for the remission of sins, as they do in many of the different churches. We believe that baptism was instituted for the remission of sins, and that having received the Spirit of God, if we humbly repent of what wrongs we have done, and earnestly seek the Lord's forgiveness, that forgiveness may come to us."[43] These thoughts are in accordance with President George Q. Cannon's statement that "if the Church observes the sacrament properly, sins are confessed and forgiveness is obtained *before* partaking of the bread and the contents of the cup."[44]

Elder James E. Talmage of the Quorum of the Twelve Apostles writes along similar lines. He explains that "the sacrament has not been established as a specific means of securing remission of sins; nor for any other special blessing aside from that of a continuing endowment of the Holy Spirit, which, however, comprises all needful blessings." Elder Talmage also makes the observation that "were the sacrament ordained specifically for the remission of sins, it would not be forbidden to those who are in greatest need of forgiveness; yet participation in the ordinance is restricted to those whose consciences are void of serious offense, those, therefore, who are acceptable before the Lord, those indeed who are in as little need of special forgiveness as mortals can be."[45]

PRIESTHOOD CONFERRAL

"What is the Priesthood?" asked President Joseph F. Smith. He replied that "it is nothing more nor less than the power of God delegated to man by which man can act in the earth for the salvation of the human family, in the name of the Father and the Son and the Holy Ghost, and act legitimately."[46] Elder LeGrand Richards explains that John the Baptist restored the Aaronic Priesthood to the earth, and Peter, James, and John "restored the Melchizedek Priesthood with the holy apostleship." With the bestowal of this authority, said Elder Richards, the Lord's people "were again empowered by ordination to perform holy ordinances here upon the earth necessary for the salva-

tion and exaltation of men." The Priesthood is required so that ordinances will be "binding in the heavens" as well as on the earth.[47] It
was President Wilford Woodruff's teaching that "everything that God
has caused to be done for the salvation of man, from the coming of
man upon the earth to the redemption of the world, has been and
will be by virtue of the everlasting Priesthood."[48]

"All [of the] ordinances of the gospel are necessary to salvation,"
said Elder George F. Richards, "and no ordinances are administered
without the Priesthood. There is no salvation, therefore, but by the
Priesthood."[49] It is the Melchizedek Priesthood which holds the power
and authority to "administer in spiritual things," and without the
authority and ordinances of that particular Priesthood "the power of
godliness is not manifest unto men in the flesh" (D&C 107:8). And
without the power of godliness no person will be able to enter into
the presence of the Lord (D&C 84:19–22). The Prophet Joseph
Smith taught that "if you wish to go where God is, you must be like
God or possess the principles which God possesses."[50] Hence the need
for the Priesthood and its rites.

Elder George F. Richards informs us that "a man cannot attain to
[the] highest exaltation without his holding the Priesthood [and] a
woman may not be exalted without being the sealed wife of a man
who holds the Priesthood."[51] Elder Bruce R. McConkie concurs with
this statement and he specifies that "brethren whose calling and election is made sure always hold the holy Melchizedek Priesthood.
Without this delegation of power and authority they cannot be sealed
up unto eternal life."[52] It should be noted that those persons who
reach the highest level of salvation obtain the *fullness* of the
Melchizedek Priesthood. Indeed, said Joseph Fielding Smith, "there is
no exaltation in the kingdom of God without the fullness of the
Priesthood."[53]

The Prophet Joseph Smith told a group of Latter-day Saints in
Nauvoo, Illinois, that the "fullness of the . . . Priesthood" constitutes
a man "a king and priest after the order of Melchizedek."[54] Brigham
Young taught the very same doctrine. He said that "for any person to
have the fullness of [the Melchizedek] Priesthood, he must be a king
and priest."[55] For some elaboration on this point we turn to the writings of President Joseph Fielding Smith:

When [a man] has proved himself by a worthy life, having been faithful in all things required of him, then it is his privilege to receive other covenants and to take upon himself other obligations which will make of him an heir, and he will become a member of the "Church of the Firstborn." Into his hands "the Father has given all things." He will be a priest and a king, receiving of the Father's fullness and of His glory. . . . *[T]he fullness of these blessings can only be obtained in the temple of the Lord!*[56]

TEMPLE CEREMONIES

The first principles and ordinances of the gospel will only grant a person partial salvation in the heavenly kingdom of God. Elder Bruce D. Porter of the Second Quorum of the Seventy notes that while baptism and the gift of the Holy Ghost are "mandatory prerequisites" for entrance into the celestial kingdom, "those who would enter into the *highest* degree of that kingdom, inheriting exaltation and 'all that my Father hath' (D&C 84:38), must further receive the higher ordinances of exaltation found only in the holy temple. The first principles and ordinances of the gospel, therefore, are not only requirements of salvation but also preparatory steps to entering the temple and fulfilling the conditions of exaltation. To receive those temple ordinances and live worthy of their promise should be the aspiration of every righteous Latter-day Saint."[57]

President Joseph Fielding Smith explained the nature of temple ordinances in the following words:

The Lord has given unto us privileges, and blessings, and the opportunity of entering into covenants, of accepting ordinances that pertain to our salvation beyond what is preached in the world; beyond the principles of faith in the Lord Jesus Christ, repentance from sin, and baptism for the remission of sins, and the laying on of hands for the gift of the Holy Ghost; and these principles and covenants are received nowhere else but in the temple of God.

If you would become a son or a daughter of God and an heir of the kingdom, then you must go to the house of the Lord and receive blessings which there can be obtained and which cannot be obtained elsewhere. . .

The ordinances of the temple, the endowment and sealings, pertain to exaltation in the celestial kingdom, where the sons and daughters are. The sons and daughters are not outside in some other kingdom. The sons and daughters go into the house, belong to the household, have access to the home. . . . And you cannot receive that access until you go to the temple. Why? Because you must receive certain key words as well as make covenants by which you are able to enter.[58]

The ordinances of the House of God include baptism (for the dead), washings and anointings, the endowment, and various sealing rituals. On the pages that follow we will briefly examine each of these essential rites.

Baptism for the Dead

As mentioned on the preceding pages, baptism is an ordinance of salvation that pertains only to the celestial kingdom of God. When this ordinance is performed for and in behalf of the dead it will only have a benefit for those persons who meet certain criteria. The Prophet Joseph Smith said that baptism for the dead applies specifically to those "who have not heard the gospel or [the] fullness of it" during their mortal lives.[59] Elder Bruce R. McConkie writes that "those who do not have opportunity in this life to receive the gospel, but who would have accepted its saving truths with all their hearts had the glad tiding been offered to them, will hear and accept it in the spirit world. They will then repent of their sins, gain forgiveness through baptism for the dead, and become heirs of the celestial kingdom itself."[60] The Lord, who is the great judge of all, will ultimately decide who qualifies for the blessings of proxy baptism, and who does not.

An editorial that appeared on the pages of the *Times and Seasons* newspaper—during Joseph Smith's stint as editor—made a connection between an Old Testament scripture and the dispensation of the fullness of times. It said that "we are commanded to be baptized for our dead thus fulfilling the words of Obadiah [who,] when speaking of the glory of the Latter Day [said,] 'And saviors shall come up upon Mount Zion' (Obad. 1:21)."[61] Elder George Q. Cannon explained that these "saviors in the last days" are "acting in a lesser capacity, it is true, but still somewhat in the capacity of our Lord and Savior Jesus Christ, for their dead." They do this not by "shedding their blood" in an act of Atonement but by "going forth and being baptized for [individuals] and receiving the ordinances of salvation in their behalf."[62] Joseph Smith emphasized that it was an obligation on the part of Latter-day Saints to seek after and save their dead through proxy baptism. And he cautioned that "those Saints who neglect it, in behalf of their deceased relatives, do it at the peril of their own salvation."[63]

Washings and Anointings

Those Latter-day Saints who receive an endowment in the House of the Lord must first participate in a ceremonial washing and anointing. In the *Encyclopedia of Mormonism* it is stated that "washings and anointings are preparatory or initiatory ordinances in the temple. They signify the cleansing and sanctifying power of Jesus Christ applied to the attributes of the person and to the hallowing of all life. They have biblical precedents." It is further stated that "women are set apart to administer the ordinances to women, and men are set apart to administer the ordinances to men. . . . A commemorative garment is given with these ordinances and is worn thereafter by the participant."[64]

During the Nauvoo era of Church history these rituals were referred to as "the holy washings [and] the holy anointing."[65] The Saints "receive the washings and anointings," said President Brigham Young, "preparatory to their becoming heirs of God and joint-heirs with Christ."[66] Heber C. Kimball had a solemn warning for those who would indulge in evil practices after the reception of these sacred rites. He said that "if they do not repent of their follies and sins, their washings and anointings will prove a curse instead of a blessing, and will expedite their condemnation."[67]

The Endowment

An endowment is a gift, "but in a specialized sense it is a course of instruction, ordinances, and covenants given only in dedicated temples of The Church of Jesus Christ of Latter-day Saints. The words 'to endow' (from the Greek *enduein*), as used in the New Testament, mean to dress, clothe, put on garments, put on attributes, or receive virtue." The temple endowment "is a course of instruction by lectures and representations. These include a recital of the most prominent events of the creation, a figurative depiction of the advent of Adam and Eve and of every man and every woman, the entry of Adam and Eve into the Garden of Eden, the consequent expulsion from the garden, their condition in the world, and their receiving of the plan of salvation leading to the return to the presence of God."[68]

One of the main purposes of the endowment ceremony is to allow initiates to enter into covenants with God the Father. Elder John A. Widtsoe says that "the temple endowment . . . requires covenants or agreements of those participating, to accept and use the laws of progress."[69] An entry in the *Encyclopedia of Mormonism* indicates that these laws pertain to "sacrifice, obedience, righteousness, chastity, and consecration."[70] President James E. Faust admonished the Saints saying, "We must do all in our power to ensure that no member of the Church departs this earth without having received the necessary ordinances and covenants of the temple." He said that "as we keep our temple covenants, we place the Savior at the center of our lives, develop greater love for others, receive protection from evil influences, and obtain spiritual strength, happiness, peace of mind, and eternal life."[71] Joseph Fielding Smith says that "after we have received these covenants we should observe them sacredly, even if it should cost us the association and good will of all the world. Why? *Because we have found the pearl of great price, the kingdom of God.* We are on the road to receive all that the Father has, all that He can give—exaltation. If others are not willing to receive these blessings, let them take their course, but for us, let us walk in the light of the truth and forsake the world."[72]

Some of the other aspects of the endowment ceremony were outlined by the Prophet Joseph Smith and President Brigham Young. When Joseph Smith introduced the temple endowment in Nauvoo he instructed a small group of Church leaders "in the principles and order of the Priesthood, attending to washings, anointings, endowments and the communication of keys pertaining to the Aaronic Priesthood, and so on to the highest order of the Melchizedek Priesthood, setting forth the order pertaining to the Ancient of Days, and all those plans and principles by which anyone is enabled to secure the fullness of those blessings which have been prepared for the Church of the Firstborn, and come up and abide in the presence of the Elohim in the eternal worlds."[73] Brigham Young said that the endowment, overall, is "to receive all those ordinances in the House of the Lord, which are necessary for you, after you have departed this life, to enable you to walk back to the presence of the Father, passing the angels who stand as sentinels, being enabled to give them the key words, the signs and tokens, pertaining to the Holy Priesthood and gain your eternal exaltation."[74]

Sealing Ordinances

Joseph Smith informs us that when Elijah appeared to him and Oliver Cowdery in the Kirtland Temple on 3 April 1836, the ancient Israelite prophet gave them the sealing power of the Priesthood (see D&C 110:13–16). By way of explanation, Joseph Smith said that "the spirit of Elijah is that degree of power which holds the sealing power of the kingdom to seal the hearts of the fathers to the children and [the hearts] of the children [to] their fathers not only on earth but in heaven, both the living and the dead to each other, for they (the dead) cannot be made perfect without us (Heb. 11:40). . . . By [the power of Elijah] we are sealed with the Holy Spirit of promise. . . . To obtain this sealing is to make our calling and election sure."[75] Furthermore, said the Prophet, "what you seal on earth by the keys of Elijah is sealed in heaven," meaning that ordinances performed by this power will be efficacious or valid in eternity.[76]

With the sealing power of Elijah in hand the Prophet proceeded to administer ordinances among the Saints that pertained both to time and eternity. Those ordinances included sealing men and women together in the new and everlasting covenant of marriage, sealing parents and children together (whether living or dead), and sealing married couples up to eternal life—thereby making their calling and election sure. Let us briefly examine each of these ordinances.

Marriage Sealing: President Joseph Fielding Smith stated unequivocally that "*a man must have a wife, and a woman a husband, to receive the fullness of exaltation. They* must be sealed for time and for all eternity in a temple; then their union will last forever, and they cannot be separated because God has joined them together."[77] He also said, "If you want salvation in the fullest, that is exaltation in the kingdom of God, so that you may become His sons and His daughters, you have got to go into the temple of the Lord and receive these holy ordinances which belong to that house, which cannot be had elsewhere. *No man shall receive the fullness of eternity, of exaltation, alone; no woman shall receive that blessing alone; but man and wife, when they receive the sealing power in the temple of the Lord, if they thereafter keep all the commandments, shall pass on to exaltation, and shall continue and become like the Lord.* And that is the destiny of men; that is what the Lord desires for His children."[78]

Elder Bruce R. McConkie of the Quorum of the Twelve Apostles made particular note of the fact that "making one's calling and election sure is in *addition* to celestial marriage and results from undeviating and perfect devotion to the cause of righteousness. Those married in the temple can never under any circumstances gain exaltation unless they keep the commandments of God and abide in the covenant of marriage which they have taken upon themselves."[79] Indeed, "every person married in the temple for time and for all eternity has sealed upon him, *conditioned upon his faithfulness,* all of the blessings of the ancient patriarchs, including the crowning promise and assurance of eternal increase, which means, literally, a posterity as numerous as the dust particles of the earth."[80]

Family Sealing: President Brigham Young taught the Saints that "when a man and woman have received their endowments and sealings, and then had children born to them afterwards, those children are legal heirs to the kingdom [of heaven] and to all its blessings and promises, and they are the only ones that are on this earth." Those who do not fit into this category can only amend the situation by adhering to "the law of adoption."[81] President George Q. Cannon expounded upon this doctrine. He stated that "it is not necessary, where parents are . . . sealed together by the authority of the Holy Priesthood for time and for eternity, that their children should be adopted or be sealed to them. They are legitimate heirs of the Priesthood and of the blessings of the new and everlasting covenant. But not so with those who have been born outside of this covenant. There has to be some ordinance performed in order to make them legitimate; and that ordinance, the Prophet Joseph [Smith] revealed, was the ordinance of adoption; that is, that which covers the ordinance or law, although we do not use the word adoption when we seal children to parents; we call that sealing. But to illustrate the principle and explain the law, the word 'adoption' is used."[82]

Joseph Fielding Smith provided some additional insight into the purpose of sealing family generations together. From the general conference pulpit he declared that there is no marriage or family organization in the terrestrial and telestial kingdoms. Sealing ordinances (husbands to wives, parents to children, the living to the dead) pertain to the "great family of God which is in heaven," meaning in the celestial kingdom.[83] On another occasion he explained:

> When everything gets finished, we will all be one family— every member of the Church a member of one family, *the family of God.* And we will all be subject to our first progenitor, Adam, Michael, the archangel, who has been appointed and given authority under Jesus Christ to stand at the head and preside over all his posterity [see D&C 78:16]. We are one family. And we all have to be joined to that family. So it is not merely enough that we be baptized for our dead or for ourselves, but also we have to be sealed to our parents. We must have the parents sealed to their parents and so on, as far back as we can go, and eventually back to Adam.
>
> There will be cases where some of our ancestors will not be worthy and will drop out, but the links will have to be joined without them. So when the Prophet [Joseph Smith] says we cannot be saved or exalted without our dead, he had this in mind. . . . We may be born under the covenant and thus belong to our parents, but where there are breaks in that lineage we are not united. . . .

Why do we go into the temples to be sealed, husbands and wives, and children to parents, and why are we commanded to have this work done, not only for ourselves, but also to be sealed to our fathers and mothers, and their fathers and mothers before them, back as far as we can go? Because we want to belong to that great family of God which is in heaven, and, so far as the Church is concerned, on earth. That is why. . . .

We are taught in the gospel of Jesus Christ that the family organization will be, so far as celestial exaltation is concerned, one that is complete—an organization linked from [the] father and mother and children of one generation, to the father and mother and children of the next generation, thus expanding and spreading out down to the end of time. If we fail to do the work, therefore, in the temples for our dead . . . our links in this chain—genealogical chain—will be broken; we will have to stand aside at least until that is remedied.

We could not be made perfect in this organization unless we [were] brought in by this selective or sealing power. . . .[84]

Sealing to Eternal Life: Elder Bruce R. McConkie declared that "we have power to make our calling and election sure, so that while we yet dwell in mortality, having overcome the world and been true and faithful in all things, we shall be sealed up unto eternal life and have the unconditional promise of eternal life in the presence of Him whose we are."[85] This most precious of all earthly blessings, explained Elder McConkie, is obtained when "a person has advanced in righteousness, light, and truth to the point that the fullness of the ordinances of the house of the Lord have been received so that he has been sealed up unto eternal life, and his calling and election has been made sure."[86]

Joseph Smith told the members of the Church in his day that even though they "might hear the voice of God and know that Jesus was the Son of God, this would be no evidence that their . . . calling and election was made sure, that they had part with Christ, and [would be] a joint-heir with Him. They then would want that more sure word of prophecy that they were sealed in the heavens and had the promise of eternal life in the kingdom of God." They would want "this promise sealed unto them," he said.[87] He also explained that "the more sure word of prophecy means a man's knowing that he is sealed up unto eternal life, by revelation and the spirit of prophecy, through the power of the Holy Priesthood" (D&C 131:5).[88] Most importantly, he encouraged all Latter-day Saints to strive to receive this great blessing. He said, "Make your calling and election sure. Go on from grace to grace until you obtain a promise from God for yourselves that you shall have eternal life. This is eternal life, to know God and His Son Jesus Christ [see John 17:3]; it is to be sealed up unto eternal life and obtain a promise for [y]our posterity."[89]

NOTES: CHAPTER 5

1. Daniel H. Ludlow, ed., *Encyclopedia of Mormonism* (New York: Macmillan, 1992), 3:1032, hereafter cited as *EM*.

2. Andrew F. Ehat and Lyndon W. Cook, eds., *The Words of Joseph Smith: The Contemporary Accounts of the Nauvoo Discourses of the Prophet Joseph* (Orem, Utah: Grandin Book, 1991), 215, hereafter cited as *WJS*.

3. George D. Watt, comp., *Journal of Discourses* (London, England: F. D. and S. W. Richards and Sons, 1854–1886), 21:354, hereafter cited as *JD*. Joseph Smith confirms this concept. He says, "The question is frequently asked, 'Can we not be saved without going through with all these ordinances?' I would answer, No, not the fullness of salvation. . . . Any person who is exalted to the highest mansion [in the Father's kingdom] has to abide a celestial law, and the whole law too" (*WJS*, 319).

4. *WJS*, 108. Joseph Smith asked, "Will everybody be damned, but Mormons?" He answered, "Yes, and a great portion of them, unless they repent and work righteousness" (B. H. Roberts, ed., *History of the Church*, rev. ed. [Salt Lake City: The Church of Jesus Christ of Latter-day Saints, 1932–1951], 3:28, hereafter cited as *HC*).

5. *WJS*, 43.

6. Ibid., 348–49. President Charles W. Penrose said, "Ordinances performed by those divinely appointed are as though attended to by Deity in person" (*The Contributor*, vol. 2, no. 11, August 1881, 338). Priesthood authority is essential in the administration of all gospel ordinances. On 15 May 1829 John the Baptist was sent as an angelic messenger to visit Joseph Smith and Oliver Cowdery and confer upon them the Aaronic Priesthood by the laying on of hands. The angel stated that the authority he had bestowed upon these men held the keys of "baptism by immersion for the remission of sins" but "not the power of laying on hands for the gift of the Holy Ghost" (JS—H, 1:69–70; cf. Matt. 3:11). The Prophet reports that John specifically ordained him and Oliver to the office of a "priest" within the Aaronic Priesthood (*WJS*, 327). After this angel had carried out his assignment the Lord commanded the Latter-day Saints to act "in the authority which [He had] given [them], baptizing in the name of the Father, and of the Son, and of the Holy Ghost" (D&C 68:8). "The Melchizedek Priesthood," says D&C section 107 verse 8, "has power and authority . . . to administer in spiritual things." Thus, it is the higher "Priesthood of Melchizedek" that holds "the power of laying on hands for the gift of the Holy Ghost" (JS—H, 1:70, 72). "The elders of the Church" have been "ordained and sealed unto this power" (D&C 76:52; 49:14). It is specified in the D&C that an "elder [of the Melchizedek Priesthood] or a priest [of the Aaronic Priesthood] shall administer" the emblems of the sacrament to the Saints. Whoever officiates in this administration is to kneel and offer a solemn prayer unto God the Father, asking Him to "bless and sanctify" these emblems of "remembrance" (D&C 20:75–79). This same pattern is seen in the Book of Mormon. "[W]hen the disciples had come [to Jesus] with bread and wine, He took of the bread and brake and *blessed* it [He being a "High Priest" (see Heb. 3:1; 6:20)]. . . . [And Jesus] said unto the disciples: 'Behold there shall one be *ordained* among you, and *to him will I give power* that he shall break bread and *bless* it and give it unto the people of my Church, unto all those who shall believe and be baptized in my name. And this shall ye always observe to do, even as I have done, even as I have broken bread and *blessed* it and given it unto you'" (3 Ne. 18:3, 5–6, emphasis added).

7. *WJS*, 12.

8. *The Contributor*, vol. 1, no. 3, December 1879, 57.

9. President Joseph Fielding Smith taught, "We have good reason to believe that all spirits while in the preexistence were perfect in form, having all their facul-

ties and mental powers unimpaired. It is difficult to believe that in that existence spirits were deficient, for that was a perfect world notwithstanding each spirit had his or her free agency. The reason for these deformities in body and mind are therefore physical. In other words they are confined to the mortal existence, and they are due to physical injury or impairment which comes because of accident or sickness before birth. . . . The Lord has made it known by revelation that children born with retarded minds shall receive blessings just like little children who die in infancy. They are free from sin, because their minds are not capable of a correct understanding of right and wrong. . . . Therefore The Church of Jesus Christ of Latter-day Saints considers all deficient children with retarded capacity to understand, just the same as little children under the age of accountability. They are redeemed without baptism and will go to the celestial kingdom of God, there, we believe, to have their faculties or other deficiencies restored according to the Father's mercy and justice" (*Improvement Era*, February 1959, 80–81, hereafter cited as *IE*).

10. Conference Report, April 1967, 31–32, hereafter cited as CR.

11. James E. Talmage, *Articles of Faith* (Salt Lake City: Deseret Book, 1984), 124.

12. Joseph F. Smith, *Gospel Doctrine* [Salt Lake City: Deseret Book, 1986], 101, hereafter cited as *GD*.

13. *IE*, March 1951, 190.

14. CR, October 1938, 61. President Brigham Young stated: "A great many of you have had your endowments, and you know what a vote with uplifted hands means. It is a sign which you make in token of your covenant with God and with one another, and it is for you to perform your vows. When you raise your hands to heaven and let them fall and then pass on with your covenants unfulfilled, you will be cursed" (*JD*, 3:332).

15. CR, April 1945, 129; cf. Mosiah 18:8–16; Alma 7:15.

16. Joseph Fielding Smith, *Doctrines of Salvation* (Salt Lake City: Bookcraft, 1999), 2:329, emphasis in original, hereafter cited as *DS*. In general conference this same author proclaimed that "when [the Lord] speaks of His kingdom, He has reference not to the great, broad kingdom which will embrace all humanity save the few who become sons of perdition, but speaks of that place where He and His Father dwell. . . . Baptism is of two-fold nature; primarily for the remission of sins, and then, entrance into the kingdom of God, not the telestial kingdom, not into the terrestrial kingdom, but entrance into the celestial

kingdom, where God dwells. That is what baptism is for" (CR, April 1922, 60–61). "The scriptures are very clear in declaring that baptism is for the celestial kingdom *only*. For a place in the terrestrial or the telestial kingdom, baptism is not required" (Joseph Fielding Smith, *Answers to Gospel Questions* [Salt Lake City: Deseret Book, 1998], 5:147, emphasis in original, hereafter cited as *AGQ*).

17. Cited in *DS*, 2:330. "The [members of the] First Presidency have answered the question, 'Is baptism necessary to salvation in any of the degrees of glory, except the celestial?'" as follows. "Baptism is the doorway into the celestial kingdom of God, as well as for the remission of sins. When the Savior said to His disciples, 'He that believeth and is baptized shall be saved,' it is quite evident that He had reference to the celestial kingdom and those who are not baptized and consequently 'damned' would have to enter some other kingdom. The gospel, as it has been revealed, is for the purpose of preparing mankind for the celestial glory. The Lord has not revealed to us what principles are required of those who enter the other degrees of glory, or kingdoms. Each kingdom is governed by law, and those who enter will do so because of obedience to the law governing in that particular kingdom" (*Our Lineage: Lessons 31 to 40 of the Course for First Year Genealogical Classes* [Salt Lake City: Genealogical Society of Utah, 1933], 7).

18. Bruce R. McConkie, *Doctrinal New Testament Commentary* (Salt Lake City: Bookcraft, 1965), 1:869, hereafter cited as *DNTC*. It was the teaching of George Albert Smith that "the gospel has been restored in these latter days to prepare men for the celestial kingdom. This gospel has not been given to qualify men for any other kingdom, but has been given to us to prepare us that we may dwell upon this earth when it has been celestialized, when our Redeemer will dwell here and He will be our lawgiver and our king" (CR, October 1926, 103).

19. Clyde J. Williams, ed., *The Teachings of Harold B. Lee* (Salt Lake City: Bookcraft, 1996), 95. Joseph Smith said that "baptism by water is but half a baptism and is good for nothing with[out] the other [half], the [baptism of the] Holy Ghost" (*WJS*, 230).

20. *IE*, January 1930, 218.

21. *DS*, 3:246, emphasis in original.

22. Joseph Fielding Smith, *Church History and Modern Revelation* (Salt Lake City:

The Church of Jesus Christ of Latter-day Saints, 1947), 2:120–21.

23. The Prophet said, the "Holy Ghost has no other effect than pure intelligence. It is more powerful in expanding the mind, enlightening the understanding, and storing the intellect with present knowledge, [in] man who is of the literal seed of Abraham, than one that is a Gentile, though it may not have half as much visible effect upon the body. For as the Holy Ghost falls upon one of the literal seed of Abraham, it is calm and serene; and his whole soul and body are only exercised by the pure spirit of intelligence; while the effect of the Holy Ghost upon a Gentile is to purge out the old blood, and make him actually of the seed of Abraham. That man that has none of the blood of Abraham (naturally) must have a new creation by the Holy Ghost. In such a case there may be more of a powerful effect upon the body and visible to the eye than upon an Israelite, while the Israelite at first might be far before the Gentile in pure intelligence" (*WJS*, 4; cf. 2 Cor. 5:17; Abr. 2:9–11).

24. *IE*, November 1900, 52–53, emphasis in original.

25. This idea of being "born of the Spirit" is the same as being born again. The Prophet Joseph Smith taught that "being born again comes by the Spirit of God through ordinances" (*WJS*, 12). Gospel scholar Robert J. Matthews makes the point that "redemption comes to a person through a change of heart [see Alma 5:14], through being born again and being sanctified by the Holy Ghost. Unless a person experiences this change of heart and spiritual rebirth, he is never quite ready for a righteous existence. In fact, he might not even desire such an existence. The Holy Ghost must touch and temper that person's spirit and disposition. Spirit must speak to spirit; that is, the Holy Spirit must act upon a person's spirit to purify his desires and actions" (Robert J. Matthews, *A Bible! A Bible!* [Salt Lake City: Bookcraft, 1990], 283).

26. Richard O. Cowan, "Instructions on Baptism for the Dead (D&C 127 and 128)," in Robert L. Millet and Kent P. Jackson, eds., *Studies in Scripture: Volume 1, The Doctrine and Covenants* (Salt Lake City: Deseret Book, 1989), 493. For further reading on the laying on of hands see *EM*, 2:813–14.

27. Heber J. Grant says that the Lord's representatives "seal the Holy Ghost upon a person" (CR, April 1902, 46–47). George Q. Cannon says of the recipient of this ordinance, "the hands of the servants of God were laid upon him to confirm him a member of the Church and to seal upon him the blessing of the Holy Ghost, that he might be led and guided by it into all truth" (*JD*, 15:117). Wilford Woodruff states, "We lay hands upon the heads of those who embrace

the gospel and we say unto them, 'In the name of the Lord Jesus Christ receive ye the Holy Ghost.' We seal this blessing upon the heads of the children of men" (*JD*, 13:157).

28. CR, April 1921, 17.

29. *BYU Speeches of the Year*, 1961, 7, emphasis in original. President Joseph F. Smith relates that "the presentation or 'gift' of the Holy Ghost simply confers upon a man the right to receive at any time, when he is worthy of it and desires it, the power and light of truth of the Holy Ghost, although he may often be left to his own spirit and judgment. . . . [I]t does not follow that a man who has received the presentation or gift of the Holy Ghost shall always receive the recognition and witness and presence of the Holy Ghost himself, or he may receive all these, and yet the Holy Ghost not tarry with him, but visit him from time to time" (*GD*, 60–61).

30. *JD*, 23:350.

31. Bruce R. McConkie, *A New Witness for the Articles of Faith* (Salt Lake City: Deseret Book, 1985), 290, hereafter cited as *NWAF*. Elder McConkie also writes that "whenever faithful Saints gain the companionship of the Holy Spirit, they are clean and pure before the Lord, for the Spirit will not dwell in an unclean tabernacle. Hence, they thereby receive a remission of those sins committed after baptism" (Bruce R. McConkie, *The Mortal Messiah* [Salt Lake City: Deseret Book, 1980], 3:40–41, n. #1).

32. Some people classify the sacrament as an ordinance of edification but President Brigham Young identified it as an ordinance of salvation. He said that "its observance is as necessary to our salvation as any other of the ordinances" (*JD*, 19:92). For similar statements see Bruce R. McConkie, *The Promised Messiah* (Salt Lake City: Deseret Book, 1978), 384; *NWAF*, 294; *DS*, 2:338–50.

33. Brigham Young had the following to say on the use of water in the sacrament. "The Lord has said to us that it mattereth not what we partake of when we administer the cup to the people, inasmuch as we do it with an eye single to the glory of God [see D&C 27:2–3]; it is then acceptable to Him. Consequently we use water as though it were wine; for we are commanded to drink not of wine for this sacred purpose except it be made by our own hands" (*JD*, 19:92).

34. David O. McKay, *Gospel Ideals* (Salt Lake City: Improvement Era, 1953), 71.

35. B. H. Roberts, *Defense of the Faith and the Saints* (Salt Lake City: Deseret News Press, 1907), 2:515.

36. CR, October 1926, 123–24.

37. *DS*, 2:350. President Joseph F. Smith taught that Latter-day Saints should attend their Sabbath day meeting "prepared to partake of the sacrament of the Lord's supper; having first confessed [their] sins before the Lord and [their] brethren and sisters, and forgiven [their] fellows as [they] expect the Lord to forgive [them]" (*GD*, 245).

38. *JD*, 25:62.

39. CR, April 1989, 50. For further reading see *New Era*, September 1983, 46–48; ibid., March 1997, 16–18.

40. CR, April 1946, 39–40.

41. Ibid., April 1985, 105, emphasis in original.

42. *Ensign,* March 1983, 67–68, emphasis in original; see also *AGQ*, 1:154–58; *DS*, 3:107–108.

43. CR, October 1916, 14.

44. Jerreld L. Newquist, ed., *Gospel Truth: Discourses and Writings of President George Q. Cannon* (Salt Lake City: Deseret Book, 1987), 138, emphasis added.

45. Talmage, *Articles of Faith*, 175. Gospel scholar Roy W. Doxey notes that "mistakenly, some members of the Church seem to believe that by partaking of the sacrament one receives forgiveness of sins. On the contrary, forgiveness is received upon the principle of genuine repentance. A purpose of the sacrament is to allow the Church member to self-examine himself that he may strive diligently to overcome his feelings and weaknesses. Partaking of the sacrament does not remit sins, but it will give spiritual strength to worthy members who are sincerely endeavoring to live the commandments" (Roy W. Doxey, *The Doctrine and Covenants Speaks* [Salt Lake City: Deseret Book, 1964], 1:134–35). In the writings of Joseph Fielding Smith we find the following. "*Question*: . . . Does the partaking of the sacrament forgive one of his sins? *Answer*: The forgiveness of sins comes through faith and sincere repentance. If a member of the Church has committed sin, the correct procedure is repentance and a sincere desire to right the wrong. . . . Partaking of the sacrament is one of the most sacred ordinances given to the Church. It is given in order that we may be brought in[to] closer communion with the Spirit of the Lord and thus renew three most sacred covenants. They are: first, that we will take upon us the name of Jesus Christ; second, that we will always remember Him; third, that we will always keep His commandments which

He has given us. We are promised if we will do this that we will be blessed with the constant companionship of His Spirit. If we have violated any one of these covenants, then there should be sincere repentance through which we receive forgiveness of the Church *before* we partake of the sacrament" (*AGQ*, 1:84–85, emphasis added).

46. CR, October 1904, 97.

47. Ibid., October 1963, 58.

48. G. Homer Durham, ed., *The Discourses of Wilford Woodruff* (Salt Lake City: Bookcraft, 1969), 64. Joseph Smith explained that the "Melchizedek Priesthood . . . is the channel through which all knowledge, doctrine, the plan of salvation and every important matter is revealed from heaven" (*HC*, 4:207).

49. *IE*, February, 1939, 74.

50. *WJS*, 113.

51. *IE*, February 1939, 74.

52. McConkie, *The Promised Messiah*, 587.

53. CR, April 1970, 58.

54. *WJS*, 246.

55. *HC*, 5:527.

56. Joseph Fielding Smith, *The Way to Perfection* (Salt Lake City: Genealogical Society of Utah, 1949), 208, emphasis in original. Elder Orson Hyde remarks, "Such as have not received the fullness of the Priesthood, (for the fullness of the Priesthood includes the authority of both king and priest) and have not been anointed and ordained in the temple of the Most High, may obtain salvation in the celestial kingdom, but not a celestial crown" (*Millennial Star*, vol. 9, no. 2, 15 January 1847, 23).

57. *Ensign*, October 2000, 15, emphasis in original.

58. *DS*, 2:40, emphasis in original.

59. *WJS*, 110.

60. *DNTC*, 1:275.

61. *Times and Seasons*, vol. 3, no. 12, 15 April 1842, 761, hereafter cited as *T&S*. "Saviors on Mount Zion" are those who receive proxy "baptisms, confirmations, washings, anointings, ordinations, and sealing powers . . . in behalf of all [their] progenitors who are dead" (*WJS*, 318).

62. *JD*, 14:318–19. In relation to proxy temple work Joseph F. Smith said, "We will not finish our work until we have saved ourselves, and then not until we shall have saved all depending upon us; for we are to become saviors upon Mount Zion, as well as Christ. We are called to this mission. The dead are not perfect without us, neither are we without them. We have a mission to perform for and in their behalf; we have a certain work to do in order to liberate those who, because of their ignorance and the unfavorable circumstances in which they were placed while here, are unprepared for eternal life; we have to open the door for them, by performing ordinances which they cannot perform for themselves, and which are essential to their release from the 'prison-house,' to come forth and live according to God in the spirit, and be judged according to man in the flesh" (ibid., 19:264).

63. *WJS*, 78.

64. *EM*, 4:1444. "There are special areas inside each temple for the various ordinances. . . . [In one of these] areas are cubicles in which individuals are ritually washed and anointed before endowments can be performed" (ibid., 4:1448).

65. *T&S*, vol. 5, no. 23, 15 December 1844, 743.

66. *JD*, 13:330. Heber C. Kimball explains further. He says, "After receiving the Priesthood, when a person receives his endowment, he is an heir to the Priesthood—an heir of God, and a joint-heir with Jesus Christ; that is, he has commenced his heirship" (ibid., 6:125).

67. Ibid., 3:269.

68. *EM*, 2:454–55.

69. John A. Widtsoe, *Program of The Church of Jesus Christ of Latter-day Saints* (Salt Lake City: The Church of Jesus Christ of Latter-day Saints, 1937), 176.

70. *EM*, 1:332.

71. *Church News,* 9 April 1988, 5.

72. *DS*, 2:255, emphasis in original.

73. *HC*, 5:2.

74. *JD*, 2:31.

75. *WJS*, 334–35.

76. Ibid., 330.

77. *DS*, 2:43–44, emphasis in original. President Smith makes these important observations: "If a man or a woman who has been sealed in the temple for time and eternity should sin and lose the right to receive the exaltation in the celestial kingdom, he or she could not retard the progress of the injured companion who had been faithful. Everyone will be judged according to his works, and there would be no justice in condemning the innocent for the sins of the guilty" (ibid., 2:177). "If a man and his wife are saved in separate kingdoms, for instance, the celestial and terrestrial, automatically the sealing is broken; it is broken because of the sins of one of the parties. *No one can be deprived of exaltation who remains faithful.* In other words, an undeserving husband cannot prevent a faithful wife from an exaltation and vice versa. In this case the faithful servant would be given to someone who is faithful" (ibid., 2:65, emphasis added).

78. Ibid., 2:44, emphasis in original. President Charles W. Penrose of the First Presidency addressed the issue of polygamy and exaltation in an official Church publication. "Question 4: Is plural or celestial marriage essential to a fullness of glory in the world to come? Answer: Celestial marriage is essential to a fullness of glory in the world to come, as explained in the revelation concerning it; but it is not stated that plural marriage is thus essential" (*IE*, September 1912, 1042). Elder Bruce R. McConkie takes the same position. "Plural Marriage is not essential to salvation or exaltation" (Bruce R. McConkie, *Mormon Doctrine*, 2d ed. [Salt Lake City: Bookcraft, 1966], 578, hereafter cited as *MD*). Elder James E. Talmage writes that the idea "that plural marriage is a vital tenet of the Church is not true. What the Latter-day Saints call celestial marriage is characteristic of the Church, and is in very general practice; but of celestial marriage, plurality of wives was an incident, never an essential" (*IE*, October 1901, 909).

79. *MD*, 118, emphasis in original.

80. Bruce R. McConkie, *The Millennial Messiah* (Salt Lake City: Deseret Book, 1982), 264, emphasis added.

81. *JD*, 11:118.

82. Brian H. Stuy, ed., *Collected Discourses* (Burbank, California: B. H. S. Publishing, 1991), 4:77.

83. CR, October 1948, 153–54.

84. *DS*, 2:173–75, emphasis in original. This same author states, "In order that we may be saved we, of necessity, must save our dead. We must be sealed to our parents, and each generation to the one which goes before it. And there shall finally be a great sealing of families, the joining together of the children of Adam, those who are worthy, in one great family, all related, and that is what the Lord intended, and that is why we must seal the dead as well as the living who are worthy to receive His blessing. Fathers will have claim upon their children, and that applies to every generation. Adam will stand at the head of his posterity and preside over them, and we will all be his children and grandchildren from generation to generation down to the end of time" (*Utah Genealogical and Historical Magazine*, vol. 13, April 1922, 58).

85. *Ensign*, November 1977, 34.

86. *MD*, 24. Elder McConkie indicates that it is in the "temples" that "men are sealed up unto eternal life—all to the end that man may become as his Maker" (Bruce R. McConkie, *The Mortal Messiah* [Salt Lake City: Deseret Book, 1979], 1:99). The Holy of Holies of the Salt Lake Temple, says Elder James E. Talmage, "is reserved for the higher ordinances in the Priesthood relating to the exaltation of both [the] living and [the] dead" (James E. Talmage, *The House of the Lord* [Salt Lake City: Deseret Book, 1968], 163).

87. *WJS*, 201. On page 202 of this same source the Prophet says, "I would exhort you to go on and continue to call upon God until you make your calling and election sure for yourselves by obtaining this more sure word of prophecy, and wait patiently for the promise until you obtain it."

88. Joseph Smith said that "the more sure word of prophecy" is "to obtain a promise from God for myself that I shall have eternal life" (ibid., 209).

89. Ibid., 334. President Brigham Young taught that the Father "has designed that we should become gods—the sons of God—fathers of eternal lives, like Abraham. This is the promise he received—to be the father of endless lives, that his posterity and generation should never cease, in time nor eternity" (*JD*, 8:179; see Genesis 22:15–17; Hebrews 6:13–15; Abraham 3:14; D&C 132:30–31).

SECTION 3

WHERE AM I GOING?

CHAPTER 6

THE SPIRIT WORLD

When a person dies their spirit is separated from their physical body and it enters into a spiritual realm, there to remain until the Day of Resurrection. Several passages in the New Testament make it clear that the spirit world is not the same location as the "heaven" where God the Father dwells (Matt. 16:17). When Jesus Christ died on the cross His spirit entered into a realm where there was both a "paradise" (Luke 23:43) and a "prison" (1 Pet. 3:18–19). Yet, after He had been resurrected the Savior said, "I am not yet ascended to my Father: but go to my brethren, and say unto them, I ascend unto my Father" (John 20:17). Elder Parley P. Pratt taught the same doctrine that is evident in these New Testament texts. He explained that "the spirit world is not the heaven where Jesus Christ, His Father, and other beings dwell who have, by resurrection or translation, ascended to eternal mansions and been crowned and seated on thrones of power." Instead, said Elder Pratt, "it is an intermediate state, a probation, a place of preparation, improvement, instruction, or education, where spirits are chastened and improved, and where, if found worthy, they may be taught a knowledge of the gospel." Also, for some deserving individuals, "it is a place of punishment, a purgatory or hell, where spirits are buffeted till the day of redemption."[1]

According to Elder Pratt "the earth and other planets of a like sphere have their inward or spiritual spheres as well as their outward, or temporal. The one is peopled by temporal tabernacles, and the other by spirits. A veil is drawn between the one sphere and the other whereby all the objects in the spiritual sphere are rendered invisible to those in the temporal."[2] President Brigham Young asked, "Where is the spirit world?" He answered, "It is right here. Do the good and evil spirits go together? Yes, they do. Do they both inhabit one kingdom? Yes, they do. . . . Do they go beyond the boundaries of this organized earth? No, they do not. . . . Where else are you going? Nowhere else, only as you are permitted."[3]

DIVISIONS WITHIN THE SPIRIT WORLD

"The righteous and the wicked all go to the same world of spirits," taught the Prophet Joseph Smith.[4] But according to President Joseph F. Smith once these beings arrive in that region a "partial judgment" takes place and a separation is made between them.[5] The righteous and obedient are allowed to enter into a pleasant area of the spirit realm called paradise while those without the proper qualifications are "shut . . . up" or confined in a place known as the "prison" (Moses 7:38).

The Paradise of the Righteous
The Book of Mormon provides a glimpse into the nature of paradise. In Alma chapter 40 verse 12 it is related that "the spirits of those who are righteous are received into a state of happiness, which is called paradise, a state of rest, a state of peace, where they shall rest from all their troubles and from all care, and sorrow." Revelation chapter 2 verse 7 hints that the paradise of the spirit realm is similar to the Garden of Eden that stood upon the earth at the beginning of human history. In this passage of scripture the Lord makes this promise: "To him that overcometh will I give to eat of the tree of life, which is in the midst of the paradise of God" (cf. Gen. 2:8–9).

President Jedediah M. Grant, who served as Second Counselor in the First Presidency of the Church, provided an eyewitness account of the spirit-world paradise. On 4 December 1856 President Heber C. Kimball related what President Grant had seen in the realm of the righteous shortly before he died:

[President Grant] said to me, "Brother Heber, I have been into the spirit world two nights in succession, and, of all the dreads that ever came across me, the worst was to have to again return to my body, though I had to do it. But Oh," says he, "the order and government that were there! When in the spirit world, I saw the order of righteous men and women; beheld them organized in their several grades, and there appeared to be no obstruction to my vision; I could see every man and woman in their grade and order. I looked to see whether there was any disorder there, but there was none; neither could I see any death nor any darkness, disorder or confusion." He said that the people he [saw] there . . . were organized in family capacities; and when he looked at them he saw grade after grade, and all were organized and in perfect harmony. He would mention one item after another and say, "Why, it is just as Brother Brigham says it is; it is just as he has told us many a time. . . ."

He saw the righteous gathered together in the spirit world, and there were no wicked spirits among them. He saw his wife; she was the first person that came to him. He saw many that he knew, but did not have conversation with any except his wife Caroline. She came to him, and he said that she looked beautiful and had their little child, that died on the plains, in her arms, and said, "Mr. Grant, here is little Margaret; you know that the wolves ate her up, but it did not hurt her; here she is all right."

"To my astonishment," he said, "when I looked at families there was a deficiency in some, there was a lack, for I saw families that would not be permitted to come and dwell together, because they had not honored their calling here."

He asked his wife Caroline where Joseph and Hyrum and Father Smith and others were; she replied, "They have gone away ahead, to perform and transact business for us. . . ."

He also spoke of the buildings he saw there, remarking that the Lord gave Solomon wisdom and poured gold and silver into his hands that he might display his skill and ability,

[but] said that the temple erected by Solomon was much inferior to the most ordinary buildings he saw in the spirit world.

In regard to gardens, [said] Brother Grant, "I have seen good gardens on this earth, but I never saw any to compare with those that were there. I saw flowers of numerous kinds, and some with from fifty to a hundred different colored flowers growing upon one stalk." We have many kinds of flowers on the earth, and I suppose those very articles came from heaven, or they would not be here.

After mentioning the things that he had seen, he spoke of how much he disliked to return and resume his body, after having seen the beauty and glory of the spirit world, where the righteous spirits are gathered together. . . .

After speaking of the gardens and the beauty of everything there, Brother Grant said that he felt extremely sorrowful at having to leave so beautiful a place and come back to earth.[6]

Latter-day prophets have made it known that when the spirits of the righteous pass through the veil and enter into paradise their capacities and abilities are greatly enhanced.

Increased Glory: In section 129 of the Doctrine and Covenants the Prophet Joseph Smith reveals that "the spirits of just men made perfect" (i.e., those who will eventually inherit the celestial kingdom) are surrounded by a radiant "glory" or light (vv. 3, 6; cf. D&C 76:69–70). He further states that "spirits can only be revealed in flaming fire, or glory." They are not like the angels who have "advanced farther—their light and glory being tabernacled" in resurrected bodies.[7] Several scriptures suggest that this radiance is a visible manifestation of the Spirit of God or the Light of Christ (see Ex. 34:29; Hel. 5:36; Matt. 17:2; Acts 12:7; D&C 84:45–46; 88:4–9; 93:9).

Increased Knowledge: Joseph Smith revealed that in the postmortal realm the knowledge of "the spirits of the just" is greatly magnified.

He said that these beings "know and understand our thoughts, feelings, and motions."[8] Furthermore, said the Prophet, "in the world of spirits no man can be exalted but by knowledge."[9] President Brigham Young said of himself, "I shall not cease learning while I live, nor when I arrive in the spirit world; but shall there learn with greater facility; and when I again receive my body, I shall learn a thousand times more in a thousand times less time; and then I do not mean to cease learning, but shall still continue my researches."[10]

Increased Visual Perception: As mentioned above, when Jedediah M. Grant visited the spirit world his visual perception was greatly enhanced. He said that he "saw the order of righteous men and women; beheld them organized in their several grades, and there appeared to be no obstruction to [his] vision; [he] could see every man and woman in their grade and order." Elder Orson Pratt believed that once a person's spirit had been separated from its physical body it might be able to "see in different directions at once." His reasoning was that when the spirit is inside the body it only receives light and images through the pupil of the physical eye. But if it were possible for the entire spirit to act as a receptor of light then the range of sight would be remarkably improved.[11]

Increased Mobility: "God has revealed some little things with regard to His movements and power," said Brigham Young, "and the operation and motion of the lightning furnish[es] a fine illustration of the ability and power of the Almighty. If you could stretch a wire from this room around the world until the two ends nearly met here again, and were to apply a battery to one end, if the electrical conditions were perfect, the effect of the touch would pass with such inconceivable velocity that it would be felt at the other end of the wire at the same moment." President Young declared that "this is what the faithful Saints are coming to; they will possess this power, and if they wish to visit different planets, they will be there. If the Lord wish[es] to visit His children here, He is here; if He wish[es] to send one of His angels to the earth to speak to some of His children, he is here," instantaneously. Brother Brigham explained, however, that even though faithful spirits will "possess a measure of this power" they will not possess it "to that degree that [they] will when resurrected and brought forth in the fullness of glory to inherit the kingdoms prepared for [them]. The power the faithful will possess then will far exceed that of the spirit world."[12]

Increased Power Over Evil: Brigham Young once said to the Saints, "If we are faithful to our religion, when we go into the spirit world, the fallen spirits—Lucifer and the third part of the heavenly hosts that came with him, and the spirits of wicked men who have dwelt upon this earth—the whole of them combined will have no influence over our spirits. Is not that an advantage? Yes. All the rest of the children of men are more or less subject to them, and they are subject to them as they were while here in the flesh." Not only does "the power of Satan ha[ve] no more influence over a faithful individual" who has died, continued President Young, but "that spirit . . . can command the power of Satan. . . . Those who have passed through the veil have power over the evil spirits to command [them], and they must obey."[13]

Additional Areas

It was the teaching of Elder Parley P. Pratt that "there are many places and degrees in [the spirit] world" just as there are in the temporal sphere.[14] President Brigham Young concurred, stating that "when we have passed into the sphere where Joseph [Smith] is, there is still another department, and then another, and another, and so on to an eternal progression."[15] Earlier in this chapter it was related that when Jedediah M. Grant met his deceased wife in paradise and asked her where some of the leaders of the Church were, he was informed that they had "gone away ahead" to transact business for the Saints. President Wilford Woodruff provides support for this idea. On one occasion he was visited by Brigham Young and Heber C. Kimball, both of whom had been dead for some time. President Young offered some counsel to President Woodruff—the very same counsel that Joseph Smith had delivered to President Young after he had been martyred. After this message had been delivered President Woodruff says that the following impression was given to him:

> Brother Joseph had left the work of watching over this Church and kingdom to others, and that *he had gone ahead, and that he had left this work to men who have lived and*

labored with us since he left us. This idea manifested itself to me, that such men *advance in the spirit world.* And I believe myself that these men who have died and gone into the spirit world had this mission left with them, that is, a certain portion of them, to watch over the Latter-day Saints.[16]

Spirits are not the only type of beings who reside behind the veil. Translated individuals (those who have been taken bodily from the earth without tasting death) and resurrected personages can also be found there. But the embodied and the disembodied inhabit different areas of the spiritual world. "Disembodied spirits . . . do not go where there are resurrected bodies, [because] they cannot live there."[17] Different types of embodied beings are separated from each other as well. The Prophet Joseph Smith made some relevant remarks about people who are translated. He said, "Many may have supposed that the doctrine of translation was a doctrine whereby men were taken immediately into the presence of God, and into an eternal fullness, but this is a mistaken idea. Their place of habitation is that of the *terrestrial* order and a place prepared for such characters."[18] Terrestrial beings do not dwell with celestial beings. In chapter 27 of the book of Matthew it is stated that "many" of the Saints received their resurrected bodies shortly after the Savior's Resurrection had taken place (vv. 52–53). Since all of these people came forth in the morning of the First Resurrection it can be said that they advanced from a terrestrial level of existence (in paradise) to a celestial level of existence (among resurrected beings).[19] But even among this group there are gradations in degrees of sanctity. Doctrine and Covenants section 132 verse 37 discloses that Abraham, Isaac, and Jacob have now entered into their exaltation, have been seated upon thrones, and have been crowned not as angels but as gods.

The Spirit Prison and Hell

It has been related on the preceding pages that when Jedediah M. Grant visited the realm behind the veil he saw that there were no wicked spirits among the righteous in paradise. When President Joseph F. Smith saw "the hosts of the dead" in a vision on 3 October 1918 he observed the same set of circumstances. He saw that "the spirits of the just," who had been "faithful" followers of Jesus Christ during mortality, "were gathered together in one place" where they enjoyed peace and light. The Lord visited this group between the time of His death and Resurrection "but unto the wicked He did not go." The sinless Son of God did not visit "the ungodly and the unrepentant who had defiled themselves while in the flesh" or "the rebellious who rejected the testimonies and the warnings of the ancient prophets. . . . Where these were, darkness reigned" (D&C 138:11–24).

Ungodly and rebellious people are not the only ones who inhabit the lower regions of the spirit realm, however. The Prophet Joseph Smith said that he would send messengers to preach to the "honest men and noble-minded men" who would be found in the "prison" portion of the spirit world.[20] He included Christian "sectarians" among this group and said, "I intend to send men to prison to preach to them."[21]

Some students of the scriptures may come to the conclusion that the spirit prison and hell are the same place. But Elder Orson Pratt disagreed with this view. It was his understanding that the "prison" and "outer darkness or hell" are two separate and distinct locations within the spiritual realm; the former being occupied by "those who never heard the gospel . . . in the flesh" and the latter by "those who will not give heed to the law of the gospel" or obey it after they have heard it.[22] Elder Pratt said that since those in this second group have rejected the truth they are destined to inherit the telestial kingdom in eternity.[23]

As mentioned above, the spirit prison is the temporary abode of multitudes of people who are both honest and noble minded. For God to consign such people to hell would be manifestly unjust. The scriptures clearly identify the types of people who will be sent to hell, but the "honest" and the "noble" are never included among this group.[24] Still, those who are confined to the prison do not qualify to enter into the paradise portion of the spiritual realm because they have not obeyed the law of God by receiving a legitimate baptism.[25] President Joseph Fielding Smith interpreted portions of section 138 of the Doctrine and Covenants to mean that only "*the righteous—meaning those who have been baptized and who have been faithful*," will be admitted into paradise. "All the others," he said, will be sent to "another part of the spirit world."[26]

SALVATION FOR THE DEAD

When the Savior was engaged in His mortal ministry He taught the covenant people that baptism was absolutely necessary for salvation in the kingdom of God (see John 3:3–5). This requirement applies to every accountable person who has ever lived upon the face of the earth or who will do so in the future. It is true that a large portion of the human family has never had the opportunity to hear the gospel of the Son of God or receive its saving ordinances from the Lord's authorized representatives. These circumstances, however, were taken into consideration during the premortal councils of heaven. The Lord "contemplated the whole of the events connected with the earth, pertaining to the plan of salvation, before it rolled into existence," said Joseph Smith. "He knows the situation of both the living and the dead and has made ample provision for their redemption according to their several circumstances and the laws of the kingdom of God, whether in this world or in the world to come."[27] President Wilford Woodruff upheld this same doctrine:

> God is no respecter of persons; He will not give privileges to one generation and withhold them from another; . . . [T]he whole human family, from father Adam down to our day, have got to have the privilege, somewhere, of hearing the gospel of Christ; . . . [T]he generations that have passed and gone without hearing that gospel in its fullness, power, and glory will never be held responsible by God for not obeying it, neither will He bring them under condemnation for rejecting a law [that] they never saw or understood; and if they live up to the light [that] they had they are justified so far, [but] they have to be preached to in the spirit world.[28]

In the New Testament it is revealed that after Jesus Christ died on the cross His spirit left His body, passed through the veil into the spirit world, and inaugurated the preaching of His gospel to the spirits who were in "prison" (1 Pet. 3:18–19; see also 4:6). When President Joseph F. Smith was shown a vision of this tremendously important event in 1918 he learned some essential truths:

> [T]he Lord went not in person among the wicked and the disobedient who had rejected the truth, to teach them;
>
> But behold, from among the righteous, He organized His forces and appointed messengers, clothed with power and authority, and commissioned them to go forth and carry the light of the gospel to them that were in darkness, even to all the spirits of men; and thus was the gospel preached to the dead.
>
> And the chosen messengers went forth to declare the acceptable day of the Lord and proclaim liberty to the captives who were bound, even unto all who would repent of their sins and receive the gospel.
>
> Thus was the gospel preached to those who had died in their sins, without a knowledge of the truth, or in transgression, having rejected the prophets (D&C 138:29–32).

Questions about salvation for the dead frequently arise among Latter-day Saints and also among those who seek to understand their faith. On the following pages an attempt will be made to provide answers to some of these questions. The answers that are presented here have been drawn from the scriptures, the teachings of Church authorities, and the writings of recognized gospel scholars.

Who will be taught the gospel in the spirit world?

It is apparent from a reading of John chapter 5 verses 25 and 28 that the message of Christ's gospel will be presented to *all* of those who are "in the graves," meaning those who are dead. President George Q. Cannon taught that "every soul born on the earth must hear the glad tidings of salvation, either in this life or in the life to come. This gospel will be preached to everyone, and all the inhabitants of the earth will have the opportunity of believing in Jesus Christ, of repenting of their sins, and of obeying the principles of the gospel."[29] President Cannon said, however, that there is one exception to this rule. The gospel is "sent to the entire spirit world, except . . . to [the] sons of perdition who [have] committed the unpardonable sin, or the sin against the Holy Ghost."[30]

Does this mean that people who have heard and rejected the gospel in mortality will have it presented to them again in the spiritual realm? The scriptures seem to verify that they will indeed have such an opportunity. Elder Jonathan C. Cutler said, "Men may reject the gospel here, and it seems that even they are going to have another chance of hearing it." Elder Cutler supported this claim by an appeal to 1 Peter 3:18–20 and 4:6 which says that those people who rejected the gospel at the hand of Noah still had it preached unto them when they were "in the spirit." Elder Cutler stresses that "even that class of people had the privilege of hearing the sound of the gospel in the spirit world, and were given another chance to receive it."[31] However, even if this particular group accepted the gospel in the spirit world such a course of action would not open the gates of the celestial kingdom to them. According to Elder George F. Richards the highest reward that they would qualify for would be in the terrestrial world.[32]

Why must the gospel be preached in the spirit world?

The gospel is preached to those who have passed beyond the veil because it is a prerequisite for judgment. It was Elder Bruce R. McConkie's teaching that "sometime after birth into this life and before the Resurrection and judgment, every living soul will hear the gospel message and be *judged by his reaction thereto*. The millions who pass to the spirit world without receiving an opportunity during mortality to hear the truths of salvation will receive their chance subsequent to what men call death."[33] The Prophet Joseph Smith taught along the same lines. He said that "all those who have not had an opportunity of hearing the gospel, and being administered unto by an inspired man in the flesh, must have it hereafter, before they can be finally *judged*."[34]

Who will preach the gospel to the dead?

Joseph Smith answered this question when he said that "all those [who] die in the faith go to the prison of spirits to preach to the dead in body (but they are alive in the spirit) and those spirits preach to the spirits that they may live according to God in the spirit"[35] (cf. 1 Pet. 4:6). The Prophet also stated that the dead have access to "the blessings pertaining to the gospel" and they will "possess the same privilege that we here enjoy, through the medium of the everlasting Priesthood, which not only administers on earth but in heaven."[36] Thus, faithful Priesthood holders will continue to build God's kingdom after they have passed from the mortal stage of existence.

Is a person more likely to accept the gospel once they are in the spirit world?

Some people assume that after a person discovers the reality of life after death they will be much more willing to accept the gospel of Jesus Christ when it is offered to them. This idea is not tenable for two reasons. First, there is no evidence that the veil of forgetfulness is completely removed after a person enters into the spirit world. It is logical to conclude that this shroud over the past will remain intact so that each individual can exercise their faith until the Day of Judgment. The Apostle Peter indicates that the spirits who hear the gospel will be "judged according to men in the flesh" (1 Pet. 4:6)—presumably because they exercise their faith like men in the flesh (who are in a state of forgetfulness). Without faith there is no trial. Second, as revealed in the following eyewitness account by Heber C. Kimball, the outlook and attitudes of a person do not automatically change for the better at the time of death.

> [W]hen righteous persons die, their spirits . . . go into the spirit world, [and] they go to work with the servants of God to help to do good, and to bring about the purposes of the Almighty pertaining to this earth; while wicked spirits, those who have been wicked in this probation, take the opposite course, just the same as they did here. I have said, a great many times, that that spirit which possesses us here will possess us when our spirits leave our bodies [see Alma 34:34], and we shall there be very much the same as we are here.
>
> If you are subject to rebellious spirits, or to a spirit of apostasy here, will you not have the same spirit beyond the veil

that you had on this side? You will, and it will have power over you to lead you to do wrong, and it will control your spirits. If, then, you are opposed to the truth while you are here, you will be occupied in that opposition hereafter, for the spirit that is opposed to the work of God here, will be opposed to that work when beyond the veil. I do not guess at this, because I have been at the other side of the veil, in vision, and have seen a degree of its condition with the eyes that God gave me. I have seen it and have seen those that lived in the faith and had the privilege of seeing Jesus, Peter, James, and the rest of the ancient apostles, and of hearing them preach the gospel. I have also seen those who rebelled against them, and they still had a rebellious spirit, fighting against God and His servants.[37]

Which ordinances can be performed vicariously?

The Prophet Joseph Smith listed proxy temple ordinances as follows: baptism, confirmation, bestowal of the Holy Ghost, ordination to the Priesthood, washings, anointings, the endowment, and the use of "sealing powers" to unite husbands to wives and parents to children. In addition to these sealings, said the Prophet, the Saints can "seal those who dwell on earth to those who dwell in heaven" and also "seal up [their] dead to come forth in the First Resurrection." By this latter ordinance the dead are "sealed . . . unto the day of their redemption" and "ordained kings and priests."[38]

Who may serve as a proxy in temple ordinance work?

"Every man that has been baptized and belongs to the kingdom, has a right to be baptized for those who [have] gone before," said Joseph Smith.[39] This concept applies to all of the other ordinances of the gospel as well. Once a person has received an ordinance for themselves they are eligible to act as a proxy in that particular rite. In all of the proxy ordinances, from baptism through the rituals of the temple, worthy men minister for deceased males and women for deceased females.[40] Even though it is desirable for family members to perform proxy temple rites for their own relatives[41] the Lord revealed through President Wilford Woodruff that it is acceptable for the Saints to receive the ordinances of salvation and exaltation for those who are outside of their immediate lineage.[42]

Why must living persons act as proxies for deceased individuals?

President Daniel H. Wells explained that "the ordinances of the gospel pertain to this [earthly] existence, and they have to be attended to in the flesh or by those in this state of existence."[43] In a related statement, President Joseph Fielding Smith said that the Latter-day Saints "are only presenting to the dead such ordinances and privileges as pertain to those who are living here and now. So far as faith is concerned, [the dead] exercise that where they are. So far as repentance is concerned, they repent where they are. We are baptized for them because they cannot be baptized there. We are confirmed and ordained for them. Why? Because they cannot receive those ordinances there. Why? Because these ordinances pertain to mortal life."[44]

What qualifications must be met before a person can leave the spirit prison?

President Joseph F. Smith made some remarks that pertain to this matter. He said that "in relation to the deliverance of spirits from their prison house, of course, we believe that can only be done after the gospel has been preached to them in the spirit, and they have accepted the same, and *the work necessary to their redemption by the living be done for them*. . . . It stands to reason that, while the gospel may be preached unto all . . . in the spirit world . . . redemption will only come to those who repent and obey."[45] The Prophet Joseph Smith made it known that "God has administrators in the eternal world to release those spirits from prison. [With] the ordinances being administered by proxy upon them, the law is fulfilled."[46]

Which kingdom do proxy temple ordinances pertain to?

A reply to this question can be found in the sermons and writings of Joseph Fielding Smith. This Church leader specifically connected the ordinances of the temple with the third or highest degree of glory. He said, "The Lord has given us the opportunity to perform in the temples the necessary labor for the *righteous and repentant dead*. The Lord is not going to save all the world in the celestial kingdom. But all who would have received the gospel had it been declared to them in the flesh, shall receive it in the spirit world, and they [will] become heirs of the celestial kingdom."[47] In a more pointed statement, President Smith remarked that "salvation for the dead is for those who died without a knowledge of the gospel so far as the celestial glory is concerned. And those who have rejected the truth and who have fought the truth, who would not have it, are not destined to receive celestial glory."[48]

Are proxy temple ordinances valid for everyone for whom they are performed?

Evidently, this is not the case. "If we perform labor in the temples for those who are unworthy," said Joseph Fielding Smith, "they shall not be entitled to those blessings simply because we have worked for them."[49]

Are the dead required to accept the work that is performed in their behalf?

No, absolutely not. There is no compulsion in the plan of salvation. Jay M. Todd, managing editor of the *Ensign* magazine, writes that "no earthly activity interferes in any way with the right of choice exercised by persons in the spirit world. They are free to accept or reject [proxy] ministrations in their behalf. If they choose to accept the ordinances performed for them, exercise faith in the Lord Jesus Christ, and repent, they are released from their spiritual bondage." However, "if they choose not to accept those conditions," says Brother Todd, "they remain in their spiritual bondage. Their right to choose remains inviolate. Agency is an eternal inheritance we each have from God our Father, and it is fundamental to our personal development. The Lord's work goes on in the spirit world as it goes on here in mortality, in that all mankind are graciously *invited*, not forced, to receive the fullness of the gospel and to use it to ennoble their lives."[50]

Is proxy temple work a second chance at celestial salvation?

The foundation for the answer to this question is laid in the Doctrine and Covenants. On 21 January 1836 the Prophet Joseph

Smith was shown a vision of the celestial kingdom and he heard the voice of the Lord proclaim that "all who have died *without a knowledge of [the] gospel*, who would have received it if they had been permitted to tarry, shall be heirs of the celestial kingdom of God" (D&C 137:7, emphasis added). Then the Lord added a second qualification. He said that all of those who die "without a knowledge" of the gospel will become heirs of the celestial kingdom only if they "would have received it *with all their hearts*" during mortality (v. 8, emphasis added). The Lord then declared that He would indeed "judge all men . . . according to *the desire of their hearts*" (v. 9, emphasis added).

Joseph Fielding Smith made several comments that, when combined with these scriptural citations, serve to more fully answer the question that has been posed.

> [T]he Lord did *not* offer to those who had *every* opportunity while in this mortal existence the privilege of another chance in the world of spirits.

> *The endowment and sealing work for the dead is for those who died without having had the opportunity to hear and receive the gospel; also, for those who were faithful members of the Church who lived in foreign lands or where, during their lifetime, they did not have the privilege to go to a temple, yet they were converted and were true members of the Church.* The work for the dead is not intended for those who had every opportunity to receive it, who had it taught to them, and who then refused to receive it, or had not interest enough to attend to these ordinances when they were living.[51]

Do proxy temple ordinances need to be performed for everyone?

Referring again to the writings of Joseph Fielding Smith we find the following insight: "Some people think we have got to do the work in the temple for everybody. *Temple work belongs to the celestial kingdom, not to the other kingdoms.* There will be millions of people, countless as the sands upon the seashore, who will not enter into the celestial kingdom. That we are told in these revelations [see D&C 76:109].

There will be no need to do temple work for them. To be exalted in the celestial kingdom one must be endowed and receive the sealing blessings. There will be many who will enter that kingdom as servants, but only those who comply with all the laws and covenants will be exalted."[52]

What will vicarious temple work be like during the Millennium?

As long as the earth remains in its fallen or telestial condition there will be a thick veil between the mortal and immortal worlds. On rare occasions those on the other side of the veil make it known that proxy temple work has been joyously accepted by those for whom it has been performed. But for the most part, proxy work is done by faith and the results are left in the hands of the Lord.

These circumstances will change dramatically during the Savior's millennial reign. The "powers of the Holy Priesthood" on the earth are "inseparably connected" with those that are in the spirit world, said Charles W. Penrose. "They are working together in harmony, and the time will come and it is not far distant, when the veil will be taken away which separates us from our brethren who have gone before, and we will work with them, and they with us. We will be in perfect harmony; and the Priesthood behind the veil will reveal to the Priesthood in the flesh, in the holy temples of God where these conversations will take place, the names of those for whom we must officiate which we cannot obtain by the means now at our command."[53] President Brigham Young assured the Saints that not only would "the names of those who have received the gospel in the spirit [world] . . . be revealed by the angels of God and the spirits of just men made perfect" but "also the places of their birth, the age in which they lived, and everything regarding them that is necessary to be recorded on earth."[54]

Thus will the grand and glorious work of salvation go forward at an excellerated pace. And because of this work men and women from all of the dispensations of the gospel will be prepared to rise from their graves and give an accounting before their King.

NOTES: CHAPTER 6

1. Parley P. Pratt, *Key to the Science of Theology* (Salt Lake City: Deseret Book, 1978), 80. On another occasion Elder Pratt taught that "the world of resurrected beings, and the world of spirits, are two distinct spheres, as much so as our own sphere is distinct from that of the spirit world. Where then does the spirit go, on its departure from its earthly tabernacle? It passes to the next sphere of human existence, called the world of spirits, a veil being drawn between us in the flesh, and that world of spirits. Well, says one, is there no more than one place in the spirit world? Yes, there are many places and degrees in that world, as in this. Jesus Christ, when absent from His flesh, did not ascend to the Father, to be crowned, and enthroned in power. Why? Because He had not yet a resurrected body, and had therefore a mission to perform in another sphere. Where then did He go? To the world of spirits" (George D. Watt, comp., *Journal of Discourses* [London, England: F. D. and S. W. Richards and Sons, 1854–1886], 1:9, hereafter cited as *JD*). Heber C. Kimball spoke along similar lines. He said, "As for my going into the immediate presence of God when I die, I do not expect it, but I expect to go into the world of spirits and associate with my brethren, and preach the gospel in the spiritual world, and prepare myself in every necessary way to receive my body again, and then enter through the wall into the celestial world. I never shall come into the presence of my Father and God until I have received my resurrected body, neither will any other person" (*JD*, 3:112–13). It is not uncommon for those who read Alma 40:11 to conclude that the spirits of all men and women return to the presence of God directly after death. But President George Q. Cannon explains that "Alma, when he says that 'the spirits of all men, as soon as they are departed from this mortal body, . . . are taken home to that God who gave them life,' has the idea, doubtless, in his mind that our God is omnipresent—not in His own personality but through His minister, the Holy Spirit. He does not intend to convey the idea that they are immediately ushered into the personal presence of God. He evidently uses that phrase in a qualified sense" (Jerreld L. Newquist, ed., *Gospel Truth: Discourses and Writings of President George Q. Cannon* [Salt Lake City: Deseret Book, 1987], 58).

2. Pratt, *Key to the Science of Theology*, 80.

3. *JD*, 3:369. Brigham Young asked, "Is the spirit world here? It is not beyond the sun, but is on this earth that was organized for the people that have lived and

that do and will live upon it" (ibid., 3:372).

4. Andrew F. Ehat and Lyndon W. Cook, eds., *The Words of Joseph Smith: The Contemporary Accounts of the Nauvoo Discourses of the Prophet Joseph* (Orem, Utah: Grandin Book, 1991), 213–14, hereafter cited as *WJS*.

5. Brian H. Stuy, ed., *Collected Discourses* (Burbank, California: B. H. S. Publishing, 1991), 4:224, hereafter cited as *CD*; see also *JD*, 21:10; Joseph F. Smith, *Gospel Doctrine* (Salt Lake City: Deseret Book, 1986), 448, hereafter cited as *GD*.

6. *JD*, 4:135–36.

7. *WJS*, 253.

8. Ibid., 253–54. Mary Ellen Jensen—who died on 3 March 1891 and was brought back to life through the administration of President Lorenzo Snow— was allowed to meet with several of her departed relatives in the spirit world. She learned from her experience with them that "people in the other world know to a great extent what happens here on the earth" (*Improvement Era*, October 1929, 974, hereafter cited as *IE*). Joseph F. Smith noted that "if we can see, by the enlightening influence of the Spirit of God . . . beyond the veil that separates us from the spirit world, surely those who have passed beyond, can see more clearly through the veil back here to us than it is possible for us to see to them from our sphere of action. I believe we move and have our being in the presence of heavenly messengers and of heavenly beings. . . . If this is the case with us in our finite condition . . . how much more certain it is and reasonable and consistent to believe that those who have been faithful, who have gone beyond . . . can see us better than we can see them; that they know us better than we know them. . . . We live in their presence, they see us, they are solicitous for our welfare, they love us now more than ever. For now they see the dangers that beset us" (James R. Clark, comp., *Messages of the First Presidency of The Church of Jesus Christ of Latter-day Saints* [Salt Lake City: Bookcraft, 1971], 5:6–7).

9. B. H. Roberts, ed., *History of the Church*, rev. ed. (Salt Lake City: The Church of Jesus Christ of Latter-day Saints, 1932–1951), 6:314, hereafter cited as *HC*. According to President Brigham Young the righteous who go "behind the veil . . . shall go on from step to step, from rejoicing to rejoicing, and from one intelligence and power to another, [their] happiness becoming more and more exquisite and sensible as [they] proceed in the words and powers of life" (*JD*, 6:349). On

another occasion President Young said that in the "next state" righteous spirits will be "learning, increasing, growing in grace and in the knowledge of the truth" (*JD,* 7:333).

10. Ibid., 8:10; cf. D&C 130:18–19.

11. *JD*, 2:243–44; The Prophet Joseph Smith reported after seeing the vision of the three degrees of glory (D&C 76): "My whole body was full of light and I could see even out at the ends of my fingers and toes" (Nels B. Lundwall, comp., *The Vision* [Salt Lake City: Bookcraft, 1951], 11; cf. D&C 88:67).

12. *JD*, 14:231.

13. Ibid., 7:240–41.

14. Ibid., 1:9.

15. Ibid., 3:375.

16. Ibid., 21:317–18.

17. Ibid., 6:293.

18. *WJS*, 41, emphasis added.

19. A "vast assembly" of Saints were resurrected after the Savior had risen from the grave and were allowed to "enter into [the] Father's kingdom" (meaning the celestial kingdom) and there they "continue[d] . . . their labor" (D&C 138:49–52; cf. 132:37). It is evident that these beings progressed from a terrestrial level of existence in paradise to a celestial level of existence in the presence of God.

    Lorenzo Dow Young (brother of President Brigham Young) had an intriguing spiritual experience which suggests that the levels of the postmortal world correspond with the four resurrections or four rewards of outer darkness and three degrees of glory. His experience is as follows:

    "I had a remarkable dream or vision. I fancied that I died. In a moment I was out of the body, and fully conscious that I had made the change. At once, a heavenly messenger, or guide, was by me. I thought and acted as naturally as I had done in the body, and all my sensations seemed as complete without as with it. The personage with me was dressed in the purest white. For a short time I remained in the room where my body lay. My sister Fanny (who was living with me when I had this dream) and my wife were weeping bitterly over my death. I sympathized with them deeply in their sorrow, and desired to comfort them. I realized that I was under the control of the man who was by me. I begged of him the privilege of speaking to them, but he said he could not grant it. My guide, for so I will call him, said 'Now let us go.'

Space seemed annihilated. Apparently we went up, and almost instantly were in another world. It was of such magnitude that I formed no conception of its size. It was filled with innumerable hosts of beings, who seemed as naturally human as those among whom I had lived. With some I had been acquainted in the world I had just left. My guide informed me that those I saw had not yet arrived at their final abiding place. All kinds of people seemed mixed up promiscuously, as they are in this world. Their surroundings and manner indicated that they were in a state of expectation, and awaiting some event of considerable moment to them.

As we went on from this place, my guide said, 'I will now show you the condition of the damned.' Pointing with his hand, he said, 'Look!'

I looked down a distance which appeared incomprehensible to me. I gazed on a vast region filled with multitudes of beings. I could see everything with the most minute distinctness. The multitude of people I saw were miserable in the extreme. 'These,' said my guide, 'are they who have rejected the means of salvation, that were placed within their reach, and have brought upon themselves the condemnation you behold.'

The expression of the countenances of these sufferers was clear and distinct. They indicated extreme remorse, sorrow and dejection. They appeared conscious that none but themselves were to blame for their forlorn condition.

This scene affected me much, and I could not refrain from weeping.

Again my guide said, 'Now let us go.'

In a moment we were at the gate of a beautiful city. A porter opened it and we passed in. The city was grand and beautiful beyond anything that I can describe. It was clothed in the purest light, brilliant but not glaring or unpleasant.

The people, men and women, in their employments and surroundings, seemed contented and happy. I knew those I met without being told who they were. Jesus and the ancient apostles were there. I saw and spoke with the Apostle Paul.

My guide would not permit me to pause much by the way, but rather hurried me on through this place to another still higher but connected with it. It was still more beautiful and glorious than anything I had before seen. To me its extent and magnificence were incomprehensible.

My guide pointed to a mansion which excelled everything else in perfection and beauty. It was clothed with fire and intense light. It appeared a fountain of light, throwing brilliant scintillations of glory all around it, and I could conceive of no limit to which these emanations extended. Said my guide, 'That is where God resides.' He permitted me to enter this glorious city but a short distance. Without speaking, he motioned that we would retrace our steps.

We were soon in the adjoining city. There I met my mother, and a sister who died when six or seven years old. These I knew at sight without an introduction.

After mingling with the pure and happy beings of this place a short time, my guide said again, 'Let us go.'

We were soon through the gate by which we had entered the city. My guide then said, 'Now we will return.'

I could distinctly see the world from which we had first come. It appeared to be a vast distance below us. To me, it looked cloudy, dreary and dark. I was filled with sad disappointment, I might say horror, at the idea of returning there. I supposed I had come to stay in that heavenly place, which I had so long desired to see; up to this time, the thought had not occurred to me that I would be required to return.

I plead with my guide to let me remain. He replied that I was permitted to only visit these heavenly cities, for I had not filled my mission in yonder world; therefore I must return and take my body. If I was faithful to the grace of God which would be imparted to me, if I would bear a faithful testimony to the inhabitants of the earth of a sacrificed and risen Savior, and His Atonement for man, in a little time I should be permitted to return and remain.

These words gave me comfort and inspired my bosom with the principle of faith. To me, these things were real. I felt that a great mission had been given me, and I accepted it in my heart. The responsibility of that mission has rested on me from that time until now.

We returned to my house. There I found my body, and it appeared to me dressed for burial. It was with great reluctance that I took possession of it to resume the ordinary avocations of life, and endeavor to fill the important mission I had received. I awoke and found myself in my bed. I lay and meditated the remainder of the night on what had been shown me.

Call it a dream, or vision, or what I may, what I saw was as real to every sense of my being as anything I have passed through" (*Fragments of Experience* [Salt Lake City: Juvenile Instructor Office, 1882], 27–30).

The following vision, which was seen by Sarah Smith of Hanley, Staffordshire, England, also supports the idea that the levels of the postmortal world correspond with the four resurrections or four levels of eternal reward. This vision was recorded by Elder Parley P. Pratt on 15 June 1842 and published in the *Millennial Star* shortly thereafter.

"In 1835, on the 26th of December, being carried away in a vision, I was in a beautiful garden, interspersed with gravel walks, green pasture, and beautiful fruit-trees; looking towards the east, I saw the rays of the sun piercing among the shades, the heavens clear and bright, and myself dressed in white, with a hymn-book in my hand, and was singing hymns. I then saw the Lord Jesus coming to meet me; He was arrayed in white, and His countenance as the sun; He had twelve angels before him, and twelve behind Him, with harps in their hands, and were singing and playing music [cf. Rev. 5:8; 14:2–3; 15:2–4]; they were all in white, with long hair hanging in beautiful ringlets down their shoulders. The Lord took me by the hand, and said unto me, 'Follow thou me'; He led me through a place like unto a prison, and said, 'Behold on thy left'; and I looked and beheld the flames of hell; and I cried, 'Lord save me,' and He said, 'Surely from this hour thy soul is saved.' We then came to the bottom of a steep hill, and I saw at my right hand, as it were, a temple built of pure gold, mingled with glass. We then ascended the hill, hand-in-hand, the twelve angels before and the twelve behind: at the top of the hill were the gates of heaven, as it were, of pearl, cut in beautiful figures, and clear as crystal. At the gates stood two angels with trumpets in their hands, the Lord spoke to them, and the gates flew open; I saw within, the Lord sitting on His throne, which was of pearl, beautifully wrought in figures and ornaments. His countenance was as the lightning, almost too bright to behold; legions of angels were round about Him, all singing, and playing on musical instruments. He had in His left hand a roll of parchment, while His right hand was extended to His Son, and He said unto His Son, 'Sit thou at my right hand;' and He was then seated at His right hand. He said unto me, 'Enter into the joy of thy Lord' and I was seated at His right hand" (*Millennial Star*, vol. 3, no. 4, August 1842, 69–70, hereafter cited as *MS*).

20. *WJS*, 368.

21. Ibid., 371. Brigham Young listed three groups of "spirits . . . that the devil has power over": (1) "the spirits of those who were as good in the flesh as they knew how to be" (residents of prison), (2) "the spirits of the wicked" (residents of hell), and (3) "the spirits of devils" (residents of hell) (*JD*, 3:368).

22. *JD,* 15:322.

23. Elder Pratt's views are supported by section 76 of the D&C, which reveals that those who will inherit the terrestrial kingdom (First Resurrection) are "kept in prison" (vv. 71–73) while those who will inherit the telestial kingdom (Second Resurrection) are "thrust down to hell" (vv. 81–84). The Prophet Joseph Smith clearly distinguished between the spirit world "prison," where "honest men and noble-minded men" wait for the gospel to be preached unto them, and "hell," where "the murderer and adulterer" are confined (*WJS*, 368). An article called "In the World of Spirits," which was published by Janne M. Sjodahl in both the *Improvement Era* and the *Millennial Star,* offers evidence that "paradise," "prison," and "the region of the spirit world at present occupied by the devil and his subjects" are all separate areas (*IE*, December 1916, 111–21; *MS*, vol. 79, no. 1, 4 January 1917, 1–7, 11–13). The glossary in the *Encyclopedia of Mormonism* includes this notable entry: "spirit world: The place where the spirits of the dead await resurrection and judgment; it consists of paradise, prison, and hell" (Daniel H. Ludlow, ed., *Encyclopedia of Mormonism* [New York: Macmillan, 1992], 4:1772, hereafter cited as *EM*).

24. A convenient list can be found in Duane S. Crowther, *Life Everlasting,* rev. ed. (Bountiful, Utah: Horizon Publishers, 1997), 351. Joseph Smith warned that those who "do not repent" will "go down to hell" (*WJS*, 122) and specifically stated that a "great portion" of the Latter-day Saints would be "damned . . . unless they repent, and work righteousness" (*HC*, 3:28). President George Q. Cannon likewise said that "Latter-day Saints especially who commit sin, if they die in their sin, will go to hell, and they will suffer torment there until the day of redemption" (Newquist, ed., *Gospel Truth: Discourses and Writings of President George Q. Cannon,* 67).

25. The Lord told Joseph Smith in the spring of 1820 that He did not acknowledge any of the existing Christian denominations as His Church and kingdom because they had all apostatized from the true doctrines and ordinances of the gospel and lost the authority of the Priesthood (see *HC*, 4:536). The Lord then restored His gospel to the earth in its purity and proclaimed The Church of Jesus Christ of Latter-day Saints to be "the only true and living Church upon the face of the whole earth" (D&C 1:30). Because of these facts, baptisms from other Christian churches are not considered valid (see D&C 22:1–4; *HC*, 3:29; *WJS*, 78).

26. Joseph Fielding Smith, *Doctrines of Salvation* (Salt Lake City: Bookcraft, 1999),

2:230, emphasis in original, hereafter cited as *DS.* "It seems that a requirement for entrance to what Alma calls the spirit world paradise is the ordinance of baptism" (Monte S. Nyman, "The State of the Soul Between Death and the Resurrection," in Monte S. Nyman and Charles D. Tate, Jr., eds., *The Book of Mormon: Alma, the Testimony of the Word* [Provo, Utah: BYU Religious Studies Center, 1992], 180).

27. *Times and Seasons,* vol. 3, no. 12, 15 April 1842, 760, hereafter cited as *T&S.* The Lord, in His infinite justice and mercy, "ordained, before the world was, that which would enable us to redeem [the dead] out of their prison" (D&C 128:22) and designated the dispensation of the fullness of times as the main "dispensation to meet the promises made by Jesus Christ before the foundation of the world for the salvation of man" (*WJS,* 346).

28. *JD,* 18:190.

29. *CD,* 5:373.

30. *JD,* 26:83.

31. Conference Report, October 1918, 97, hereafter cited as CR.

32. See CR, April 1922, 57–58; Bruce R. McConkie, *Mormon Doctrine,* 2d ed. (Salt Lake City: Bookcraft, 1966), 686, hereafter cited as *MD.*

33. *MD,* 673, emphasis added.

34. *HC,* 3:29, emphasis added.

35. *WJS,* 370.

36. *T&S,* vol. 3, no. 12, 15 April 1842, 760. President Joseph F. Smith offered his opinion that women would preach the gospel to women in the world of spirits. "Now, among all these millions of spirits that have lived on the earth and have passed away, from generation to generation, since the beginning of the world, without the knowledge of the gospel—among them you may count that at least one-half are women. Who is going to preach the gospel to the women? Who is going to carry the testimony of Jesus Christ to the hearts of the women who have passed away without a knowledge of the gospel? Well, to my mind, it is a simple thing. These good sisters who have been set apart, ordained to the work, called to it, authorized by the authority of the Holy Priesthood to minister for their sex, in the House of God for the living and for the dead, will be fully authorized and empowered to preach the gospel and minister to the women while the elders and prophets are preaching it to the men. The things

we experience here are typical of the things of God and the life beyond us" (*GD*, 461).

37. *JD*, 4:273–74. Heber C. Kimball also said that "the separation of body and spirit makes no difference in the moral and intellectual condition of the spirit[.] When a person, who has always been good and faithful to his God, lays down his body in the dust, his spirit will remain the same in the spirit world. It is not the body that has control over the spirit, as to its disposition, but it is the spirit that controls the body. When the spirit leaves the body the body becomes lifeless. The spirit has not changed one single particle of itself by leaving the body" (ibid., 3:108).

38. These ordinances are listed in *WJS*, 78, 318, 329, 363–65, 371.

39. Ibid., 368.

40. See *EM*, 1:96; 4:1458.

41. In referring to proxy baptism Joseph Smith warned that "those Saints who neglect it, in behalf of their deceased relatives, do it at the peril of their own salvation" (*WJS*, 78).

42. See *EM*, 4:1455. The revelation to President Woodruff on this subject is mentioned in Elder Abraham H. Cannon's journal under the date of 5 April 1894.

43. *JD*, 16:240. Several other Church authorities have taught this doctrine. Brigham Young: "You may ask if they are baptized there [in the spirit world]. No. Can they have hands laid upon them for the gift of the Holy Ghost? No. None of the outward ordinances that pertain to the flesh are administered there" (ibid., 2:138). Charles W. Penrose: "The ordinances which belong to the sphere of mortality cannot be received in a spiritual estate; they belong to the flesh and must be attended to in the flesh" (*The Contributor*, vol. 2, no. 8, May 1881, 233). Joseph Fielding Smith: "Baptism is an ordinance which pertains to mortal life and those who have passed beyond, whether they were in the spirit world or had passed through the Resurrection, no longer belong to mortality, and therefore cannot be baptized in person. If this could be done, there would be no need for us to officiate for the dead by proxy now, for they could act for themselves after the Resurrection" (*IE*, September 1920, 1029). Wilford Woodruff: "They will not baptize anybody in the spirit world; there is no baptism there; there is no marrying or giving in marriage there. All these ordinances have to be performed on the earth" (*JD*, 18:114). Orson Pratt: "If you

wish to obtain a great many blessings pertaining to the future world, you have to secure these blessings here. You cannot be baptized in the next state of existence for the remission of sins; that is an ordinance pertaining to the flesh, which you must attend to here. And so with all other ordinances which God has ordained, you have to partake of them here in order to have a claim on the promises hereafter. . . . [T]his is the world for all these ordinances to be attended to. Here is the place to secure all the blessings for the next world. We have to show in this probation that we will be obedient in obeying the commandments of heaven so that we may have a claim on every blessing pertaining to the next life" (ibid., 15:251).

44. *DS*, 2:142.

45. *GD*, 438, emphasis added. The Prophet Joseph Smith reportedly taught the Saints in Nauvoo that "those who die without the obedience of the gospel while having a privilege here will have to [be] subject to the law they are under. But those who have not had this privilege will have it in the prison of spirits. For so long as they have not the privilege they cannot be condemned. Therefore they must come under condemnation by this wise" (*BYU Studies*, vol. 18, no. 2, Winter 1978, 173). The Prophet is also reported to have said that "those who hear the gospel . . . [and] who know the gospel and do not obey, but fight against it, will be shut up in prison [under] condemnation and shall not be visited till many days hence, Isaiah 24[:22]. Then some person has to redeem them by making a forfeit of some payment for them" (ibid., 174). Joseph Fielding Smith made some similar comments. "Every man who rejects the gospel, . . . *who rejects the testimony of Jesus, who denies the truth, who refuses to receive the testimony as it is declared unto him by the elders of Israel, shall be punished and shall be placed in the prison house, and there he shall stay until he has paid the penalty of his transgressions*" (*DS*, 2:229, emphasis in original).

46. *WJS*, 372; see also ibid., 368. Orson Pratt had the following to say about divine law. "The Lord our God is a God of law, His house is a house of order; and all blessings, and honor, and glory, and inheritance, that are to be received in the eternal worlds must be according to divine law and divine ordinances, and whosoever complies with the law of heaven has a legal claim in eternity" (*JD*, 16:257).

47. *DS*, 2:191, emphasis in original.

48. Ibid., 3:131. In another source President Smith notes that "there is a feeling existing among some members of the Church that because the Prophet [Joseph

Smith] declared that we without our dead cannot be made perfect [see D&C 128:15], the work in the temples will have to be performed for all the dead. This is an error. What is intended by this remark is that we cannot be made perfect without our dead who are worthy and entitled to salvation. There will be a great host of the dead who will not be entitled to the ordinances of exaltation and who will not be made perfect. Perfection is in the celestial kingdom only, and those who enter the other kingdoms and who are restricted will be as countless as the stars of heaven" (Joseph Fielding Smith, *Church History and Modern Revelation* [Salt Lake City: Deseret News Press, 1949], 4:135–36).

49. Ibid., 2:185.

50. *Ensign*, February 1995, 49, emphasis in original. Elder Orson Pratt said much the same thing. "When these holy and sacred institutions are made known to the spirits in prison by holy messengers holding the Priesthood, they will be left to their own agency either to receive or reject these glad tidings, and will be judged according to men in the flesh who have the privilege of hearing the same things" (*The Seer*, vol. 1, no. 9, September 1853, 141–42). Elder James E. Talmage writes, "The results of such labors are to be left with the Lord. It is not to be supposed that by these ordinances the departed are in any way compelled to accept the obligation, nor that they are in the least hindered in the exercise of their free agency. They will accept or reject according to their condition of humility or hostility in respect to the gospel" (James E. Talmage, *Articles of Faith* [Salt Lake City: Deseret Book, 1984], 138; see also *EM*, 1:96).

51. *DS*, 2:184, emphasis in original. President Smith also states, "If the person had every opportunity to receive [the temple] blessings in person and refused, or through procrastination and lack of faith did not receive them, then he is not entitled to them, and it is doubtful if the work for him will be valid if done within one week [after his death] or 1,000 years. The Lord has declared that it is he who endures to the end that shall be saved, and he who rejects or neglects these blessings until death, when he has had the opportunity, is not worthy of them" (ibid., 2:179). According to President Spencer W. Kimball "vicarious work for the dead is for those who could not do the work for themselves. Men and women who live in mortality and who have heard the gospel here have had their day, their seventy years to put their lives in harmony, to perform the ordinances, to repent and to perfect their lives" (Edward L. Kimball, ed., *The Teachings of Spencer W. Kimball* [Salt Lake City: Bookcraft, 1982], 542). Elder Bruce R. McConkie taught that "there is no such thing as salvation for the

dead for those to whom the truth is offered in plainness and purity while they dwell in mortality. . . . In what is probably the greatest of all recorded visions, given 16 February 1832, the Prophet saw that those to whom Noah offered the gospel and who were then destroyed in the flood, assuming they repent and accept the gospel in their spirit prison, shall not obtain celestial rest. Theirs is an everlasting terrestrial inheritance because they rejected the truth when it was offered to them in mortality" (*Ensign*, August 1976, 9). Elder Melvin J. Ballard said, "Any man or woman who has heard the gospel and rejected it—not only those in the days of Noah, but any man or woman in this day who has had a good chance to receive and embrace the gospel and enjoy its blessings and privileges, but who has been indifferent of these things, ignoring and neglecting them—such a person need not hope or anticipate that when he is dead the work can be done for him and he can gain celestial glory. Don't you Latter-day Saints get the notion that a man can live in defiance or total indifference, having had a good chance—not just a casual chance or opportunity—to accept the gospel and that when he dies you can go and do the work for him and have him receive every blessing that the faithful ones are entitled to" (Melvin R. Ballard, ed., *Melvin J. Ballard: Crusader for Righteousness* [Salt Lake City: Bookcraft, 1966], 221). For further reading on the Second Chance Theory see *DS*, 2:181–83; Bruce R. McConkie, *Doctrinal New Testament Commentary* (Salt Lake City: Bookcraft, 1965), 1:435; DS, 2:423–24; *MD*, 685–87; Bruce R. McConkie, "The Seven Deadly Heresies," in *Brigham Young University Devotional and Fireside Addresses 1980* (Provo, Utah: Brigham Young University Press, 1981), 77–78.

52. *DS*, 2:176, emphasis in original.

53. CR, April 1906, 86. On another occasion President Penrose said, "The time will come when the Priesthood behind the veil will minister personally in the temples of God to men holding the Priesthood in the flesh, revealing matters that are needful to be known concerning the departed that the work being performed for the dead, as well as for the living, may go on and be accomplished and perfected properly" (ibid., June 1919, 35).

54. *JD*, 9:317. Joseph Fielding Smith concurs on this matter. He says, "The Lord expects of us all that we do what we can for ourselves and for our dead. He wants us to make the search for our ancestry because He does not do for us what we can do for ourselves. And after we have done all we can, then means will be furnished, or the way will be opened for the furnishing of the informa-

tion which we are unable to discover. The time will come when the dead, or at least those who have passed through the Resurrection unto life, will work hand in hand with those who are still in mortality, and they will furnish the information. There will be no mistakes about it then, and we will have the privilege of going into the temple of the Lord and doing the work, until every soul for whom this work is intended shall be ferreted out, and not one soul shall be overlooked" (*DS*, 2:149–50).

CHAPTER 7

RESURRECTION AND JUDGMENT

Latter-day Saints are accustomed to thinking that the first principles and ordinances of the gospel are limited to faith, repentance, baptism, and the gift of the Holy Ghost (A of F #4). They hold this view because Joseph Smith listed these four particular items in a letter that he wrote to Mr. John Wentworth—a Chicago newspaper editor—on 1 March 1842. These items were eventually canonized and today they are published in the Pearl of Great Price as part of the Articles of Faith.

But long before Joseph Smith wrote to Mr. Wentworth he was teaching the Latter-day Saints an expanded view of the first principles. On 27 June 1839 (after discoursing on faith, repentance, baptism, and the gift of the Holy Ghost) the Prophet informed a gathering of Saints that "the doctrine of the resurrection of the dead and eternal judgment are necessary to preach among the first principles of the gospel of Jesus Christ"[1] (cf. Heb. 6:1–2). The Prophet also listed these doctrines together in a letter that is dated 22 March 1839. In this correspondence he wrote, "We believe in the doctrine of faith, and of repentance, and of baptism for the remission of sins, and the gift of the Holy Ghost by the laying on of hands, and of [the] resurrection of the dead, and of eternal judgment."[2] This expanded list of principles is also found in an epistle that was written by members of the Quorum of the Twelve Apostles on 3 July 1839. These Church authorities instructed the Elders of the Church to "preach the first principles of the doctrine of Christ—faith in the Lord Jesus Christ, repentance towards God, baptism in the name of Jesus for the remission of sins, laying on of hands for the gift of the Holy Ghost, the resurrection of the dead, and eternal judgment."[3]

Since the Resurrection and the Judgment have such primary importance among the doctrines of the gospel it is imperative that Latter-day Saints understand something of their nature and the role that they will play in the salvation of each individual. These doctrines will be explored on the pages that follow.

THE RESURRECTION OF THE DEAD

"The greatest events of history," explained President Ezra Taft Benson, "are those which affect the greatest number for the longest periods. By this standard, no event could be more important to individuals or nations than the Resurrection of the Master."[4] President N. Eldon Tanner, Second Counselor in the First Presidency, agreed with this assessment. He affirmed that Jesus Christ's Resurrection was "the greatest event that has ever taken place in the history of mortal man."[5] The scriptures testify that Jesus of Nazareth was "the firstfruits of them that slept" (1 Cor. 15:20), meaning that He was the first mortal to ever come forth from the grave in a state of immortality.[6] Angels have borne witness to this miraculous event (see Luke 24:4–7) and so have numerous people who have had the privilege of seeing the risen Lord for themselves (see Acts 2:32; 3:15; 1 Cor. 15:3–8; 3 Ne. 11:8–17; D&C 76:12–14, 20–24; 110:1–10).[7]

The Resurrection is classified as one of the "mysteries" of God in both the Bible and the Book of Mormon (see 1 Cor. 15:51–53; Alma 40:3). Yet President Joseph F. Smith was confident that "there will be no more mystery in the Resurrection from the dead to life and everlasting light, than there is in the birth of man into the world, when we understand the truth, as we will someday."[8] In order to begin to understand this great mystery we might ask a series of short questions and search for answers among the writings of prophets and scholars.

What is the meaning of the word "resurrection"?

Gospel scholar Robert J. Matthews provides an informative answer to this question. He writes that "the term *resurrection* comes from two words: the prefix *re-*, meaning to repeat or do again, and *surgere*, meaning 'to rise,' as with a strong impulse or surge. A resurrection is to be brought back to life; to have a resurge of life or power. A resurrected person is one whose body was once alive, and which has died, and is filled again with a surge of power or life, which enables him to rise up again."[9]

Who will be resurrected?

The Bible testifies that "as in Adam *all* die, even so in Christ shall *all* be made alive" (1 Cor. 15:22, emphasis added). The Book of Mormon contains a confirmation of this teaching in Alma chapter 40 verse 4. It is stated in this passage of scripture that "there is a time appointed that *all* shall come forth from the dead" (emphasis added). President Ezra Taft Benson affirms that "the eventual resurrection of every soul who has lived and died on earth is a scriptural certainty." And he also reminds us that "there is no event for which one should make more careful preparation."[10]

President Joseph F. Smith provides an interesting perspective on mankind's eventual rise from the grave. He says that "it was decreed in the beginning that man should be, and will be, through the Atonement of Jesus, in spite of himself, resurrected from the dead. Death came upon us without the exercise of our agency; we had no hand in bringing it originally upon ourselves; it came because of the transgression of our first parents. Therefore, man, who had no hand in bringing death upon himself, shall have no hand in bringing again life unto himself."[11]

Why is the Resurrection necessary?

Those who inhabit the fallen or telestial world are cut off both spiritually and physically from the presence of the Lord. The Resurrection will redeem "all mankind" from "*spiritual* death" (Hel. 14:16, emphasis added) because each person will be "raised [with] a *spiritual* body" (1 Cor. 15:44, emphasis added). A resurrected tabernacle will also enable each individual to overcome their physical separation from God—at least temporarily. The Lord causes "the Resurrection [to] pass upon *all* men, that *all* might stand before Him at the great . . . Judgment Day" (2 Ne. 9:22, emphasis added; see also Alma 42:23; Hel. 14:15, 17). As it was pointed out in the previous chapter, spirits cannot go where resurrected beings reside.

How will the Resurrection be accomplished?

Jesus Christ took up His body again "by the power of the Spirit," says 2 Nephi chapter 2 verse 8. It appears that this same mechanism will play a part in the resurrection of each son and daughter of God. It was Joseph Smith's teaching that "God [will] bring [the dead] up again, clothed upon and quickened by the Spirit of the great God."[12] This may not be the only mechanism that plays a part in the resurrection process, however. Gospel scholar Robert J. Matthews notes:

> Any doctrine or ordinance as fundamental to man's eternal salvation as the resurrection of the dead is of necessity regulated and performed by the keys of the Melchizedek Priesthood. It is also part of the patriarchal order of the family. So far as the celestial kingdom is concerned, the resurrection is a family event. We would at first naturally suppose that Jesus would resurrect Himself, but perhaps He did not. Jesus did not baptize Himself. The clear rendering of Acts 2:22–24, 32; 3:12–15; 5:30–32 . . . represents Peter saying on three separate occasions that *God* raised up Jesus from the dead. If we read those passages literally and combine that concept with the teachings of President [Brigham] Young and Elder [Erastus] Snow, that only a resurrected being can perform a resurrection, we may gain an insight into the resurrection process as a patriarchal family order in which a righteous resurrected father would resurrect his son, and so forth.[13]

Brigham Young put forward the idea in one of his discourses that "some person holding the keys of the resurrection, having previously passed through that ordeal, will be delegated to resurrect our bodies."[14] He also explained that mortals do not currently possess "the ordinance and the keys of the resurrection. They will be given to those who have passed off this stage of action and have received their bodies again. . . . They will be ordained, by those who hold the keys of the resurrection, to go forth and resurrect the Saints."[15] Elder Erastus Snow was even more specific about who would be granted this sacred privilege. He said that those who have been "crowned *kings and priests* with God and the Lamb . . . shall . . . carry on the work of the redemption and resurrection of the Saints of God."[16] Such an idea is confirmed by Charles W. Penrose, who says that "in the resurrection [husbands and wives] stand side by side and hold dominion together. Every man who *overcomes all things* and is thereby entitled to *inherit all things*, receives power to bring up his wife to join him in the possession and enjoyment thereof."[17]

What will happen to a resurrected body once it has been raised?

The Apostle Paul informs us in the book of 1 Corinthians that when the Resurrection takes place the body "is raised in glory" (15:43). But the glory of each resurrected body will differ by degrees. "There is one glory of the sun, and another glory of the moon, and another glory of the stars: for one star differeth from another star in glory. So also is the resurrection of the dead" (vv. 41–42). Thus, President Joseph F. Smith remarks that "when we come forth out of the grave . . . our spirits shall enter into [our physical bodies] again, and they shall become living souls [see D&C 88:15–16]. . . . And then those who have not been subject and obedient to the celestial law will not be quickened by the celestial glory. And those who have not been subject and obedient to the terrestrial law will not be quickened by the terrestrial glory. And those who have not been subject and obedient to the telestial law will not be quickened by a telestial glory"[18] (cf. D&C 76:70, 78, 81; 88:22–24).

How many resurrections will take place?

The standard works speak of two general resurrections—of the "just" and the "unjust" (D&C 76:17); of "life" and "damnation" (John 5:29); of "endless life" and "endless damnation" (Mosiah 16:11); of "everlasting life" and "everlasting contempt" (Daniel 12:2). But in section 88 of the Doctrine and Covenants it is revealed that each of these resurrections are subdivided into two events. Thus, there are actually four separate resurrections that will take place, and they will correspond exactly to the three degrees of glory and outer darkness.

> And [the angel] shall sound his *trump* both long and loud, and all nations shall hear it.

> And there shall be silence in heaven for the space of half an hour; and immediately after shall the curtain of heaven be unfolded, as a scroll is unfolded after it is rolled up, and the face of the Lord shall be unveiled.

> And the Saints that are upon the earth, who are alive, shall be quickened and be caught up to meet [Jesus Christ].

> And they who have slept in their graves shall come forth, for their graves shall be opened; and they also shall be caught up to meet him in the midst of the pillar of heaven.

> They are Christ's, the first fruits, they who shall descend with him first, and they who are on the earth and in their graves, who are first caught up to meet him; and all this by the voice of the sounding of the *[first] trump* of the angel of God.

> And after this another angel shall sound, which is the *second trump;* and then cometh the redemption of those who are Christ's at his coming; who have received their part in that prison which is prepared for them, that they might receive the gospel, and be judged according to men in the flesh.

> And again, another trump shall sound, which is the *third trump;* and then come the spirits of men who are to be judged, and are found under condemnation.

> And these are the rest of the dead; and they live not again until the thousand years are ended, neither again, until the end of the earth.

And another trump shall sound, which is the *fourth trump,* saying: "There are found among those who are to remain until that great and last day, even the end, who shall remain filthy still" (D&C 88:94–102, emphasis added).

Elder Bruce R. McConkie offers some clarification on the various resurrections. He explains that all of those people who lived between Adam's day and the meridian of time, and who merited a celestial reward, were resurrected shortly after Jesus Christ arose from the grave (see Matt. 27:52–53; D&C 133:54–55). This was the beginning or morning of the First Resurrection. This resurrection has generally been put on hold (with a few exceptions—like Peter, James, and Moroni) but it will resume at the time of the Second Coming. It must be understood, however, that "those being resurrected with celestial bodies, whose destiny it is to inherit a celestial kingdom, will come forth in the *morning* of the First Resurrection" regardless of when they actually arise from the grave or are changed to their resurrected state (see 1 Cor. 15:51–52; 3 Ne. 28:4–8; D&C 63:50–53; 101:30–31). Those who are raised from death with a terrestrial body, regardless of when they actually arise, will come forth in the *afternoon* of the First Resurrection. In the forepart of the Second Resurrection (at the end of the Millennium) the heirs of the telestial world will come forth, and they will be followed thereafter by the sons of perdition.[19]

The Nature of Resurrected Bodies

The scriptures and the writings of LDS Church leaders contain a substantial amount of information on the nature of resurrected bodies. The following are a few points of interest.

Body and Spirit Reunited: The most fundamental principle associated with the Resurrection is that "the bodies and the spirits of men will be restored one to the other"(2 Ne. 9:12). President John Taylor explains that "man is an eternal being, composed of body and spirit: his spirit existed before he came here; his body exists with the spirit in time, and after death the spirit exists without the body. In the Resurrection, both body and spirit will finally be reunited; and it requires both body and spirit to make a perfect man, whether in time, or eternity."[20]

Perfect Human Form: Resurrected bodies will consist of flesh and bones just as mortal bodies do (cf. D&C 138:17; 129:1; 130:22; Ezek. 37:1–14). Alma chapter 41 verse 2 relates that "every part of the body [will] be restored to itself" and in Alma chapter 40 verse 23 the statement is made that "every limb and joint shall be restored to its body; yea, even a hair of the head shall not be lost; but all things shall be restored to their proper and perfect frame" (cf. Alma 11:44). Indeed, all resurrected beings will "receive the same body which was [their] natural body . . . [but their] glory shall be that glory by which [their] bodies are quickened" (D&C 88:28). They will "be in the same image, and have the same likeness, without variation or change in any of [their] parts or faculties," said John Taylor, "except the substitution of spirit for blood."[21]

President Spencer W. Kimball, in speaking of the condition that resurrected bodies will be in, said, "I am confident that when we come back with our bodies again, there will be no aches or pains. There will be no wrinkles or deformities. I am sure that if we can imagine ourselves at our very best, physically, mentally, spiritually, that is the way we will come back—perhaps not as a child or youth, perhaps in sweet and glorious maturity, but not in age or infirmity or distress or pain or aches."[22]

Spiritual and Immortal: According to the Apostle Paul the "natural body . . . is raised [as] *a spiritual body*" (1 Cor. 15:44, emphasis added; cf. D&C 88:27). Similarly, Amulek says in the Book of Mormon, "Now, behold, I have spoken unto you concerning the death of the mortal body, and also concerning the Resurrection of the mortal body. I say unto you that this mortal body is raised to an *immortal* body, that is from death, even from the first death unto life, that *they can die no more*; their spirits uniting with their bodies, *never to be divided*; thus the whole *becoming spiritual and immortal*, that they can no more see corruption" (Alma 11:45, emphasis added).

Why are resurrected bodies referred to as "spiritual" bodies? "The Resurrection will again unite the spirit with the body," taught Howard W. Hunter, "and the body becomes a spiritual body, one of flesh and bones but quickened by the spirit instead of blood. Thus, our bodies after the resurrection, quickened by the spirit, shall become immortal and never die. This is the meaning of the statements of Paul."[23] The Prophet Joseph Smith taught "concerning resurrection: flesh and blood cannot inherit the kingdom of God or the kingdom that God . . . inhabits [see 1 Cor. 15:50]. But the flesh without the blood and the Spirit of God flowing in the veins instead of the blood [can] for blood is the part of the body that causes corruption. . . . God dwells in flaming flames [cf. D&C 130:6–7] and He is a consuming fire [see Deut. 4:24; Heb. 12:29]. He will consume all that is unclean and unholy and we could not abide His presence unless pure Spirit's in us."[24]

Same Identical Person: President Joseph F. Smith teaches us that a resurrected personage will be "the same identical being that we associated with here in the flesh—not some other soul, some other being, or the same being in some other form, but the same identity and the same form and likeness, the same person we knew and were associated with in our mortal existence."[25]

Some people may ask, "Do not the particles that compose man's body, when returned to mother earth, go to make or compose other bodies?" President Brigham Young answered, "No, they do not. . . . Neither can the particles which have comprised the body of man become parts of the bodies of other men, or of beasts, [fowls], fish[es], insect[s], or vegetables. They are governed by divine law and though they may pass from the knowledge of the scientific world, that divine law still holds, governs and controls them. . . . [A]t the sound of the trumpet of God every particle of our physical structures necessary to make our tabernacles perfect will be assembled, to be rejoined with the spirit, every man in his order. Not one particle will be lost."[26]

Scars and Deformities Removed: President Joseph F. Smith maintained that "a person will [not] always be marred by scars, wounds, deformities, defects or infirmities, for these will be removed in their course."[27] And he offered the reassurance that once these defects and deformities are eliminated "men and women shall attain to the perfection of their spirits, to the perfection that God designed in the beginning."[28] President Smith's son, Joseph Fielding Smith, informs us that the former "never intended to convey the thought that it would require weeks or months of time in order for the defects to be removed. These changes will come naturally, of course, but *almost instantly*."[29]

Fully Formed: In speaking of those who die before reaching adulthood, President Joseph F. Smith observed that "the body will come forth as it is laid to rest, for there is no growth nor development in the grave. As it is laid down, so will it arise, and changes to perfection will come by the law of restitution. But the spirit will continue to expand and develop, and the body after the resurrection will develop to the full stature of man."[30]

Joseph Fielding Smith declared the very same doctrine. He said that "when a baby dies, it goes back into the spirit world, and the spirit assumes its natural form as an adult, for we were all adults before we were born. When a child is raised in the resurrection, the spirit will enter the body and the body will be the same size as it was when the child died. It will then *grow after the resurrection* to full maturity to conform to the size of the spirit."[31]

Higher Capabilities: Elder James E. Talmage referred in his writings to some of the higher capabilities that are possessed by those who receive the Resurrection. Said he, "A resurrected body, though of tangible substance, and possessing all the organs of the mortal tabernacle, is not bound to earth by gravitation, nor can it be hindered in its movements by material barriers. To us who conceive of motion only in the directions incident to the three dimensions of space, the passing of a solid, such as a living body of flesh and bones, through stone walls, is necessarily incomprehensible. But that resurrected beings move in accordance with laws making such passage possible and to them natural, is evidenced not only by the instance of the risen Christ [see Luke 24:36–39], but by the movements of other resurrected personages [see JS—H, 1:43]."[32]

Resurrected Status Is Final

Some Latter-day Saints have speculated that if a person were to merit a telestial resurrection they might, according to the principle of eternal progression, eventually advance to the point where they would qualify to enter into the celestial sphere.[33] Several prominent leaders of the LDS Church have addressed this issue from the general conference pulpit and have denied the validity of such a belief. President George Albert Smith, for one, said in the October conference of 1945, "There are some people who have supposed that if we are quickened telestial bodies that eventually, throughout the ages of eternity, we will continue to progress until we will find our place in the celestial kingdom, but the scriptures and revelations of God have said that those who are quickened telestial bodies cannot come where God and Christ dwell, worlds without end"[34] (see D&C 76:112). During the general conference held in April of 1922 Joseph Fielding Smith, who was then a member of the Quorum of the Twelve Apostles, said something similar:

> There has been a great deal of discussion going on in certain parts, as to whether or not those of the telestial kingdom may advance into the terrestrial, and those of the terrestrial into the celestial, and whether eventually all men enter into the kingdom where God lives and Christ reigns. Why should we worry ourselves? Why should we argue? Why should we contend? Why should we discuss a matter of that kind? When we have come out of the world and have received the gospel in its fullness, we are candidates for celestial glory; nay, we are more than candidates, if we are faithful, for the Lord has given unto us the assurance that through our faithfulness, we shall enter into the celestial kingdom, and surely, no Latter-day Saint desires a place somewhere else, there to take a chance of someday being forgiven and having the opportunity of advancing and finally reaching the place where the righteous dwell.
>
> Then again, let us keep in mind what the Lord has said; it is unnecessary for us to go outside of that which the Lord has stated in the revelations unto the Church. He has declared, speaking of those who enter into the telestial kingdom, that "where God and Christ dwell they cannot come, worlds without end" [D&C 76:112]. Then, why should we bother about it; why should we argue about it; why should we consider these things in such a serious manner?[35]

During the October general conference of 1917 Elder Melvin J. Ballard of the Council of the Twelve asked the following pointed questions of those who were seated before him:

Now, my brethren and sisters, what is your aim? To which place do you desire to go? How earnest are you in this struggle? How much are you willing to live of this precious gospel? Is your mark fixed for the celestial glory, or the telestial glory, the lowest place? Is that your ambition? Do you imagine that by living a terrestrial law you will attain the celestial glory? Some of my brethren and sisters find it very difficult to understand the words of the Prophet [Joseph Smith], wherein he said that those who gain a lower place of glory than a celestial kingdom cannot come where those who gain the highest dwell, worlds without end.

And there is an imagination on the part of some of us that we could do our work over again, that we could catch up, and finally get into the celestial kingdom. Now to help you to see it, I ask you if three men were started on an endless race, and one given a handicap of a mile and still another of two miles, and each man could run as fast as the other, would one ever catch the other? No. But there is a big difference here. Those who live the laws and attain unto the glory of the celestial [world] shall have a body whose very fineness and texture, the composition of it, the quality of flesh shall be superior, for the Lord has said, "There is a celestial body, and celestial flesh, and there shall be telestial bodies, and their flesh will not be so refined nor so pure, nor the body so capable of progress and enjoyment and exaltation which shall be enjoyed by those who gain a celestial body." So there will be a handicap. Those who gain the highest place provided shall have a very superior physical equipment, capable of more intense and rapid growth.[36]

There have been other general authorities who have dealt with the notion of progression between kingdoms. President Spencer W. Kimball, for instance, made this unambiguous statement. "After a person has been assigned to his place in the kingdom, either in the telestial, the terrestrial, or the celestial, or to his exaltation, he will *never* advance from his assigned glory to another glory. That is eternal! That is why we must make our decisions early in life and why it is imperative that such decisions be right."[37] Elder John A. Widtsoe also made his stance on this matter very clear when he wrote that progression between kingdoms is "utterly impossible."[38] And Elder Bruce R. McConkie even stated that this idea is one of the seven deadly heresies.[39]

BEFORE THE JUDGMENT SEAT

After the resurrection of the dead has taken place[40] "every soul who belongs to the whole human family of Adam . . . must stand to be judged of [their] works" (Morm. 3:20). "They must appear before the judgment seat of the Holy One of Israel," says 2 Nephi 9:15, "and then cometh the judgment, and then must they be judged according to the holy judgment of God" (cf. Rom. 14:10, 12).

According to Elder Milton R. Hunter the Final Judgment will encompass the totality of a person's existence and not just one's mortal probation. He says, "Every person who has lived and shall live in this world—every man, woman, and child—shall stand before the judgment seat of God to answer for the life he or she lived here in mortality, and also to answer for the life lived in the spirit world."[41] Gospel scholar Larry E. Dahl observes that by the time this Judgment takes place "the accumulated effect of all our decisions in the pre-earth life, mortality, and the post-earth spirit world will be an unmistakable demonstration of what we *really are*, what law we can and will obey, and therefore what measure of truth and light and glory we can abide"[42] (cf. D&C 88:22–24, 40).

Since the Final Judgment will irrevocably determine the eternal circumstances of every child of God, it would seem prudent to understand as much as possible about its purpose, nature, and administration. The following set of questions and answers are designed to start the reader down that path.

Why is the Judgment necessary?

In short, the Judgment is essential so that a person's use of the power of agency can be properly assessed and appropriately rewarded. When Adam and Eve partook of the fruit of "the tree of [the] knowledge of *good and evil*" (Gen. 2:9, emphasis added) they made the knowledge of those two opposites accessible to all of those who would come after them. "Behold, ye are free," says a passage in the Book of Mormon; "ye are permitted to act for yourselves; for behold, God hath given unto you a knowledge and he hath made you free. He hath given unto you that ye might know *good from evil*, and he hath given unto you that ye might *choose* life or death; and ye can do *good* and be restored unto that which is *good* . . . or ye can do *evil*, and have that which is *evil* restored unto you" (Hel. 14:30–31, emphasis added). Because all of Adam and Eve's descendants have been granted the agency to choose between the two opposing forces of life (see 2 Ne. 2:11, 14–16), they are required to "stand to be judged of [their] works, whether they be *good or evil*" (Morm. 3:20, emphasis added).

Who will act as our judge?

Many people believe that the answer to this question is simple— God the Father will be the judge of all mankind. But a careful examination of the scriptures demonstrates that the answer is considerably more complex. Verse 27 in the fifth chapter of the book of John states that God the Father has given Jesus Christ "authority to execute judgment." Indeed, "the Father judgeth no man, but hath committed all judgment unto the Son." Why did God grant this authority to His firstborn? The answer given in holy writ is so that "all men [will] honor the Son, even as they honor the Father" (vv. 22–23).

The forty-fourth verse in the eleventh chapter of the book of Alma states that all men and women will "be arraigned before the bar of Christ the Son, and God the Father, and the Holy Spirit, which is one Eternal God, to be judged according to their works, whether they be good or whether they be evil." From this verse it can be seen that even though Judgment takes place at the bar of the entire Godhead, Jesus Christ has been assigned the role of the primary judge. It is important to remember, however, that "Christ's judicial decisions are those of the other two members of the Godhead because all three are perfectly united as one"[43] (cf. John 17:11, 22).

Elder Orson Pratt made a noteworthy observation about the amount of work that will be involved in the Final Judgment. He said, "It seems to me that unless there were a great number [of people] engaged in judging the dead, it would require a very long period of time; . . . [F]or one being to personally investigate all the idle thoughts and words of the children of men from the days of Adam down until that time, it would require a great many millions of years." After considering this situation, Elder Pratt came to the conclusion that "God has His agents, and that through those agents the dead will be judged."[44] Elder Pratt's conclusion is supported by the words of the Savior. The Son of God told His Twelve Apostles: "in the regeneration [i.e., Resurrection] when the Son of Man shall sit [o]n the throne of His glory, ye also shall sit upon twelve thrones, judging the twelve tribes of Israel" (Matt. 19:28). God the Father has decreed that the Twelve Apostles will "judge the whole house of Israel, even as many as have loved [Him] and kept [His] commandments, *and none else*" (D&C 29:12, emphasis added; cf. 1 Ne. 12:9; Morm. 3:18–19). The scriptures also reveal that in addition to the Twelve Apostles "the Saints shall judge the world . . . [and they shall also] judge angels" (1 Cor. 6:2–3; cf. D&C 75:21).

President John Taylor summarizes what has been said thus far and also adds his own personal view on this subject. He says that "Christ is at the head, His apostles and disciples seem to take the next prominent part; then comes the actions of the Saints, or other branches of the Priesthood, who it is stated shall judge the world. This combined Priesthood, it would appear, will hold the destiny of the human family in their hands and adjudicate in all matters pertaining to their affairs; and it would seem to be quite reasonable . . . that the First Presidency and Twelve who have officiated in our age, should operate in regard to mankind in this dispensation."[45]

How will the Judgment be administered?

In the second chapter and second verse of the book of Romans it is stated that "the judgment of God is according to truth" (cf. Deut. 32:3–4; Ps. 31:5; D&C 93:26; Moses 1:6). Other scriptures teach that each of the judicial decisions of the Almighty are righteous and just (see Acts 17:31; Rev. 16:7; 19:2; Ps. 19:9; Mosiah 16:1; Alma 12:15). President Spencer W. Kimball assures us that "in the judgment of God there will be no injustice and no soul will receive any blessing, reward, or glory which he has not earned, and no soul will be punished through deprivation or otherwise for anything of which he was not guilty."[46] We will all face a "Righteous Judge," says President Harold B. Lee, and He "will take into account our capacities and our limitations, our opportunities and our handicaps."[47]

What will be the criteria for judgment?

There are several answers to this question. According to Alma 12:12–14, Matthew 12:36–37, and Doctrine and Covenants 137:9, the children of God will be required to answer on the Day of Judgment for all of their thoughts, desires, words, and works (cf. D&C 6:16; Alma 18:32).[48] It will also be "required of the Lord, at the hand of every steward, to render an account of his stewardship, both in time and in eternity" (D&C 72:3; see also 70:4). Furthermore, all men and women will be held accountable for their knowledge of the Lord's revealed word and how they responded to it (see 2 Ne. 29:11).[49] Finally, President Marion G. Romney informs us that "the verdict [of the Final Judgment] will turn on obedience or disobedience to the laws and ordinances of the gospel. If these laws and ordinances have been complied with during mortal life, the candidate will be cleansed from the stain of sin by the atoning blood of Jesus Christ and be saved in the celestial kingdom of God, there to enjoy with God eternal life. Those who have not complied with the laws and ordinances of the gospel will receive a lesser reward."[50]

There are several sources that may be drawn upon when the souls of men and women are "weighed in the balances" (Dan. 5:27). Included among these are witnesses, written records, and visual representations of a person's life.

Witnesses: The Law of Witnesses is designed to determine the truth of facts as they are laid out or presented (see Deut. 19:15; 2 Cor. 13:1; D&C 6:28). At the Final Judgment this law will be utilized in order to ensure that a person is neither accused nor rewarded unjustly. Some of the Lord's prophets may be called forward to appear "at the bar of God" during a session of judgment so that the Lord can ask the person who is being arraigned, "Did I not declare my words unto you, which were written by this man?" (Moro. 10:27). Missionaries may also be summoned to raise their voice in witness of the truth. "The missionaries of the Church who faithfully perform their duty," said Joseph Fielding Smith, "are under the obligation of leaving their testimony with all with whom they come in contact in their work. This testimony will stand as a witness against those who reject the message [of the gospel], at the judgment"[51] (cf. D&C 60:14–15; 75:18–22; 99:4–5).

Written Records: It is plainly set forth in the New Testament that written records will play a role on the Day of Judgment. "And I saw a great white throne," said John the Revelator, "and Him that sat on it. . . . And I saw the dead, small and great, stand before God; and the *books* were opened: and another book was opened, which is *the book of life*: and the dead were judged out of those things which were written in the books, according to their works" (Rev. 20:11–12, emphasis added).

Jesus Christ told His disciples in the New World that "out of the books which have been written, and which shall be written, shall this people be judged, for by them shall their works be known unto men. And behold, *all things are written by the Father;* therefore out of the books which shall be written shall the world be judged" (3 Ne. 27:25–26, emphasis added; cf. D&C 62:3). It was Elder Orson Pratt's belief that God has authorized numerous "agents" to carry out the enormous task of recording earthly events.[52]

Visual Representations: It appears from the writings of several LDS Church leaders that visual records of earth life are recorded by two different means—on the grand scale and on an individual level. Elder John A. Widtsoe said that the Spirit of God automatically records all earthly events, and he suggested that this omnipresent essence might be utilized on Judgment Day.

> So thoroughly permeated with the Holy Spirit is the immensity of space that every act and word and thought are recorded and transmitted everywhere, so that all who know how to read may read. Thus we make an imperishable record of our lives. To those whose lives are ordered well this is a blessed conception; but to those of wicked lives, it is most terrible. *He who has the receiving apparatus, in whose hands the key is held, may read from the record of the Holy Spirit, an imperishable history of all that has occurred during the ages that have passed in the world's history.* This solemn thought, that in the bosom of the

Holy Spirit is recorded the whole history of the universe—
our most secret thought and our faintest hope—helps man
to walk steadily in the midst of the contending appeals of
life. We cannot hide from the Master.[53]

John Taylor said it was his understanding that the spirit or mind
of a person acts as a register, recording every experience that a mortal
has. Human experiences are "printed" or recorded in this spiritual
"book" and those persons who have possession of their faculties can
access or "read" the information in this register as memories. Since
God holds the "keys" of the spirit of man He can read the impres-
sions made upon anyone's register whenever He desires. "When we
get into the eternal world," said Elder Taylor, "into the presence of
God our Heavenly Father, His eye can penetrate every one of us, and
our own record of our lives here [on the earth] shall develop all." The
indestructible record that is "written by the man himself in the tablets
of his own mind—that record that cannot lie—will in that day be
unfolded before God and angels, and those who shall sit as judges."
Therefore, "it would be in vain for a man to say [on the Day of
Judgment], 'I did not do so-and-so.' The command would be,
'Unravel and read the record which he has made of himself, and let it
testify in relation to these things' and all could gaze upon it."[54] This
concept was illustrated by an incident that occurred in the life of
George Albert Smith. During a very serious illness he lost consciousness of his surroundings and thought that he had "passed to the other
side." There he met his deceased grandfather and was shown a review
of his entire earthly existence in a few moments of time. "Everything
I had ever done," he said, "passed before me as though it were a flying
picture on a screen—everything I had done. Quickly this vivid retro-
spect came down to the very time I was standing there. My whole life
had passed before me."[55]

What will the Judgment be like for the righteous?
The "bar of the great Jehovah, the Eternal Judge" is a "pleasing"
place for the righteous to be (Moro. 10:34; see also Jacob 6:13). In
their resurrected state "the righteous shall have a perfect knowledge of
their enjoyment, and their righteousness, being clothed with purity,

yea, even with the robe of righteousness" (2 Ne. 9:14). Those "whose garments are cleansed and are spotless, pure and white" by virtue of the blood of the Lamb will be granted "a place to sit down in the kingdom of God, with Abraham, with Isaac, and with Jacob, and also all the holy prophets" (Alma 5:24).

After the righteous have been judged for their thoughts, their desires, their words, and their works they may hear their Redeemer exclaim, "Well done, good and faithful servant; thou hast been faithful over a few things, I will make thee ruler over many things: enter thou into the joy of thy [L]ord" (Matt. 25:23). Or they may hear the Savior of all mankind say unto them, "Come, ye blessed of my Father, inherit the kingdom prepared for you from the foundation of the world" (v. 34).

What will the Judgment be like for the wicked?

The "bar of God . . . strike[s] the wicked with awful dread and fear," says Jacob chapter 6 verse 13. They will "stand before the bar of God, having [their] garments stained with . . . all manner of filthiness" as a testimony that they are "guilty of all manner of wickedness" (Alma 5:22–23). Those whose "hearts are corrupt, and full of wickedness and abominations . . . [and who] love darkness rather than light, because their deeds are evil" will find nothing but "shame and condemnation in the Day of Judgment" (D&C 10:21, 23). They will "shrink with awful fear" because they "remember [their] awful guilt in perfectness" and will be constrained to admit to the Lord that "the devil hath obtained" them (2 Ne. 9:46). These people will be filled with "remorse" when they vividly recall the details of their sinful lives and also the fact that they "set at defiance the commandments of God" (Alma 5:18). And they "would fain be glad if [they] could command the rocks and the mountains to fall upon [them] to hide [them] from [the Lord's] presence" (Alma 12:14).

In the end, the wicked will be "found unclean before the judgment-seat of God; and [since] no unclean thing can dwell with God . . . [they] must be cast off forever" (1 Ne. 10:21). The words they will hear on this fateful day will haunt and disappoint them forever after. The Lord will command them saying, "depart from me, ye that work iniquity" (Matt. 7:23).

How can such a tragedy be avoided? King Benjamin offered these words of advice: "If ye do not watch yourselves, and your thoughts, and your words, and your deeds, and observe the commandments of God, and continue in the faith . . . of our Lord, even unto the end of your lives, ye must perish. And now, O man, remember, and perish not" (Mosiah 4:30).

NOTES: CHAPTER 7

1. Andrew F. Ehat and Lyndon W. Cook, eds., *The Words of Joseph Smith: The Contemporary Accounts of the Nauvoo Discourses of the Prophet Joseph* (Orem, Utah: Grandin Book, 1991), 4, hereafter cited as *WJS*.

2. Dean C. Jessee, ed., *The Personal Writings of Joseph Smith* (Salt Lake City: Deseret Book, 1984), 421.

3. B. H. Roberts, ed., *History of the Church*, rev. ed. (Salt Lake City: The Church of Jesus Christ of Latter-day Saints, 1932–1951), 3:396, hereafter cited as *HC*.

4. Ezra Taft Benson, *The Teachings of Ezra Taft Benson* (Salt Lake City: Bookcraft, 1988), 15.

5. Conference Report, April 1969, 116, hereafter cited as CR.

6. Joseph Fielding Smith notes that Jesus Christ "declared Himself to be the 'resurrection and the life' [John 11:25], and that He had power in Himself to lay down His life and take it up again [see John 5:26; 10:17–18]. Such power has never been the possession of any other creature upon the earth. All other creatures were under the curse of death, and Christ alone could free them" (Joseph Fielding Smith, *Doctrines of Salvation* [Salt Lake City: Bookcraft, 1999], 2:259, hereafter cited as *DS*).

7. Elder David B. Haight testified that he had been shown a vision of the Savior's Resurrection (see David B. Haight, *A Light Unto the World* [Salt Lake City: Deseret Book, 1997], 4).

8. Joseph F. Smith, *Gospel Doctrine* (Salt Lake City: Deseret Book, 1986), 216, hereafter cited as *GD*.

9. Robert J. Matthews, *Gospel Scholars Series: Selected Writings of Robert J. Matthews* (Salt Lake City: Deseret Book, 1999), 505–506, emphasis in original.

10. Benson, *The Teachings of Ezra Taft Benson*, 15–16.

11. *Improvement Era*, March 1908, 385, hereafter cited as *IE*.

12. *WJS*, 196.

13. Robert J. Matthews, *Behold the Messiah* (Salt Lake City: Bookcraft, 1994), 282, emphasis in original.

14. George D. Watt, comp., *Journal of Discourses* (London, England: F. D. and S. W. Richards and Sons, 1854–1886), 9:139, hereafter cited as *JD*.

15. Ibid., 15:137. President Young said that after the Prophet Joseph Smith had been resurrected he would be delegated "the keys of the resurrection" for the last dispensation and would then "seal this authority upon others" (ibid., 15:138–39).

16. Ibid., 25:34, emphasis added.

17. *The Contributor*, vol. 2, no. 11, August 1881, 339, emphasis added.

18. *GD*, 450–51. The Prophet Joseph Smith made it known that God had shown him a vision of the resurrection of the dead and that "great joy and glory rested upon" those who were ascending from their graves (*WJS*, 195–96, 198).

19. Bruce R. McConkie, *Mormon Doctrine*, 2d ed. (Salt Lake City: Bookcraft, 1966), 639–41, hereafter cited as *MD*.

20. John Taylor, *The Government of God* (London, England: S. W. Richards, 1852), 27.

21. John Taylor, *Mediation and Atonement* (Salt Lake City: Deseret News Co., 1882), 166.

22. Edward L. Kimball, ed., *The Teachings of Spencer W. Kimball* (Salt Lake City: Bookcraft, 1982), 45.

23. CR, April 1969, 138.

24. *WJS*, 370–71. The Prophet made several other comments that confirm his meaning on this point. "Flesh and blood cannot go there but flesh and bones quickened by the Spirit of God can" (ibid., 255); "God Almighty Himself dwells in eternal fire. Flesh and blood cannot go there for all corruption is devoured by the fire—our God is a consuming fire. When our flesh is quickened by the Spirit, there will be no blood in [our] tabernacles. . . . Immortality dwells in everlasting burnings" (ibid., 368); "All [will be] raised by the power of God having the Spirit of God in their bodies and not blood" (ibid., 109). It is interesting to note that when Wilford Woodruff was shown a vision of the

Resurrection by an angel of God he beheld "vast fields of graves" in "what is termed the Second Resurrection," and he saw that "the Spirit of God rested upon the earth like a shower of gentle rain, and when that fell upon the graves they were opened, and an immense host of human beings came forth" (*Millennial Star*, vol. 67, no. 39, 28 September 1905, 612).

25. *GD*, 23. In connection with this statement we have the declaration of the Prophet Joseph Smith that the "transmigration of soul[s]" or reincarnation is a "doctrine . . . of the devil" (*HC*, 2:307; cf. 1 Tim. 4:1; D&C 46:7).

26. *Elders' Journal*, vol. 1, no. 12, July 1904, 153.

27. *IE*, June 1909, 592.

28. *GD*, 23.

29. *DS*, 2:294, emphasis in original. "*Bodies will come up, of course, as they were laid down, but will be restored to their proper, perfect frame immediately. Old people will not look old when they come forth from the grave.* . . . Of course, children who die do not grow in the grave. They will come forth with their bodies as they were laid down, and then they will grow to the full stature of manhood or womanhood after the resurrection, but *all* will have their bodies fully restored. . . . *Deformities and the like will be corrected, if not immediately at the time of the uniting of the spirit and body, [then] so soon thereafter that it will make no difference*" (ibid., 2:292–94, emphasis in original).

30. *IE*, June 1904, 623–24.

31. *DS*, 2:56, emphasis in original.

32. James E. Talmage, *Jesus the Christ* (Salt Lake City: Deseret Book, 1962), 698.

33. Elder B. H. Roberts made an important observation about the notion of advancing from lower to higher kingdoms of glory after the Resurrection. He stated that such an idea "is *not revealed in the revelations of God*, and any statement made on the subject must partake more or less of the nature of *conjecture*" (B. H. Roberts, *Outlines of Ecclesiastical History* [Salt Lake City: Deseret Book, 1979], 417, emphasis added. This very same statement is found in B. H. Roberts, *A New Witness for God* [Salt Lake City: George Q. Cannon and Sons, 1895], 1:391).

34. *CR*, October 1945, 172.

35. Ibid., April 1922, 61. Another statement by President Smith is even more to the point.

"NO ADVANCEMENT FROM LOWER TO HIGHER. It has been asked if it is possible for one who inherits the telestial glory to advance in time to the celestial glory. The answer to this question is, *No!* The scriptures are clear on this point. Speaking of those who go to the telestial kingdom, the revelation says: 'And they shall be servants of the Most High; but *where God and Christ dwell they cannot come, worlds without end'* [D&C 76:112].

"Notwithstanding this statement, those who do not comprehend the word of the Lord argue that while this is true, that they cannot go where God is 'worlds without end,' yet in time they will get where God *was*, but He will have gone on to other heights.

"This is *false reasoning, illogical,* and creates mischief in making people think they may procrastinate their repentance, but in course of time they will reach exaltation in celestial glory.

"KINGDOMS PROGRESS IN DIFFERENT DIRECTIONS. Now let us see how faulty this reasoning is. *If* in time those who enter the telestial glory may progress till they reach the stage in which the celestial is in *now*—then they are *in* celestial glory, are they not, even *if* the celestial has advanced? That being the case (I state this for the argument only, for it is not true), then they partake of all the blessings which are *now* celestial. That means that they become gods, have exaltation, gain the fullness of the Father, and receive a continuation of the 'seeds forever.' The Lord, however, has said that these blessings, which are celestial blessings, they may *never have;* they are barred forever!

"The celestial and terrestrial and telestial glories, I have heard compared to the wheels on a train. The second and third may, and will, reach the place where the first was, but the first will have moved on and will still be just the same distance in advance of them. *This illustration is not true! The wheels do not run on the same track, and do not go in the same direction. The terrestrial and the telestial are limited in their powers of advancement, worlds without end*" (*DS,* 2:31–32, emphasis in original).

36. CR, October 1917, 110–11. On another occasion Elder Ballard said, "The question is often asked, 'Is it possible for one who attains telestial glory in time in the eternal world to live so well that he may graduate from the telestial and pass into the terrestrial, and then after a season that he may progress from that and be ultimately worthy of the celestial glory?' That is the query that has been asked. I have just read the answer, so far as the telestial group is concerned. 'Where God and Christ dwell they cannot come, worlds without end' [D&C 76:112]. I take it upon the same basis, the same argument likewise applies to

the terrestrial world. Those whose lives have entitled them to terrestrial glory can never gain celestial glory. One who gains possession of the lowest degree of the telestial glory may ultimately arise to the highest degree of that glory, but no provision has been made for promotion from one glory to another. Let us be reasonable about it. I wish to say in illustrating the subject that if three men were starting out on an endless race, one having an advantage of one mile, and the other of two miles, and each one could run as fast as the other, when would the last ever catch up to the first? If you can tell me that, I can tell you when candidates for the telestial glory will get into the celestial glory. Each will grow, but his development will be prescribed by his environment, and there is a reason for it" (Bryant S. Hinckley, *Sermons and Missionary Services of Melvin Joseph Ballard* [Salt Lake City: Deseret Book, 1949], 255–56).

37. Kimball, ed., *The Teachings of Spencer W. Kimball*, 50, emphasis added.

38. John A. Widtsoe, *The Message of the Doctrine and Covenants* (Salt Lake City: Bookcraft, 1969), 169–70. Elder Widtsoe remarks in another of his publications that "in the Final Judgment, all the earth children of the Lord will be assigned places in one or the other of the three grand divisions or degrees of salvation, known to us from modern revelation as the three glories. Each assignment will depend upon the use the candidate has made of the opportunities placed before him on earth and elsewhere. 'For they shall be judged according to their works' (D&C 76:111). By his own acts each person has shown his fitness to participate in the activities of this or that glory. It would be useless to place him higher than his capabilities would permit, and unfair to place him lower. If placed too high, he would not be competent or happy there, nor could he be content if placed too low. The degree of salvation of necessity corresponds, under the merciful justice of the Lord, with the demonstrated worthiness, capacity, and capability of each individual. The Final Judgment is individual.

"Within each glory, however, there may be advancement. The law of progress may be utilized by every intelligence in the universe. Those who inherit the telestial, terrestrial, or celestial glories may progress, and progress eternally. But, let it ever be remembered that the power to progress is greatest in the celestial glory, and is decreasingly smaller in the lower glories. There can be no talk, therefore, of those in the lower places overtaking those in the higher, any more than an automobile traveling at the rate of twenty-five miles an hour can overtake one moving at the rate of fifty miles an hour.

"They who inherit the celestial glory will dwell in the presence of the Father and the Son. They are kings and priests. From that glory issues the power of God, known to us as the Priesthood of the Lord. In that glory certain conditions of joy belong which are absent in the other glories. They who have inherited the lesser glories will receive a salvation so glorious as to be beyond the understanding of man—that has been revealed to us—but, 'where God and Christ dwell they can not come, worlds without end' (D&C 76:112)" (John A. Widtsoe, *Evidences and Reconciliations* [Salt Lake City: Bookcraft, 1960], 204).

39. Bruce R. McConkie, "The Seven Deadly Heresies," in *Brigham Young University Devotional and Fireside Addresses 1980* (Provo, Utah: Brigham Young University Press, 1981), 78.

40. Mormon 9:13–14 is one of several scriptural passages which confirm that the Final Judgment will occur *after* the Resurrection has taken place. It reads, "the trump shall sound; and they shall come forth, both small and great, and all shall stand before his bar, being redeemed and loosed from . . . temporal death. And then cometh the judgment of the Holy One upon them."

41. CR, April 1949, 69.

42. Larry E. Dahl, "The Vision of the Glories (D&C 76)," in Robert L. Millet and Kent P. Jackson, eds., *Studies in Scripture: Volume 1, The Doctrine and Covenants* (Salt Lake City: Deseret Book, 1989), 291, emphasis in original.

43. Bruce R. McConkie, *The Promised Messiah* (Salt Lake City: Deseret Book, 1978), 215–16. D&C 76:68 mentions that "in heaven . . . God and Christ are the judge of all." Other scriptures say that "the Lord Jesus Christ . . . shall judge the quick [i.e., living] and the dead" (2 Tim. 4:1; see also Acts 10:42). The Lord is called "the great Jehovah, the Eternal Judge" (Moro. 10:34). Why is Jesus Christ singled out? Perhaps because He is "the keeper of the gate" that leads into the celestial realm (2 Ne. 9:41).

44. *JD*, 17:182.

45. John Taylor, *Mediation and Atonement* (Salt Lake City: Deseret News Press, 1882), 156–57. President Charles W. Penrose said that "the time will come, according to the revelations of God, concerning the resurrection, that judgment will be given into the hands of men who hold [the] Priesthood, so that what they do in the Judgment will be as though done by the Father or by the Son. . . . The great judgment that is to come will not be altogether

performed by one individual sitting upon a great white throne and passing judgment upon the millions upon millions of the earth's inhabitants. God's house is a house of order, and the Lord will have agents appointed as He has now behind the veil as well as in the flesh, and when the great judgment comes, all will be judged according to their works, and the books will be opened, and the book of life will be scanned and the man's acts and the woman's acts upon the earth will be disclosed, and we will all confess in our souls that the judgment is just and righteous, because it will be uttered and delivered by one having authority and the seal of God will be upon it" (CR, October 1916, 21, 24). Parley P. Pratt disclosed that the Prophet Joseph Smith "will hold the keys to judge the generation to whom he was sent, and will judge my brethren that preside over me; and will judge me, together with the apostles ordained by the word of the Lord through him and under his administration. When this is done, those apostles will judge this genera-tion and the Latter-day Saints. . . . We will be judged by Brother Joseph; and he will be judged by Peter, James, and John, and their associates. Brother Brigham . . . will hold the keys under Brother Joseph; and he and his brethren, who hold the keys with him, or under his direction, will judge the people; for they will hold those keys to all eternity, worlds without end" (*JD*, 5:195–96).

46. Kimball, ed., *The Teachings of Spencer W. Kimball*, 47.

47. Harold B. Lee, *Decisions for Successful Living* (Salt Lake City: Deseret Book, 1973), 100–101. Even though all of these things will be taken into consideration during the Judgment it should not be expected that mercy will be allowed to rob justice (see Alma 42:25). Elder Bruce R. McConkie writes, "Unfortunately the professors of religion in an uninspired Christendom, along with masses of would-be Christians in general, *including many in the true Church itself,* assume that somehow or other mercy will be poured out upon the generality of Christian mankind and that eventually they will be saved in the kingdom of heaven. How common it is to hear such things as: 'Surely, if I confess the Lord Jesus with my lips and accept Him as my personal Savior, a merciful God will save me in His kingdom.' Or: 'Surely a merciful God will not deny me my family in eternity just because I wasn't married in the temple in this mortal life.' Or: 'Surely, in the mercy of God, men will be able to progress from one kingdom of glory to another in the next life, so that if I don't gain the celestial kingdom in the first instance, eventually I will.' Or: 'Even if I don't keep the commandments and work out my

salvation in this life, the Lord is merciful; He will give me another chance in the spirit world; and even those who reject it here will have a second chance there, and eventually they will be saved.' Or any of a thousand other sophistries that Satan delights to whisper into the ears of the spiritually untutored.

"But the doctrinal reality is that aside from the fact that a merciful and gracious Father created us and placed us here on earth to undergo a mortal probation; aside from the fact that 'He maketh his sun to rise on the evil and on the good, and sendeth rain on the just and on the unjust' (Matt. 5:45); aside from certain mortal blessings which come to the righteous and the wicked as a necessary part of mortality—aside from the fact that a merciful God provides immortality for all His children as a free gift—aside from such things as these, there is no such thing as mercy except for those who love the Lord and signify such by keeping His commandments. In other words, mercy is reserved for the faithful members of the Church and kingdom of God on earth, and for none else, except little children or others who have not arrived at the years of accountability" (Bruce R. McConkie, *The Promised Messiah* [Salt Lake City: Deseret Book, 1978], 243–44, emphasis added).

48. Alma 42:23 indicates that the totality of our existence will not be measured arbitrarily but will be "judged . . . according to the law and justice." What about those individuals who never become aware of various human and divine laws? Elder James E. Talmage had the following to say about people who fall into this category. "According to the technical definition of sin it consists in the violation of law, and in this strict sense sin may be committed inadvertently or in ignorance. It is plain, however, from the scriptural doctrine of human responsibility and the unerring justice of God, that in his transgressions as in his righteous deeds man will be judged according to his ability to comprehend and obey law. To him who has never been made acquainted with a higher law the requirements of that law do not apply in their fullness. For sins committed without knowledge—that is, for laws violated in ignorance—a propitiation has been provided in the Atonement wrought through the sacrifice of the Savior; and sinners of this class do not stand condemned [see 2 Ne. 9:25–26], but shall be given opportunity yet to learn and to accept or reject the principles of the gospel" (James E. Talmage, *Articles of Faith* [Salt Lake City: Deseret Book, 1984], 52).

49. In the Book of Mormon the prophet Nephi explains that his scriptural record and also the scriptural records produced by the Jews will be utilized in the work of judgment.

"And now, my beloved brethren, and also Jew, and all ye ends of the earth, hearken unto these words and believe in Christ; and if ye believe not in these words believe in Christ. And if ye shall believe in Christ ye will believe in these words, for they are the words of Christ, and he hath given them unto me; and they teach all men that they should do good.

And if they are not the words of Christ, judge ye—for Christ will show unto you, with power and great glory, that they are his words, at the last day; and you and I shall stand face to face before his bar; and ye shall know that I have been commanded of him to write these things, notwithstanding my weakness.

And I pray the Father in the name of Christ that many of us, if not all, may be saved in his kingdom at that great and last day.

And now, my beloved brethren, all those who are of the house of Israel, and all ye ends of the earth, I speak unto you as the voice of one crying from the dust: Farewell until that great day shall come.

And you that will not partake of the goodness of God, and respect the words of the Jews, and also my words, and the words which shall proceed forth out of the mouth of the Lamb of God, behold, I bid you an everlasting farewell, for these words shall condemn you at the last day.

For what I seal on earth, shall be brought against you at the judgment bar" (2 Ne. 33:10–15).

50. Marion G. Romney, *Learning for the Eternities* (Salt Lake City: Deseret Book, 1977), 43.

51. Joseph Fielding Smith, *Church History and Modern Revelation* (Salt Lake City: The Church of Jesus Christ of Latter-day Saints, 1946), 1:206.

52. *JD*, 17:182. "Men's deeds and thoughts must be recorded in heaven, and recording angels will not fail to make complete recordings of our thoughts and actions. . . . There will be no omissions in the heavenly records, and they will all be available at the Day of Judgment" (Spencer W. Kimball, *The Miracle of Forgiveness* [Salt Lake City: Bookcraft, 1988], 109). For further remarks on recording angels see *MD*, 620–21; *JD*, 7:84.

53. John A. Widtsoe, *A Rational Theology* (Salt Lake City: Deseret Book, 1965), 74, emphasis added.

54. *JD*, 11:74–80. On another occasion John Taylor said, "If I had time to enter into this subject alone I could show you upon scientific principles that man himself is a self-registering machine. His eyes, his ears, his nose, the touch, the taste, and all the various senses of the body are so many media whereby man

lays up for himself a record which perhaps nobody else is acquainted with but himself; and when the time comes for that record to be unfolded all men that have eyes to see, and ears to hear will be able to read all things as God Himself reads them and comprehends them, and all things, we are told, are naked and open before Him" (ibid., 26:31). President Spencer W. Kimball writes, "At that day we may be sure that we shall receive fair judgment. The judges will have the facts as they may be played back from our own records, and our voices and the pictures of our own acts and the recordings of our thoughts will testify [both] against and for us" (Spencer W. Kimball, *The Miracle of Forgiveness* [Salt Lake City: Bookcraft, 1969], 109).

55. Preston Nibley, comp., *Sharing the Gospel With Others* (Salt Lake City: Deseret Book, 1948), 111–12.

CHAPTER 8

REWARDS OF DARKNESS AND GLORY

Both ancient and modern scriptures testify that after the children of God have completed their mortal probation and been judged accordingly they will receive a reward of darkness or glory.[1] These rewards are referred to in scriptural texts as outer darkness, the telestial kingdom, the terrestrial kingdom, and the celestial kingdom (see JST, Matt. 8:11–12; 1 Cor. 15:40–42; D&C 76:19–113; 101:90–91). Outer darkness will be the reward of the sons of perdition, and as Elder Joseph L. Wirthlin, Second Counselor in the Presiding Bishopric, states, "the celestial [is] for those who achieved highly, the terrestrial for those who achieved partially, and the telestial for those who were indolent and careless."[2]

Elder Hugh B. Brown relates that the "rules of admittance into all these kingdoms are fixed and irrevocable. All their blessings are predicated upon the observance of law."[3] Indeed, the Lord states in section 88 of the Doctrine and Covenants that "every kingdom is given a law; and unto every law there are certain bounds . . . and conditions. All beings who abide not in those conditions are not justified" (vv. 38–39). Conversely, those who are "governed by law [are] also preserved by law and perfected and sanctified by the same" (v. 34). The Lord has revealed a substantial amount of information about the laws, bounds, and conditions that are associated with mankind's future rewards. This information will be examined on the pages that follow.

OUTER DARKNESS

Outer darkness is an appropriate description of the one "kingdom which is not a kingdom of glory" (D&C 88:24). Through latter-day revelation it has been made known that after mortals who become sons of perdition receive their resurrected bodies they will "return again to their own place" (v. 32). From this scriptural passage it can be deduced that the post-Resurrection "outer darkness" and the pre-Resurrection "hell" are the same type of state or condition.[4] According to 2 Nephi chapter 9 verse 9, the inhabitants of this horrid realm are "shut out from the presence of God." And in the book of Jude chapter 1 verse 6 we learn that they are "reserved in everlasting chains under darkness."

Those who are condemned to outer darkness will remain in a state of filthiness after the Final Judgment has taken place. This will be so because those who "breaketh a law, and abideth not by law, but seeketh to be a law unto [themselves], and willeth to abide in sin, and altogether abideth in sin, cannot be sanctified by law, neither by mercy, justice, nor judgment. Therefore, they must remain filthy still" (D&C 88:35). They will "go away into everlasting fire, prepared for them; and their torment [will be] *as a lake of fire and brimstone*, whose flame ascendeth up forever and ever and has no end" (2 Ne. 9:16, emphasis added). Alma chapter 12 verse 17 adds that "they shall be chained down to an everlasting destruction, according to the power and captivity of Satan, he having subjected them according to his will." The devil will have "all power" over them, says Alma 34:35; he will "seal" them as his own.

Throughout the dismal regions of "outer darkness" will be heard the inconsolable sounds of "weeping, and wailing, and gnashing of teeth" (D&C 101:91). Elder Orson Pratt provides an interesting and insightful perspective on why these beings will suffer so much:

> If we should inquire [as to] what constitutes the misery of the fallen angels, the answer would be, they are destitute of love; they have ceased to love God; they have ceased to have pure love one towards another; they have ceased to love that which is good. Hatred, malice, revenge, and every

evil passion have usurped the place of love; and unhappiness, wretchedness, and misery are the results.

Where there is no love, there will be no desire to promote the welfare of others. Instead of desiring that others may be happy, each desires to make all others miserable like himself [see 2 Ne. 2:18, 27]; each seeks to gratify that hellish disposition against the Almighty which arises from his extreme hatred of that which is good. For the want of love the torment of each is complete. All the wicked who are entirely overcome by these malicious spirits will have the heavenly principle of love wholly eradicated from their minds, and they will become angels to these infernal fiends, being captivated by them, and compelled to act as they act. They cannot extricate themselves from their power, nor ward off the fiery darts of their malicious tormentors. Such will be the condition of all beings who entirely withdraw themselves from the love of God.[5]

The Unpardonable Sin

The Lord Jesus Christ has declared that "all manner of sin and blasphemy shall be forgiven unto men *who receive me and repent*; but the blasphemy against the Holy Ghost . . . shall not be forgiven unto men . . . neither in this world, neither in the world to come" (JST, Matt. 12:26–27, emphasis added; see also JST, Mark 3:22–24). Those who commit this unpardonable sin are doomed to become sons of perdition. According to Elder B. H. Roberts such people "commit the same act of high treason that Lucifer in the rebellion of heaven did, and hence are condemned to the same punishment."[6]

Scriptural Criteria: In Hebrews chapter 6 verses 4 through 6 the Apostle Paul states that in order for someone to sin beyond the possibility of repentance they must first do several things: (1) they must be enlightened through the "heavenly gift . . . of the Holy Ghost," (2) they must taste "the good word of God," (3) they must taste "the powers of the world to come," and (4) they must "fall away" or apostatize.[7] Such people, says Paul, "crucify to themselves the Son of God afresh, and put Him to an open shame." In section 76 of the Doctrine and Covenants the Lord repeats several of these points but

He also adds a few that are not found in the New Testament text. According to the Lord's latter-day revelation, those who become sons of perdition must do the following:

- Know God's "power" and be made a partaker of it (v. 31).[8]
- Allow themselves through the "power" of the devil to be overcome (v. 31).[9]
- Defy God's "power" (v. 31).[10]
- Deny the truth (v. 31).[11]
- Deny the Holy Spirit after they have received it (v. 35).[12]
- Deny "the Only Begotten Son of the Father,[13] having crucified Him unto themselves and put Him to an open shame" (v. 35).[14]
- "Deny the Son after the Father has revealed Him" (v. 43).

This last point calls for some commentary. The Prophet Joseph Smith was very specific about the degree to which the Son of God needs to be revealed to a person before they are able to commit blasphemy against the Holy Ghost. He said that in order for a person "to commit the unpardonable sin" he "must receive the Holy Ghost, have the *heavens opened* unto [him], and *know God*, and then sin against Him."[15] Such a person "has got to say that the sun does not shine while he sees it. He has got to *deny Jesus Christ when the heavens are open to him* and from that time [he] begin[s] to be [an enemy]."[16] Elder Bruce R. McConkie relates how the Holy Ghost is connected with this particular type of revelation. He says that "because the Holy Ghost is a personage of spirit He has power to convey truth to the spirit within us with absolute certainty. From Him we can come to know, nothing doubting, that Jesus is Lord of all. When this revealed knowledge is received *without limit or bounds, when the heavens are opened and a mortal knows his Maker*, when a man gains this *perfect knowledge*, then, should he fall away, he commits the unpardonable sin."[17]

Prerequisite Status: It is evident from the criteria listed above that individuals must reach a very high spiritual state before they can commit the most abominable of all sins.[18] Indeed, President George Q. Cannon taught that "a man must have attained to considerable knowledge about God and eternal things before he is in a condition

where he can commit the unpardonable sin. . . . There are compara-
tively few who get so far as this. A man must have sufficient knowledge to make him a *god* in order to be a devil."[19] President Brigham
Young taught this same doctrine by using slightly different termi-
nology. He asked, "How much does it take to prepare a man, or
woman, or any being, to become angels to the devil, to suffer with
him to all eternity? Just as much as it does to prepare a man to go into
the celestial kingdom, into the presence of the Father and the Son,
and to be made an *heir* to His Kingdom, and *all* His glory, and be
crowned with crowns of glory, immortality, and *eternal lives*."[20] The
only way for a person to become a full *heir* of God, or a *god* in their
own right, is to receive all of the ordinances of the House of the Lord.
Thus President Young, while referring directly to the temple "endowments," said that "it takes almost as much knowledge to make a
complete devil as it does to fit a man to go into the celestial kingdom
of God, and become an *heir* to His kingdom."[21] Elder Charles W.
Penrose made this same connection. He said that before a person can
become a son of perdition they must first receive certain temple keys
and also become the recipient of the power of exaltation.

> The "sons of perdition" are those who have received the
> gospel, those to whom the Father has revealed the Son;
> those who know something concerning the plan of salva-
> tion; those who have had keys placed in their hands by
> which they could unlock the mysteries of eternity; those
> who received power to ascend to the highest pinnacle of
> the celestial glory; those who received power sufficient to
> overcome all things, and who, instead of using it for their
> own salvation, and in the interest of the salvation of others,
> prostituted that power and turned away from that which
> they knew to be true, denying the Son of God and putting
> Him to an open shame. . . . [T]hey are governed by Satan,
> becoming servants to him whom they list to obey; they
> become the sons of perdition, doomed to suffer the wrath
> of God reserved for the devil and his angels.[22]

Elder Orson F. Whitney was another leader of the LDS Church
who publicly taught that in order for a person to "commit the unpar-

donable sin, the sin against the Holy Ghost" he must have "knowledge and power sufficient to entitle him to celestial exaltation; and then prove utterly recreant to the great light that has come to him. Such a sin," said Elder Whitney, "can be committed only by men equipped with every qualification for the highest degree of eternal glory."[23]

When Wilford Woodruff was serving as the President of the Church, Elder Abraham H. Cannon and James E. Talmage were told by "the brethren" in the President's office that "only such can become sons of perdition who receive a testimony of the gospel—who receive the Holy Ghost, and *the highest blessings of the Church*, and then willfully deny the light they have obtained."[24] President Woodruff clarified these remarks when he told a gathering of Latter-day Saints that those who receive the "*highest blessings*" of the Church "enter the Lord's house" and have them "sealed upon their heads."[25] In even more specific terms, he said that being "ordained to the fullness of the Melchizedek Priesthood [is to be] ordained to *the highest office and gift of God* to man on the earth."[26]

Eternal Punishment

The Savior declares in a latter-day revelation that "it had been better for [the sons of perdition] never to have been born" (D&C 76:32) because for them "there is no forgiveness in this world nor in the world to come" (v. 34). They are "doomed to suffer the wrath of God, with the devil and his angels in eternity" (v. 33) and "shall not be redeemed in the due time of the Lord, after the sufferings of His wrath" (v. 38). They are the only ones who will experience the "second death" (v. 37) in "the lake of fire and brimstone, with the devil and his angels" (v. 36).

Jesus Christ "saves all except [the sons of perdition]" (v. 44) because they are "the ungodly" (v. 49). These extremely wicked individuals will suffer "everlasting punishment, which is endless punishment, which is eternal punishment" (v. 44) but the full extent or nature of their "torment" has never been revealed to anyone on the earth. Therefore, "the end, the width, the height, the depth, and the misery thereof, [mortals] understand not, neither any man except those who are ordained unto this condemnation" (vv. 45–48; cf. D&C 19:10–12).[27]

TELESTIAL KINGDOM

The telestial kingdom is typified by the "glory" or light that radiates from the stars (D&C 76:81).[28] When Joseph Smith and Sidney Rigdon saw the vision that is now recorded in section 76 of the Doctrine and Covenants, they learned that even though the telestial world is the lowest of the three kingdoms of light its glory still "surpasses all understanding" (v. 89).

Those who inhabit the telestial kingdom will be "as innumerable as the stars in the firmament of heaven, or as the sand upon the seashore" (v. 109). There will be many different levels of light radiating from the beings who reside in this sphere; "for as one star differs from another star in glory, even so differs one [person] from another in glory in the telestial world" (v. 98).

The residents of this realm will merit their place within it due to the following reasons:

- They did not receive "the prophets" (v. 101).
- They did not receive "the testimony of Jesus" (vv. 82, 101).
- They did not receive "the gospel" (vv. 82, 101). Joseph Smith relates in a poetic rendition of section 76 of the Doctrine and Covenants that the inhabitants of the telestial world "went their own way" and "worshiped in darkness." These individuals may have subscribed to the teachings of various biblical personalities—such as Moses, Peter, and Paul—or even formally joined themselves with a religious denomination, but they "*never* received the [true] gospel of Christ" (stanzas 70–72, emphasis added).[29]
- They did not receive "the everlasting covenant" (v. 101). The Prophet's poetic version of D&C 76 indicates that this is a reference to "the covenant . . . which Jacob once had," meaning the Abrahamic covenant (stanza 71).
- They were liars, sorcerers, adulterers, and whoremongers (v. 103). Joseph Smith adds in his poetic rendition that hypocrites, thieves, the mean-spirited, the materialistic, and the proud will share the fate of the "sinful" and the "wicked" in the lowest kingdom of glory (stanzas 60, 73).

The Prophet Joseph Smith reports that those who fit themselves for a telestial reward will "suffer the wrath of God on earth" and "suffer the vengeance of eternal fire" (vv. 104–105). This is probably a reference to the fact that such people will be burned as stubble at the Second Coming (see D&C 29:9; 64:23–24). They will not be permitted to remain on a planet that is to become a terrestrial or paradisiacal kingdom during the Lord's millennial reign (see A of F #10).

Those who live a telestial type of lifestyle are "thrust down to hell" after they die (D&C 76:84, 105–106) and are not "redeemed from the devil until the last resurrection" (vv. 85, 106). Nevertheless, since they "deny not the Holy Spirit" (v. 83) they are not consigned to outer darkness after their resurrection has taken place. They will be "heirs of salvation," albeit in the least possible degree (v. 88).

In Doctrine and Covenants 76:86–88 it is stated that telestial beings will receive "of the Holy Spirit through the ministration of the terrestrial" kingdom; they will "receive it of the administering of angels who are appointed to minister for them." Gospel scholar Richard O. Cowan believes that these verses mean that "those in the telestial glory receive the influence of the Holy Ghost—and that, only indirectly—by means of visitors from the terrestrial degree."[30] This manifestation of the Holy Ghost is evidently the mechanism which enables telestial beings to understand and acknowledge that Jesus is the Christ, the Son of the living God (vv. 106–110; cf. John 15:26; 2 Ne. 31:18).

Those who reside in the telestial world will become "servants of the Most High," but their abilities and opportunities will be considerably limited. For the rest of eternity they will not be allowed or able to go where God and Christ dwell (D&C 76:112).[31] While progress will certainly be possible for those in the lowest kingdom of light, their growth and development will be encumbered by restrictions. Elder Melvin J. Ballard of the Quorum of the Twelve Apostles said that "one who gains possession of the lowest degree of the telestial glory may ultimately arise to the highest degree of that glory, but no provision has been made for promotion from one glory to another."[32]

TERRESTRIAL KINGDOM

The terrestrial kingdom is typified by the "glory" or light that radiates from the moon (D&C 76:71), yet it "excels in all things the glory of the telestial [realm], even in glory, and in power, and in might, and in dominion" (v. 91). The Prophet added to this with his poetic rendering of the same scriptural passage, writing that terrestrial beings possess more "knowledge, and wisdom, and joy" than those in the telestial world and have greater access to the Lord's "blessings and graces" (stanza 65). Terrestrial individuals will receive "the ministration of the celestial" sphere (v. 87) and will also be privileged to enjoy "the presence of the Son" of God (v. 77).

Those who will be granted a terrestrial abode for eternity will include:

- Those who "died without law" (v. 72). Joseph Smith indicates in his poetic version of Doctrine and Covenants 76 that this has reference to the "heathen" nations (stanza 54; cf. D&C 45:54). The Prophet also had the following to say about what it means for a person to be without law:

  To say that the heathen would be damned because they did not believe the gospel would be preposterous; and to say that the Jews would all be damned that do not believe in Jesus, would be equally absurd; for "how can they believe on Him of whom they have not heard; and how can they hear without a preacher; and *how can he preach except he be sent*" [Romans 10:14–15]; consequently neither Jew, nor heathen, can be culpable for rejecting the conflicting opinions of [Christian] sectarianism, nor for rejecting any testimony but that which is sent of God, for as the preacher cannot preach except he be sent, so the hearer cannot believe [unless] he hear[s] a sent preacher; and cannot be condemned for what he has not heard; and being without law, will have to be judged without law.[33]

Elder Bruce R. McConkie provides the clarification that those who will obtain an inheritance in the terrestrial kingdom will be "accountable persons who die without law (and who, of course, do not accept the gospel in the spirit world under those particular circumstances which would make them heirs of the celestial kingdom)."[34]

- Those who did not receive "the testimony of Jesus in the flesh" but did so in the spirit "prison" when they heard it again (D&C 76:73–74; stanza 56). In Joseph Smith's poetic rendition he equates this group with the "honorable men of the earth" who were blinded and duped by the cunning or craftiness of men (v. 75; stanza 56; cf. D&C 123:12).
- Those who were "not valiant in the testimony of Jesus" (D&C 76:79).[35] Elder Bruce R. McConkie believes that this last category includes "those who are lukewarm members of the true Church . . . who have testimonies, but who are not true and faithful in all things."[36] Spencer W. Kimball concurs with this viewpoint. He interprets verse 79 of section 76 of the Doctrine and Covenants to mean that "many [Latter-day Saints] who have received baptism by proper authority, many who have received other ordinances, even temple blessings, will not reach the celestial kingdom of glory unless [they] live the commandments and are valiant."[37]

CELESTIAL KINGDOM

The celestial kingdom is typified by the "glory" or light that radiates from the sun (D&C 76:70). The splendor of this realm "excels in all things" because it is here that "God, even the Father, reigns upon his throne" (v. 92). Latter-day scripture relates that the Almighty resides on "a globe like a sea of glass and fire,[38] where all things . . . are manifest, past, present, and future" (D&C 130:7). This heavenly orb, said the Prophet Joseph Smith, "is a great Urim and Thummim" and "this earth, in its sanctified and immortal state, will be made like unto crystal and will be a Urim and Thummim to the inhabitants who dwell thereon, whereby all things pertaining to an inferior kingdom, or all kingdoms of a lower order, will be manifest to those who dwell on it" (vv. 8–9). The Prophet also explained that "a white stone is given to each of those who come into the celestial kingdom, whereon is a new name written, which no man knoweth save he that receiveth it. The new name is the key word" (v. 11). This stone "is a small representation of [the] globe" where God resides.[39] It "will become a Urim and Thummim to each individual who receives one, whereby things pertaining to a higher order of kingdoms will be made known" (v. 10). By utilizing these two devices (the globe and the stone) celestial beings will be able to "see as they are seen, and know as they are known" (D&C 76:94; cf. Mosiah 8:16–17).

Three Degrees

Joseph Smith revealed that "in the celestial glory there are three heavens or degrees" (D&C 131:1). Elder John A. Widtsoe notes that "naturally, those who enter the celestial kingdom are of various attainments. There is not absolute uniformity anywhere among the children of God. Their innate capacities and their use of the law of free agency makes them different, often widely so. Therefore, the members of the highest kingdom are also grouped, according to the Prophet Joseph Smith, into three 'degrees.'"[40]

What are the minimum requirements for entering into even the lowest level or degree of the celestial world? From several sections of the Doctrine and Covenants, and Joseph Smith's poetic rendition of section 76 in particular, it is evident that a person must do the following:

- Receive "the testimony of Jesus" and believe on His name (D&C 76:51).
- Repent (stanza 41).
- Be "baptized after the manner of [Jesus Christ's] burial" (v. 51).[41]
- "Receive the Holy Spirit by the laying on of the hands of him who is ordained and sealed unto [that] power" (v. 52).[42]
- Be "cleansed from *all* their sins" (v. 52, emphasis added). This means that they must become "sanctified" (D&C 88:2, 18).[43]
- "Abide the law of a celestial kingdom" which is "the law of Christ" (D&C 88:21–22). "For if you will that I give unto

you a place in the celestial world," says the Lord, "you must prepare yourselves by doing the things which I have commanded you and required of you" (D&C 78:7).

- "Overcome [the world] by faith" (D&C 76:53). The Prophet adds that celestial candidates "overcome by . . . their works" while they are "being tried in their lifetime, as purified gold" (stanza 43).

Even though these sources make it clear that baptism and the gift of the Holy Ghost are required for entrance into the celestial kingdom, they do not indicate if these ordinances qualify or enable someone to pass beyond the lowest level of that realm. Aside from the requirements listed above, "there is no scriptural explanation of those who go to the two lower categories of the celestial kingdom except that they 'are not gods, but are angels of God forever and ever,' ministering servants who 'remain separately and singly, without exaltation'" (D&C 132:16–17).[44] President Joseph Fielding Smith made some remarks that *may* provide an insight on this issue. His comments are presented here simply for the reader's careful consideration without any pretense of providing an authoritative or final answer. He said, "People baptized, and who are not endowed in the temple of the Lord, may enter the celestial kingdom. But that does not mean that a baptized person is going to get the exaltation in that kingdom. He is not going to pass on to the fullness just by being *baptized*. He will not pass on to the fullness even after he has been baptized and received an *endowment* in the temple. He has also to receive the *other ordinances* so that he can become, through his faithfulness and obedience, a son of God."[45]

One of the "other ordinances" that is necessary for exaltation in the celestial kingdom is referred to in section 131 of the Doctrine and Covenants. Verses 1 through 4 of this revelation read:

> In the celestial glory there are *three heavens or degrees*. And in order to obtain the *highest,* a man must enter into this order of the Priesthood [meaning the new and everlasting covenant of marriage]; And if he does not, he cannot obtain it.
>
> He may enter into the other,[46] but that is the end of his kingdom; he cannot have an increase (emphasis added).

Thus, in order to ascend to the highest heaven of the celestial world a man and a woman must be joined together in the everlasting covenant of temple marriage. The Lord is very specific about this requirement in section 132 of the Doctrine and Covenants. There He states that "the new and everlasting covenant . . . was instituted for the fullness of [His] glory, and he that receiveth a fullness thereof must and shall abide the law" (D&C 132:6; cf. 76:56, 71).

But even after a man and a woman have entered into this covenant with each other they will not be exalted unless that covenant is "sealed by the Holy Spirit of promise . . . by revelation and commandment through the medium of [the Lord's] anointed, whom [the Lord has] appointed on the earth to hold this power" (D&C 132:7; cf. 76:53). Joseph Smith expounded upon this concept in his poetic rendition of Doctrine and Covenants 76 when he said that those who achieve exaltation are "sealed by the [Holy] Spirit of promise, to [eternal] life, by men called of God, as was Aaron" (stanza 43)—meaning by those who hold "the power of the Holy Priesthood" (D&C 131:5). To those who are thus sealed it is proclaimed that they "shall come forth in the First Resurrection . . . and shall inherit thrones, kingdoms, principalities, and powers, dominions, all heights and depths" (D&C 132:19; cf. 76:64–65).

> [Then] they shall pass by the angels, and the gods, which are set there, to their exaltation and glory in all things, as hath been sealed upon their heads, which glory shall be a fullness and a continuation of the seeds forever and ever.[47] Then shall they be gods [cf. D&C 76:58], because they have no end. . . . Then shall they be gods, because they have all power, and the angels are subject unto them (D&C 132:19–20).[48]

The section 76 of the Doctrine and Covenants and the Prophet's poetic rendition of that revelation provide further details on the nature of exalted beings. These sources indicate the following concerning these individuals:

- God makes them "perfect" through the atoning blood of Jesus Christ (D&C 76:69).[49]

- God gives "all things" into their hands (v. 55), "whether life or death, or things present, or things to come" (v. 59).
- God makes them "equal in power, and in might, and in dominion" (v. 95).
- They "overcome all things" (v. 60).
- They receive "a fullness of . . . light" (stanza 45).
- They "hold the keys of the kingdom of heaven" (stanza 44).

Many of the steps that need to be taken on the way to exaltation have been conveniently summarized by Elder Vaughn J. Featherstone of the First Quorum of the Seventy. He writes, "Those who are baptized, receive the Priesthood (if male), receive the temple endowment, are sealed as husbands and wives, and remain true and faithful throughout their lives—these will inherit the highest degree of glory in the celestial kingdom. They will become like God and have eternal lives (that is, eternal increase), 'which glory shall be a fullness and a continuation of the seeds forever and ever. Then shall they be gods, because they have no end' (D&C 132:19–20)."[50] Elder Delbert L. Stapley of the Quorum of the Twelve Apostles provides similar information on the prerequisites for godhood:

> As sons and daughters of God, we are required to purify and perfect ourselves in righteousness; otherwise, we cannot be with Him nor enjoy eternal lives and glory in His kingdom. To become like God we must possess the powers of godhood. For such preparation there are important covenants, obligations, and ordinances for mankind to receive beyond the requirement of baptism and the laying on of hands for the reception of the Holy Ghost. Every person is to receive his or her endowments in the house of the Lord which permit them, if faithful and true, to pass by the angels who stand as sentinels guarding the way to eternal glory in the mansions of God. The everlasting covenant of marriage, ordained of God for man and woman, also is to be entered into and the marriage contract sealed eternally by the authority of the Holy Priesthood of God. Otherwise, the highest degree of the celestial kingdom cannot be attained nor godhood

acquired, which exalted condition assures continuation of the lives forever.[51]

The "gods" of the celestial glory (D&C 76:58) are "priests and kings" (v. 56) and members of "the Church of the Firstborn" (vv. 54, 67, 71). The "Church of the Firstborn," explains Elder Bruce R. McConkie, "is the Church which exists among exalted beings in the celestial realm. But it has its beginning here on earth. Members of The Church of Jesus Christ of Latter-day Saints who so devote themselves to righteousness that they receive the higher ordinances of exaltation become members of the Church of the Firstborn. Baptism is the gate to the Church itself, but celestial marriage is the gate to membership in the Church of the Firstborn, the inner circle of faithful Saints who are heirs of exaltation and the fullness of the Father's kingdom."[52] Those who become "kings and priests," says Elder McConkie, have been "converted, baptized, endowed, married for eternity, and finally sealed up unto eternal life, having their calling and election made sure."[53]

It is appropriate to end this chapter with a few words concerning the key to reaching the pinnacle of salvation. President Spencer W. Kimball reminded all Latter-day Saints that "exaltation requires diligence." He asked, "Why will only a few reach exaltation in the celestial kingdom? Not because it was not available to them, not because they did not know of its availability, not because the testimony was not given to them, but because they would not put forth the effort to pattern their lives and make them like the Savior's life and establish them so well that there would be no deviation until the end."[54]

NOTES: CHAPTER 8

1. Lorenzo Snow said that "God loves His offspring, the human family. His design is not simply to furnish happiness to the few here, called Latter-day Saints. The plan and scheme that He is now carrying out is for universal salvation; not only for the salvation of the Latter-day Saints, but for the salvation of every man and woman on the face of the earth, for those also in the spirit world, and for those who may hereafter come upon the face of the earth. It is

for the salvation of every son and daughter of Adam. They are the offspring of the Almighty, He loves them all and His plans are for the salvation of the whole, and He will bring all up into that position in which they will be as happy and as comfortable as they are willing to be" (George D. Watt, comp., *Journal of Discourses* [London, England: F. D. and S. W. Richards and Sons, 1854–1886], 14:30, hereafter cited as *JD*).

2. Conference Report, October 1944, 38, hereafter cited as CR.

3. *Brigham Young University Speeches of the Year*, 17 May 1961, 4.

4. It should be noted that even though hell is currently located in the immediate vicinity of the earth (see Rev. 12:9) outer darkness will not be in the same locale since this planet will eventually become a celestial world (see D&C 88:17–18). For an article that discusses the concepts of a temporary hell and a permanent hell see H. Donl Peterson, "What Is the Meaning of the Book of Mormon Scriptures on Eternal Hell for the Wicked?" *Ensign*, April 1986, 36–38. For an insightful study on the Book of Mormon's teachings about hell see Larry E. Dahl, "The Concept of Hell," in Bruce A. Van Orden and Brent L. Top, eds., *Doctrines of the Book of Mormon: The 1991 Sperry Symposium* (Salt Lake City: Deseret Book, 1992), 42–56.

5. *The Seer*, vol. 1, no. 10, October 1853, 156.

6. B. H. Roberts, *New Witnesses for God* (Salt Lake City: Deseret News Press, 1911), 389. Moses 5:18–41 relates that Adam's son Cain became a son of perdition. Elder Bruce R. McConkie listed the steps that Cain took on the way to his extreme condemnation. "He understood the gospel and the plan of salvation, was baptized, received the Priesthood, had a *perfect knowledge* of the position and perfection of God, and *talked personally with Deity*. Then he came out in open rebellion, fought God, worshiped Lucifer, and slew Abel" (Bruce R. McConkie, *Mormon Doctrine*, 2d ed. [Salt Lake City: Bookcraft, 1966], 109, emphasis added, hereafter cited as *MD*). Joseph Fielding Smith said, "All who partake of . . . the greatest of sins, sell themselves as did Cain to Lucifer. They learn to hate the truth with an eternal hatred, and they learn to love wickedness. They reach a condition where they will not and cannot repent. The spirit of murder fills their hearts and they would, if they had the power, crucify our Lord again, which they virtually do by fighting His work and seeking to destroy it and His prophets" (Joseph Fielding Smith, *Doctrines of Salvation* [Salt Lake City: Bookcraft, 1999], 1:49, hereafter cited as *DS*). For an intriguing story related by Elder David W. Patten about Cain and his

"mission . . . to destroy the souls of men" see Spencer W. Kimball, *The Miracle of Forgiveness* (Salt Lake City: Bookcraft, 1969), 127–28.

7. It is evident from this scripture, as Elder Melvin J. Ballard expresses it, that "members of the Church are . . . the only ones who can commit [the] unpardonable sin" (Bryant S. Hinckley, *Sermons and Missionary Services of Melvin Joseph Ballard* [Salt Lake City: Deseret Book, 1949], 211). D&C 76:29–32 indicates that Satan makes "war with the *Saints* of God," and those who allow themselves to be "overcome" during this assault become "sons of perdition" (emphasis added).

8. Some students of the scriptures believe that this verse refers to the Holy Priesthood. Several LDS Church leaders and scholars support this view. President Brigham Young, for instance, taught that "men in the flesh are clothed with the Priesthood [and] with its blessings, the apostatizing from which and turning away from the Lord prepares them to become sons of perdition" (*JD*, 8:279). President Joseph Fielding Smith once said that "no man can become a son of perdition until he has known the light . . . [I]t is only those who have the light through the Priesthood and through the power of God and through their membership in the Church who will be banished forever from His influence into outer darkness to dwell with the devil and his angels" (CR, October 1958, 21). Dr. Sidney B. Sperry, in speaking about the sons of perdition, was even more specific. "It is obvious that only a member of the Church, a man holding the Melchizedek Priesthood who has taken upon himself sacred covenants and who knows the power of God and has been made a partaker thereof, can become such" (Sidney B. Sperry, *Doctrine and Covenants Compendium*, 2d ed. [Salt Lake City: Bookcraft, 1960], 343). It may be argued from quotations like these that since LDS women are not ordained to offices in the Priesthood they cannot possibly become daughters of perdition. Yet, Brigham Young once stated that both a "man" and a "woman" could become "angels to the devil" (*JD*, 3:93). Furthermore, Elder Abraham H. Cannon and James E. Talmage were told by "the brethren" in "the President's office" (Wilford Woodruff being President of the Church) that they had "no doubt" that "there will also be daughters of perdition" (Abraham H. Cannon Journal, 29 November 1893, Harold B. Lee Library, Special Collections, Brigham Young University, Provo, Utah). In considering the connection between women and the Priesthood one might bear in mind statements like the following one found in the *Encyclopedia of Mormonism*. "In the temples of the Lord, sacred Priesthood ordinances (e.g., washings, anointings, clothings) are

administered to men by men and to women by women who have received the
endowments of the Priesthood in the temple . . . and have been given that
specific Priesthood responsibility. Women thus may act in Priesthood power
when called, set apart, and authorized by those who hold the keys; however,
women officiators are not ordained to the Priesthood or to an office in the
Priesthood to do this work" (Daniel H. Ludlow, ed., *Encyclopedia of
Mormonism* [New York: Macmillan, 1992], 3:1137, hereafter cited as *EM*).
Two statements made by Joseph Fielding Smith also call for consideration. He
said, "Women do not hold the Priesthood, but if they are faithful and true,
they will become *priestesses* and queens in the kingdom of God, and that
implies that they will be given authority" (*DS*, 3:178, emphasis added). Those
who end up "possessing the fullness of the blessings of the celestial kingdom"
will be "kings and priests and queens and *priestesses*" (Joseph Fielding Smith,
Answers to Gospel Questions [Salt Lake City: Deseret Book, 1998], 4:61,
emphasis added, hereafter cited as *AGQ*; see also *EM*, 1:276; *MD*, 594, 613).

9.   Elder Charles W. Penrose stated that those who become sons of perdition
     "become imbued with [Satan's] spirit, which is the spirit of destruction, in
     opposition to the spirit which brings life. . . . The spirit of murder enters their
     hearts; they are ready to put to death even the Son of God, if His existence in
     life comes in their way" (CR, October 1911, 51).

10. Those who defy God's power challenge it, confront it, resist it, and rebel
     against it. Joseph Fielding Smith warned that "for men who have had the light
     of the Holy Ghost to turn away and fight the truth with murderous hate, and
     those who are authorized to proclaim it, there is no forgiveness in this world,
     neither in the world to come" (*AGQ*, 1:69). His reasoning was that "those who
     have known the truth and then fight against the authorized servants of Jesus
     Christ also fight against Him, for they who fight against His servants also do it
     unto Him, and thus are guilty of His blood" (ibid., 1:64; cf. Matt. 25:40).

11. The fundamental nature of the unpardonable sin is apostasy. Joseph Smith
     relates that "all sin . . . [may be] forgiven except the sin against the Holy
     Ghost." To commit this sin a person has "got to deny the plan of salvation,
     etc., with his eyes open—like many of the apostates . . . of The Church of Jesus
     Christ [in the] last days" (Andrew F. Ehat and Lyndon W. Cook, eds., *The
     Words of Joseph Smith: The Contemporary Accounts of the Nauvoo Discourses of
     the Prophet Joseph* [Orem, Utah: Grandin Book, 1991], 342, hereafter cited as
     WJS). In his poetic rendition of section 76 of the D&C the Prophet declared

that "the torment apostates receive" is to "reign with the devil in hell" along with the rest of the "Sons of Perdition" (Lawrence R. Flake, *Three Degrees of Glory: Joseph Smith's Insights on the Kingdoms of Heaven* [American Fork, Utah: Covenant Communications, 2000], 45).

12. The Prophet Joseph Smith made it clear that "no man can commit the unpardonable sin until he receives the Holy Ghost" (*WJS*, 347). "*Why* should blasphemy against the Holy Ghost be a greater evil than to blaspheme the name of God or Jesus Christ?" asked Joseph Fielding Smith. "The answer is, because the Father and the Son are not our constant companions. Moreover, the Holy Ghost is Spirit speaking to spirit. When a man has the manifestation from the Holy Ghost, it leaves an indelible impression on his soul, one that is not easily erased. It is Spirit speaking to spirit, and it comes with convincing force. . . . When a person denies the truth which has been made manifest to him by the power of the Holy Ghost, and which, perhaps, has been repeated time and time again, and then he denies Christ and turns away from the truth and puts Christ to open shame, there can be no forgiveness" (*AGQ*, 2:151, emphasis in original). "This sin is [known as] blasphemy against the Holy Ghost," said Elder Bruce R. McConkie, "because the sure and perfect knowledge of God and Christ and their laws can come only by revelation from the Holy Ghost" (Bruce R. McConkie, *A New Witness for the Articles of Faith* [Salt Lake City: Deseret Book, 1985], 279, hereafter cited as *NWAF*). This particular form of blasphemy "is a scurrilous and evil declaration against the Holy Ghost, against the sole and only source of absolute and sure knowledge" (Bruce R. McConkie, *The Mortal Messiah* [Salt Lake City: Deseret Book, 1980], 2:216).

13. In the Book of Mormon Sherem feared that he had "committed the unpardonable sin" because he had "denied the Christ" (Jacob 7:19).

14. In D&C 132:27 the Lord explains that "the blasphemy against the Holy Ghost, which shall not be forgiven in the world nor out of the world, is in that ye commit murder wherein ye shed innocent blood, and assent unto my death." Elder Bruce R. McConkie provides the following commentary on this doctrine: "The unpardonable sin consists in denying Christ, in fighting the truth, in joining hands with those who crucified Him, knowing full well, and with a perfect knowledge, that He is the Son of God; it means pursuing this course after gaining a perfect knowledge, given of the Holy Ghost, that He is the Lord of all. *The innocent blood thus shed is His blood; those who so sin become murderers by assenting unto His death*, an assent that is given with a full and

perfect knowledge of His divinity" (*NWAF*, 233, emphasis added). It appears that a person can also become a son of perdition by murdering another human being under certain circumstances. During the administration of President Wilford Woodruff "the brethren" in "the President's office"—after speaking of those "who receive the Holy Ghost"—taught that "murderers who crucify Christ anew, or consent to His death, in that they shed innocent blood knowing at the time that they are thereby preventing the spread of the truth, will be subject to [the] penalty" of becoming "sons of perdition" (Abraham H. Cannon Journal, 29 November 1893, Harold B. Lee Library, Special Collections, Brigham Young University, Provo, Utah). President Woodruff once publicly connected "apostates" who "labor to shed innocent blood and to destroy the Church and kingdom of God on the earth" to "the sons of perdition" (*JD*, 13:168). It would appear from the writings of Elder McConkie that those who are not in the category of murdering with the intent of destroying God's kingdom, but who nevertheless commit premeditated murder *after* making their calling and election sure, will go to the telestial kingdom (see Bruce R. McConkie, *Doctrinal New Testament Commentary* [Salt Lake City: Bookcraft, 1973], 3:347, hereafter cited as *DNTC*). He notes that "murderers shall eventually go to the telestial kingdom, unless of course there are some among those destined to be sons of perdition who are also murderers" *(DNTC,* 3:584).

15. *WJS*, 347. Joseph Smith also taught, "No one can truly say he *knows God* until he has handled something, and this can only be in the Holiest of Holies" (ibid., 120, emphasis added; cf. John 17:3; 1 Jn. 1:1–3; 3 Ne. 11:13–17; D&C 45:51–53; 50:45; 93:1; 132:22–24). This statement is clarified in a discourse the Prophet delivered on 27 June 1839. After speaking of making one's "calling and election sure," the "sealing power," being "sealed with [the] Holy Spirit of promise," and being "sealed up unto the day of redemption" he paraphrased Jeremiah 31:34, which reads, "And they shall teach no more every man his neighbor, and every man his brother, saying, *Know the Lord*: for they shall all *know me*, from the least of them unto the greatest of them, saith the Lord" (emphasis added). The Prophet then asked, "How is this to be done? It is to be done by this sealing power and the other comforter spoken of which will be manifest by revelation." He then explained, "There [are] two comforters spoken of [in the New Testament]. . . . [The] first comforter [is the] Holy Ghost. . . . The other comforter spoken of is a subject of great interest and perhaps understood by few of this generation. After a person ha[s] faith in

Christ, repents of his sins and is baptized for the remission of his sins and receive[s] the Holy Ghost (by the laying on of hands), which is the first comforter, then let him continue to humble himself before God, hungering and thirsting after righteousness and living by every word of God. And the Lord will soon say unto him, 'Son, thou shalt be exalted,' etc. When the Lord has thoroughly proved him and finds that the man is determined to serve him at all hazard[s], then the man will find his calling and election made sure. Then it will be his privilege to receive the other comforter which the Lord ha[s] promised the Saints [see John 14:16–18, 21, 23]. . . . Now what is this other comforter? It is no more or less than the Lord Jesus Christ Himself. And this is the sum and substance of the whole matter—that when any man obtains this last comforter he will have the personage of Jesus Christ to attend him or appear unto him from time to time. And . . . he will [even] manifest the Father unto him and they will take up their abode with him, and the visions of the heavens will be opened unto him and the Lord will teach him face to face and he may have a perfect knowledge of the mysteries of the kingdom of God" (*WJS*, 4–5). On another occasion the Prophet said, "To *know God* learn to become gods" (ibid., 361, emphasis added).

16. Ibid., 353 emphasis added. The Prophet taught that mortals "cannot commit the unpardonable sin after the dissolution of the body. . . . [They] must commit the unpardonable sin in this world" (ibid., 342).

17. *NWAF*, 279, emphasis added.

18. On this point we have the statement of Brigham Young, who said that the "sin against the Holy Ghost is a sin against God the Father, the Son, and the Holy Ghost that bears record of them. *A man cannot sin against the Holy Ghost until the Holy Ghost has revealed unto Him the Father and Son and a knowledge of eternal things in a great degree.* When he has a knowledge of these things, [and] with his eyes open, he rebels against God and defies His power, he sins against all three" members of the Godhead (Scott G. Kenney, ed., *Wilford Woodruff's Journal* [Midvale, Utah: Signature Books, 1983], 4:95, emphasis added). Elder B. H. Roberts concurs, saying that "only those who attain to *a very great knowledge of the things of heaven* are capable of committing [this crime]; and the number among such is few indeed who become so recklessly wicked as to rebel against and defy the power of God" (B. H. Roberts, *New Witnesses for God* [Salt Lake City: Deseret News, 1911], 389, emphasis added). President Spencer W. Kimball taught that "the sin against the Holy Ghost requires such

knowledge that it is manifestly impossible for the rank and file to commit such a sin" (Kimball, *The Miracle of Forgiveness*, 123). Elder John A. Widtsoe specifies what type of knowledge is necessary before one can be consigned to outer darkness. "Very few will be so condemned because very few have the knowledge required. Denial of the truth by those who have not a *perfect knowledge* does not merit the greatest punishment, to be classed as sons of perdition" (John A. Widtsoe, *Joseph Smith: Seeker after Truth, Prophet of God* [Salt Lake City: Deseret News Press, 1951], 177, emphasis added). He also said that "there will be few [sons of perdition], for few know so much as to fall so low" (John A. Widtsoe, *Evidences and Reconciliations* [Salt Lake City: Bookcraft, 1987], 201).

19. Jerrald L. Newquist, ed., *Gospel Truth: Discourses and Writings of George Q. Cannon* (Salt Lake City: Deseret Book, 1987), 94, emphasis added. Even though Latter-day Saints were aware in 1832 that they could become "gods" or "priests and kings" who had received a "fullness" of the Father's glory (D&C 76: 56, 58), they did not become acquainted with all of the ordinances associated with obtaining that "fullness" until a decade later (D&C 124:28; see also vv. 39–40). The Prophet Joseph Smith spent part of 4 May 1842 instructing a small group of men "in the principles and order of the Priesthood, attending to washings, anointings, endowments and the communication of keys pertaining to the Aaronic Priesthood, and so on to the highest order of the Melchizedek Priesthood, setting forth the order pertaining to the Ancient of Days, and all those plans and principles by which anyone is enabled to secure *the fullness of those blessings* which have been prepared for the Church of the Firstborn" (B. H. Roberts, ed., *History of the Church*, rev. ed. [Salt Lake City: The Church of Jesus Christ of Latter-day Saints, 1932–1951], 5:2, emphasis added, hereafter cited as *HC*). Joseph F. Smith said, "[H]e that believes, is baptized and receives the light and testimony of Jesus Christ, and walks well for a season, *receiving the fullness of the blessings of the gospel in this world*, and afterwards turns wholly unto sin, violating his covenants . . . will taste the second death, and be banished from the presence of God eternally" (*JD*, 18:93, emphasis added). Elder Bruce R. McConkie taught that the "sons of perdition are those who have known the *fullness of light* and have then come out in open rebellion against the Author of light" (*MD*, 445, emphasis added). Elder Boyd K. Packer notes that the sons of perdition receive their extreme condemnation "after having known a *fullness*" (*Ensign*, November 1995, 19, emphasis added).

20. *JD*, 3:93, emphasis added. The Prophet Joseph Smith equated those who become "an *heir* of God and *joint-heir* . . . with Jesus Christ" with those who "arrive at the station of a *god*" (*WJS*, 345, emphasis added). President Joseph Fielding Smith likewise taught that "exalted beings, because they have proved themselves by obedience to 'every word that proceedeth forth from the mouth of God,' will become perfect and be like Him, and as *heirs* will become *gods* themselves" (Joseph Fielding Smith, *Man, His Origin and Destiny* [Salt Lake City: Deseret Book, 1954], 532–33, emphasis added).

21. *JD*, 4:372, emphasis added.

22. Ibid., 24:93. Similar statements by Elder Penrose can be found in *The Contributor*, vol. 2, no. 12, September 1881, 363–64; CR, October 1914, 41–42; CR, April 1917, 17. Gospel scholar Robert L. Millet and Elder Bruce R. McConkie of the Quorum of the Twelve Apostles have made statements which support the interpretation that those mortals who become sons of perdition must first make their calling and election sure and then fall from that spiritual height. "Once one has been sealed by the Holy Spirit of Promise," said Brother Millet, "he is in a position to either rise to exaltation or (through rebellion and apostasy) fall to perdition. . . . One who has been sealed up unto eternal life and *thereafter* proves to be a total enemy to the cause of righteousness is guilty of 'shedding innocent blood,' the innocent blood of Christ, and assenting unto His death [see *DNTC*, 3:161, 345; McConkie, *The Mortal Messiah*, 2:216]. Such a vicious disposition would lead the transgressor to reject and crucify the Son of God afresh" (Robert L. Millet, "A New and Everlasting Covenant (D&C 132)," in Robert L. Millet and Kent P. Jackson, eds., *Studies in Scripture: Volume 1, The Doctrine and Covenants* [Salt Lake City: Deseret Book, 1989], 520, emphasis added). Elder McConkie writes that "even though a person has his calling and election made sure and is sealed up unto eternal life, he still has his agency; he can still fall; he can still choose to serve Satan; but if he does—having had a perfect knowledge of the truth and *now* choosing to defy God; to trample His Son under foot; and to do [insult] to the Spirit of grace—he is damned eternally as a son of perdition" (*DNTC*, 3:191, emphasis added).

23. Orson F. Whitney, *Saturday Night Thoughts* (Salt Lake City: Deseret News Press, 1921), 321–22. A similar statement is found in Orson F. Whitney, *Gospel Themes* (Salt Lake City: The Church of Jesus Christ of Latter-day Saints, 1914), 40.

24. Abraham H. Cannon Journal, 29 November 1893, Harold B. Lee Library,

Special Collections, Brigham Young University, Provo, Utah, emphasis added.

25. *JD*, 22:208, emphasis added. John Taylor stated that "being ordained to eternal life after sin is overcome" is the "*highest* honor of the Priesthood" (*Times and Seasons*, vol. 5, no. 18, 1 October 1844, 670, emphasis added, hereafter cited as *T&S*). The Prophet Joseph Smith wrote that the "*highest* reward" that can be received from the Savior is to be made a king and a priest "of the order of Melchizedek" (Flake, *Three Degrees of Glory: Joseph Smith's Insights on the Kingdoms of Heaven*, 47, emphasis added). President Brigham Young proclaimed that to be "sealed up to the day of redemption and have the promise of eternal lives, is the *greatest* gift of all." Such blessings, he said, are "sealed upon our heads" (*JD*, 2:301, emphasis added).

26. Brian H. Stuy, ed., *Collected Discourses* (Burbank, California: B. H. S. Publishing, 1992), 5:102, emphasis added, hereafter cited as *CD*. Brigham Young taught that "for any person to have the *fullness* of [the Melchizedek] Priesthood, he must be a king and priest" (*HC*, 5:527, emphasis added). Students of the D&C will notice that section 84 verse 41, which speaks of the oath and covenant of the Melchizedek Priesthood, utilizes language that is normally associated with the unpardonable sin. Joseph Fielding Smith offers an interesting perspective on this passage of scripture. He says, "Every man who is ordained to an office in the Melchizedek Priesthood should realize fully just what that ordination means. He receives the Priesthood with an oath and covenant that he will magnify his calling and be faithful therein. This oath and covenant *when received in the fullness* will entitle a man to become a member of *the Church of the Firstborn*, and the elect of God. He receives the fullness of the Father's kingdom and is entitled, if faithful to the end, 'to all that the Father hath.' This oath and covenant cannot be treated lightly, and if broken and altogether turned from, the man thus guilty has no forgiveness, that is to say, he will not again have these privileges granted to him which bring exaltation, or 'all that the Father hath.' He will stand aside without these blessings, but does not become a son of perdition because of this serious offense" (Joseph Fielding Smith, *Church History and Modern Revelation* [Salt Lake City: The Church of Jesus Christ of Latter-day Saints, 1947], 2:104, emphasis added; see also *NWAF*, 232). Marion G. Romney said, "I do not think [D&C 84:41] means that all who fail to magnify their callings in the Priesthood will have committed the unpardonable sin" (*Ensign*, July 1972, 99).

27. The Lord specifically states in D&C 43:33 that "their end *no man* knoweth

on earth, nor ever shall know, until they come before me in judgment" (emphasis added). Even with this revelation at hand, Brigham Young and Heber C. Kimball voiced their opinion that the sons of perdition would eventually be destroyed as entities and reduced to the elementary particles from which their bodies and spirits had been created. A few of the statements made by these men make it clear that they were *not* announcing revelations from the Lord but were drawing their own conclusions based upon their interpretation of certain scriptures. For example, President Young said that a son of perdition "will be decomposed, and the particles which compose his body and spirit will return to their native element. I told you some time ago what would become of such men. But I will quote the scriptures on this point, and you can make what you please of it. Jesus says he will DESTROY *death* and *him* that hath the power of it [see Heb. 2:14]. What can you make of this but decomposition, the returning of the organized particles to their native element, after suffering the wrath of God until the time appointed? That appears a mystery, but the principle has been in existence from all eternity, only it is something you have not known or thought of. When the elements in an organized form do not fill the end of their creation, they are thrown back again, like Brother Kimball's old pottery ware, to be ground up, and made over again [cf. Jer. 18:1–8]. All I have to say about it is what Jesus says—I will *destroy* death, and him that hath the power of it, which is the devil. And if He ever makes 'a *full end* of the wicked,' [incorrect paraphrase of Jer. 30:11 and Ps. 37:37–38?] what else can He do than entirely disorganize them, and reduce them to their native element? Here are some of the mysteries of the kingdom" (*JD*, 1:275, emphasis in original).

Apostle Orson Pratt, for one, took issue with this idea. Said he, the "second death [is] not a dissolution of body and spirit like that of the first death, but a banishment from the presence of God, and from the glory of His power" (*JD*, 1:330). President Joseph F. Smith held a similar view. In speaking of "spiritual death" he said, "I do not understand it to be the separation of the body and the spirit again. I do not understand it to be the dissolution of the spirit into its native element" (*CD*, 4:227–28).

President Joseph Fielding Smith offered the following reasons for rejecting the notion that the sons of perdition will be dissolved into their fundamental particles:

"NO DEATH AFTER RESURRECTION. Will any after receiving the

Resurrection ever die, or have the dissolution of the spirit and body? The answer to this is obviously, *no!* What reason could there be in calling them forth and uniting their spirits and bodies only to cause death to intervene the second time and dissolve their souls? The words of the Prophet already quoted are to the effect that the sons of perdition, who concocted scenes of bloodshed, shall dwell in hell 'worlds without end' [*TPJS*, 361]. According to the word of the Lord—and that we must accept as final, no matter what may have been, or what may be now the opinions of men—we are told:

'And they who remain shall also *be quickened*; nevertheless, *they shall return again to their own place*, to enjoy that which they are willing to receive, because they were not willing to enjoy that which they might have received' [D&C 88:32].

They who 'remain' must refer to *those who are not included in any of the three kingdoms*, and in another place, section 76:33, the Lord has said: 'For they are vessels of wrath, doomed to suffer the wrath of God, with the devil and his angels in eternity.' These are they who remain 'filthy still' [D&C 88:35, 102].

"NO CORRUPTION AFTER RESURRECTION. Amulek said: 'Now, this restoration shall come to *all*, both old and young, both bond and free, both male and female, *both the wicked and the righteous*; and even there shall not so much as a hair of their heads be lost; but everything shall be restored to its perfect frame, as it is now, or in the body, and shall be brought and be arraigned before the bar of Christ the Son, and God the Father, and the Holy Spirit, which is one Eternal God, to be judged according to their works, whether they be good or whether they be evil.

"'Now, behold, I have spoken unto you concerning the death of the mortal body, and also concerning the resurrection of the mortal body. I say unto you that this mortal body is raised to an immortal body, that is from death, even from the first death unto life, that *they can die no more; their spirits uniting with their bodies, never to be divided; thus the whole becoming spiritual and immortal, that they can no more see corruption*' [Alma 11:44–45].

"In this statement it is shown that Amulek is speaking of the dead, both good and bad, and in the next, or 12th chapter, Alma confirms this doctrine in relation to the wicked who are cast out in the following words: 'I say unto you, *they shall be as though there had been no redemption made; for they cannot be redeemed according to God's justice; and they cannot die, seeing there is no more corruption'* [Alma 12:18]" (*DS*, 2:278–79, emphasis in original).

28. The word "telestial" is perplexing to some readers of LDS scripture because it is not found in modern English dictionaries. The editors of the Oxford English Dictionary, however, note that in ancient times the words "tele" and "teles" meant "to speak evil of . . . to revile . . . to mock, scorn, deride. . . . to deceive, entrap . . . to betray." In direct connection with these words is "teling" which means "deception, sorcery, [and] witchcraft." Therefore, it could be said that someone who lives a *teles*–tial type of lifestyle engages in evil speaking, mockery, deception, sorcery, or witchcraft. Verses 98 and 103 of section 76 of the D&C confirm that "liars" and "sorcerers" will inhabit the "telestial" kingdom after the Resurrection. In modern English the prefix "tele" means "afar, far off" and, indeed, the telestial kingdom is the degree of glory that is farthest from God's presence (J. A. Simpson and E. S. C. Weiner, *The Oxford English Dictionary*, 2d ed. [Oxford: Clarendon Press, 1989], 17:720–21).

29. Flake, *Three Degrees of Glory: Joseph Smith's Insights on the Kingdoms of Heaven*, 55.

30. Richard O. Cowan, *Answers to Your Questions About the Doctrine and Covenants* (Salt Lake City: Deseret Book, 1996), 92.

31. Since Jesus Christ dwells in both the celestial and terrestrial kingdoms (see D&C 76:62, 77) it is logical to conclude from a reading of D&C 76:112 that those who inherit the telestial kingdom cannot dwell in, inherit, or eventually advance to either of those higher realms—"worlds without end." Elder Melvin J. Ballard said that "we must not overlook the fact that those who attain to the higher glories may minister unto and visit and associate with those of the lesser kingdoms. While the lesser may not come up, they may still enjoy the companionship of their loved ones who are in higher stations" (Hinckley, *Sermons and Missionary Services of Melvin Joseph Ballard*, 257).

32. Ibid., 255.

33. *T&S*, vol. 3, no. 12, 15 April 1842, 760, emphasis in original. Gospel scholar Kent P. Jackson notes that "the phrase 'died without law' (D&C 76:72) seems to imply an unwillingness to accept the law, not a lack of opportunity. An 1836 revelation makes it clear that lack of opportunity in this life will not be a hindrance to an inheritance in the celestial kingdom (D&C 137:5–9)" (Kent P. Jackson, *From Apostasy to Restoration* [Salt Lake City: Deseret Book, 1996], 193, n. 8). Along these same lines Elder Melvin J. Ballard said, "Now, I wish to

say to you that those who died without law, meaning the pagan nations, for lack of faithfulness, for lack of devotion, in the former life, are obtaining all that they are entitled to. I don't mean to say that all of them will be barred from entrance into the highest glory. Any one of them who repents and complies with the conditions might also obtain celestial glory, but the great bulk of them will only obtain terrestrial glory" (Hinckley, *Sermons and Missionary Services of Melvin Joseph Ballard*, 251).

34. *MD*, 784.

35. For an extensive statement on what it means to be "valiant in the testimony of Jesus" see Elder Bruce R. McConkie's comments in the *Ensign,* November 1974, 35.

36. *NWAF*, 146. See also *DNTC*, 2:394; *MD*, 784; Melvin J. Ballard, *Three Degrees of Glory* (Salt Lake City: Joseph Lyon and Associates, 1975), 27. President Charles W. Penrose, First Counselor in the First Presidency, said of "the terrestrial kingdom" that "there are several degrees in that one glory" (CR, April 1922, 29–30).

37. CR, April 1951, 104.

38. On 21 January 1836 the Prophet Joseph Smith saw a vision of "the celestial kingdom of God, and the glory thereof." Said he, "I saw the transcendent beauty of the gate through which the heirs of that kingdom will enter, which was *like unto circling flames of fire.* [I] also [saw] the *blazing* throne of God, whereon was seated the Father and the Son. I saw the beautiful streets of that kingdom, which had the appearance of being paved with gold" (D&C 137:1–4, emphasis added). The Prophet taught that "God Almighty Himself dwells in eternal fire. Flesh and blood cannot go there for all corruption is devoured by the fire—'Our God is a consuming fire' [Heb. 12:29]. . . . Immortality dwells in everlasting burnings [see Isa. 33:14]" (*WJS*, 368–69).

39. Ibid., 169.

40. John A. Widtsoe, *Evidences and Reconciliations* (Salt Lake City: Bookcraft, 1987), 200–201.

41. Joseph Smith taught that "a man may be saved, after the judgment, in the terrestrial kingdom, or in the telestial kingdom, but he can never see the celestial kingdom of God without being born of the water and the Spirit" (*HC*, 1:283). Elder Richard G. Scott of the Quorum of the Twelve Apostles makes this straightforward observation. "Time and time again at funerals, statements

are made that the deceased will inherit all blessings of celestial glory when that individual has in no way qualified by obtaining the necessary ordinances and by keeping the required covenants. That won't happen. Such blessings can only be earned by meeting the Lord's requirements. His mercy does not overcome the requirements of His law. They must be met" (*Ensign*, May 2001, 9).

42. Elder John A. Widtsoe relates that "the concern of the Church is to bring all men into the celestial kingdom. It has no interest in the other, lower kingdoms. Every doctrine, principle, and item of organization within the Church pertains to the celestial glory. The manner of entrance into this, the highest kingdom, is therefore made clear. Any person who wishes to enter it must have faith and repent from his sins. Then he must be baptized, and receive the gift of the Holy Ghost by one who has divine authority to perform such ordinances. The[s]e are principles and ordinances which in their entirety belong peculiarly to the higher kingdom" (Widtsoe, *Evidences and Reconciliations*, 200).

43. "No unclean thing can dwell with God" (1 Ne. 10:21; see also Alma 40:26; 3 Ne. 27:19; Moses 6:57).

44. *EM*, 1:368.

45. *DS*, 2:45, emphasis added. Alvin R. Dyer, who served as an assistant to the Quorum of the Twelve Apostles, had similar views about the ritual qualifications of those who inherit the three degrees within the celestial sphere.

"They who are to be assigned to the celestial kingdom, which kingdom will be upon the regenerated and sanctified earth, will be bodies that have been sanctified by obedience to celestial law (see D&C 88:18–20). As to the characteristics of and the powers to be inherited by those who will be assigned to dwell in this kingdom of glory, we have this description from the Lord: 'They are they who received the testimony of Jesus, and believed on his name and were baptized after the manner of his burial, being buried in the water in his name, and this according to the commandment which he has given. That by keeping the commandments they might be washed and cleansed from all their sins, and receive the Holy Spirit by the laying on of the hands of him who is ordained and sealed unto this power' (D&C 76:51–52).

"Since the celestial kingdom will have three heavens or degrees (see D&C 131:1), no doubt all who will inherit the second degree, in addition to possessing all of the qualities of those who will possess the first, or lowest degree, will receive an endowment in the temples of God for this purpose, and will have 'overcome by faith,' and be sealed by the Holy Spirit of Promise, which the Father sheds forth upon all those who are just and true (D&C 76:53). They attained this by obedience to the sacred obligations of the endowment which they received by covenant.

"As to exaltation, or the inheritance of the third heaven or degree in the celestial kingdom, we have the following revelation which gives the dominions and powers of the spiritual bodies (D&C 88:27), who, in addition to possessing all the qualities of those who possess the first and second degrees of this kingdom, will also be: 'They are they into whose hands the Father has given all things. They are they who are priests and kings, who have received of his fullness, and of his glory. And are priests of the Most High, after the order of Melchizedek, which was after the order of Enoch, which was after the order of the Only Begotten Son. Wherefore, as it is written, they are gods, even the sons of God. Wherefore, all things are theirs, whether life or death, or things present, or things to come, all are theirs and they are Christ's, and Christ is God's. And they shall overcome all things' (D&C 76:55–60).

"Concerning the bodies who will be exalted in the celestial kingdom, the Lord has given this further identification: 'In the celestial glory there are three heavens or degrees. And in order to obtain the highest, a man must enter into this order of the Priesthood (meaning the new and everlasting covenant of marriage). And if he does not, he cannot obtain it. He may enter into the other, but that is the end of his kingdom; he cannot have an increase' (D&C 131:1–4)" (Alvin R. Dyer, *Who Am I?* [Salt Lake City: Deseret Book, 1966], 547–48).

The understanding of gospel scholar Victor L. Ludlow is that "those who are endowed but not sealed in marriage and family lines to other endowed Saints will be 'ministering servants' in the celestial kingdom . . . 'to minister for those who are worthy of a far more, and an exceeding, and an eternal weight of glory' (D&C 132:16)" (Victor L. Ludlow, *Principles and Practices of the Restored Gospel* [Salt Lake City: Deseret Book, 1992], 368).

46. Taken in context, it appears that this reference is to the "other[s]" or the lower two levels of the celestial kingdom. Even though D&C 131:1–4 speaks specifically of conditions "*in* the celestial glory" (v. 1, emphasis added) some people have argued that these verses do not refer to three degrees or levels within the celestial kingdom but rather to the three degrees of glory in general (i.e., celestial, terrestrial, telestial). However, this view is not supported by the available

evidence. The material in D&C 131:1–4 was copied from William Clayton's journal, and in the sentences directly before this material Joseph Smith reportedly refers to exalted beings having children "in the celestial glory" (George D. Smith, ed., *An Intimate Chronicle: The Journals of William Clayton* [Salt Lake City: Signature Books, 1995], 102). Thus, it would appear that on 16 May 1843 the Prophet equated the "celestial glory" with the celestial kingdom. And this is not the only time that he made such an equation (see *HC*, 2:8; *WJS*, 347). It should also be noted that on 17 May 1843 the Prophet said that "Paul had seen the third heavens and I more"—possibly meaning that he had seen multiple levels within the third heaven or celestial kingdom (Smith, ed., *An Intimate Chronicle: The Journals of William Clayton*, 103). It is clear from numerous statements by Church leaders who personally knew Joseph Smith that they believed there would be different levels of reward in the celestial kingdom. For example, Elder Orson Hyde wrote that, "Such as have not received the fullness of the Priesthood, (for the fullness of the Priesthood includes the authority of both king and priest) and have not been anointed and ordained in the temple of the Most High, may obtain salvation in the celestial kingdom, but not a celestial crown. Many are called to enjoy a celestial glory, yet few are chosen to wear a celestial crown, or rather, to be rulers in the celestial kingdom" (*Millennial Star*, vol. 9, no. 2, 15 January 1847, 23–24). Elder Orson Pratt said that "some will inherit . . . the highest or celestial glory . . . while others, though celestial, will be subject to them, inheriting a less[er] degree of celestial glory" (*JD*, 7:90). President Brigham Young declared that some people in the celestial kingdom would act in the capacity of servants (see *JD*, 11:297, 301; cf. D&C 132:15–16).

47. It was Joseph Fielding Smith's teaching that "*in both [the terrestrial and telestial] kingdoms there will be changes in the bodies and limitations. They will not have the power of increase, neither the power or nature to live as husbands and wives, for this will be denied them and they cannot increase.* Those who receive the exaltation in the celestial kingdom will have the 'continuation of the seeds forever' [D&C 132:19]. *They will live in the family relationship.* In the terrestrial and in the telestial kingdoms there will be no marriage. Those who enter there will remain 'separately and singly' forever [D&C 132:15–32]. Some of the functions in the celestial body will not appear in the terrestrial body, neither in the telestial body, and *the power of procreation will be removed*" (*DS*, 2:287–88, emphasis in original). "Restrictions will be placed upon those who enter the terrestrial and telestial kingdoms, and even those in the celestial kingdom who

do not get the exaltation; *changes will be made in their bodies to suit their condition;* and there will be no marrying or giving in marriage, nor living together of men and women, because of these restrictions" (ibid., 2:73, emphasis in original).

48. The nature of godhood can be glimpsed in the following quotations from leaders of the LDS Church:

Brigham Young: "After men have got their exaltations and their crowns—have become gods, even the sons of God—are made Kings of kings and Lords of lords, they have the power then of propagating their species in spirit; and that is the first of their operations with regard to organizing a world. Power is then given to them to organize the elements, and then commence the organization of tabernacles" (*JD*, 6:275).

First Presidency and Quorum of the Twelve: "We are to understand that only resurrected and glorified beings can become parents of spirit offspring. Only such exalted souls have reached maturity in the appointed course of eternal life; and the spirits born to them in the eternal worlds will pass in due sequence through the several stages or estates by which the glorified parents have attained exaltation" (*Improvement Era*, August 1916, 942, hereafter cited as *IE*).

Melvin J. Ballard: "When the power of endless increase shall come to us, and our offspring grow and multiply through ages that shall come, they will be in due time, as we have been, provided with an earth like this wherein they too may obtain earthly bodies and pass through all the experiences through which we have passed. . . . [W]e shall stand in our relationship to them as God our Eternal Father does to us" (Melvin R. Ballard, ed., *Melvin J. Ballard: Crusader for Righteousness* [Salt Lake City: Bookcraft, 1966], 211–12).

Lorenzo Snow: "The time will come" when faithful Latter-day Saints "will progress and develop in knowledge, intelligence and power, in future eternities, until they shall be able to go out into space where there is unorganized matter and call together the necessary elements, and through their knowledge of and control over the laws and powers of nature, to organize matter into worlds on which their posterity may dwell, and over which they shall rule as gods" (*IE*, June 1919, 658–59).

49. Moroni 10:32–33 speaks of the key to attaining perfection. "Yea, come unto Christ, and be perfected in him, and deny yourselves of all ungodliness; and if

ye shall deny yourselves of all ungodliness, and love God with all your might, mind and strength, then is his grace sufficient for you, that by his grace ye may be perfect in Christ; and if by the grace of God ye are perfect in Christ, ye can in nowise deny the power of God. And again, if ye by the grace of God are perfect in Christ, and deny not his power, then are ye sanctified in Christ by the grace of God, through the shedding of the blood of Christ, which is in the covenant of the Father unto the remission of your sins, that ye become holy, without spot." In August of 1916 the First Presidency and Quorum of the Twelve Apostles published a doctrinal exposition which included the statement that those who achieve perfection or "obtain exaltation and even reach the status of godhood . . . are still subject to Jesus Christ as their Father in this exalted relationship [see D&C 76:59]" (James R. Clark, comp., *Messages of the First Presidency of The Church of Jesus Christ of Latter-day Saints* [Salt Lake City: Bookcraft, 1971], 5:31).

50. Vaughn J. Featherstone, *The Incomparable Christ: Our Master and Model* (Salt Lake City: Deseret Book, 1995), 42.

51. CR, April 1961, 66.

52. *DNTC,* 3:230.

53. Ibid., 3:491.

54. Edward L. Kimball, ed., *The Teachings of Spencer W. Kimball* (Salt Lake City: Bookcraft, 1982), 51–52.

APPENDIX I

THE SALVATION OF CHILDREN

When children die, questions naturally arise about the reasons for their passing, their condition in the spirit world, their circumstances in the Resurrection, and the degree of salvation that they will ultimately receive. This appendix will attempt to provide meaningful answers to these and other related questions by drawing upon the scriptures and the teachings of Church leaders.

What is the nature of a child before it is born?

The answer to this question is provided by Patriarch Hyrum Smith, brother of the Prophet Joseph Smith. Hyrum made note of the fact that "the spirit of Jesus Christ was full-grown before He was born into the world [see Ether 3:6–16]; and so our children were full-grown and possessed their full stature in the spirit, before they entered mortality."[1] Elder Melvin J. Ballard of the Quorum of the Twelve Apostles taught the same doctrine. He said that "long before we were born into this earth we were tested and tried in our preexistence. . . . There are no infant spirits born. They had a being ages before they came into this life. They appear in infant bodies, but they were tested, proven souls."[2]

What is the status of a child before it reaches the age of accountability?

The revelations that are contained in the Doctrine and Covenants state that "every spirit of man was innocent in the beginning; and . . .

men bec[o]me again, in their infant state, innocent before God" (D&C 93:38). Little children are, therefore, "holy" and "sanctified" in the eyes of the Lord (D&C 74:7). They are redeemed through the Atonement of Jesus Christ, and "they cannot sin, for power is not given unto Satan to tempt little children, until they begin to become accountable" before the Lord (D&C 29:46–47).

What happens to a child who dies before it reaches eight years of age?

The Prophet Joseph Smith had a reassuring answer to this particular question. He said that "the moment . . . children leave this world they are taken to the bosom of Abraham,"[3] meaning that they dwell among the righteous in the spirit world (see Luke 16:22). On 21 January 1836 the Prophet saw, in vision, the ultimate destiny of "all children who die before they arrive at the years of accountability," and he reported that they are "saved in the celestial kingdom of heaven" (D&C 137:10).

Why do some children die?

There are several answers to this question. To begin with, no mortals are immune from the accidents and vicissitudes of the fallen or telestial world. The Prophet Joseph Smith pointed out that "it is a false idea that the Saints will escape all the judgments [that are described in the scriptures], whilst the wicked suffer; for all flesh is subject to suffer, and 'the righteous shall hardly escape' [D&C 63:32–34]; . . . [M]any of the righteous shall fall . . . prey to disease, to pestilence, etc., by reason of the weakness of the flesh, and yet be saved in the kingdom of God."[4]

It appears that some children die because of the stage that they have reached in their eternal progression; they are evidently only required to be on the earth for a short period of time. Joseph Smith prefaced the following doctrine with a question:

> Why is it that infants [or] innocent children are taken away from us, especially those that seem to be most intelligent beings? . . . The Lord takes many away even in infancy that they may escape the envy of man—the sorrows and evils of this present world. . . . [T]hey were too pure and too lovely to live on earth. Therefore, if rightly considered, instead of

mourning we have reason to rejoice, as they are delivered
from evil and we shall soon have them again. . . . The only
difference between the old and [the] young dying is one
lives longer in heaven and eternal light and glory than the
other and was freed a little sooner from this miserable,
wicked world.[5]

When Elder Bruce R. McConkie was serving in the Quorum of
the Seventy he asserted that "there are certain spirits who come into
this life only to receive bodies; for reasons that we do not know, but
which are known in the infinite wisdom of the Eternal Father, they do
not need the testing, probationary experiences of mortality. We come
here for two great reasons—the first, to get a body; the second, to be
tried, examined, schooled, and tested under mortal circumstances, to
take a different type of probationary test than we underwent in the
premortal life. There are some of the children of our Father, however,
who come to earth to get a body—for that reason solely. They do not
need the testings of this mortality."[6]

Some children may be taken to the other side of the veil so that
they can help to fulfill a heavenly law. President Wilford Woodruff
related the following story about the loss of his own son:

> While in the St. George Temple I had a son, who was in
> the north country, drowned. He was 21 years of age, and
> was a faithful young man. He had a warning of this. In a
> dream he was notified how he would die. We had testi-
> mony of that after his death. I asked the Lord why he was
> taken from me. The answer to me was, "You are doing a
> great deal for the redemption of your dead; but the law of
> redemption requires some of your own seed in the spirit
> world to attend to work connected with this." That was a
> new principle to me; but it satisfied me why he was taken
> away. I name this because there are a great many instances
> like it among the Latter-day Saints. This was the case with
> Brother Abraham Cannon. He was taken away to fulfill
> that mission. And where we have anything of this kind, we
> should leave it in the hands of God to reconcile.[7]

What is the nature of a child after it dies?

President Joseph F. Smith answered this question in the following manner. He said, "The spirits of our children are immortal before they come to us, and their spirits, after bodily death, are like they were before they came. They are as they would have appeared if they had lived in the flesh, to grow to maturity, or to develop their physical bodies to the full stature of their spirits."

President Smith also offers this interesting insight. He relates that "if you see one of your children that has passed away it may appear to you in the form in which you would recognize it, the form of child-hood; but if it came to you as a messenger bearing some important truth, it would perhaps come as the spirit of Bishop Edward Hunter's son (who died when a little child) came to him, in the stature of full-grown manhood, and revealed himself to his father, and said: 'I am your son.'"[8] Elder Melvin J. Ballard reported that he experienced a manifestation of this type. He said, "I lost a son six years of age, and I saw him a man in the spirit world after his death."[9]

Will those who die as children need to be taught the gospel of Jesus Christ?

President Joseph Fielding Smith explained that "it is not the fault of innocent children who die that their parents do not come into the Church and refuse to accept the gospel. Through the mercy and justice of our Eternal Father, every soul is entitled to hear the gospel. If they do not have the privilege in this mortal life, then they will have it in the spirit world, where it is preached to the dead."[10]

Will those who die as children need to receive any of the ordinances of the gospel?

President Joseph Fielding Smith explains that the celestial kingdom "has different degrees in it, and to obtain the highest there are many blessings and commandments which have to be kept. The children who die in infancy or early childhood must comply with all of these, just the same as do those who gain their maturity in this mortal life."[11] President Smith added a few instructive details on this matter.

Little children who die before they reach the years of accountability will automatically inherit the celestial kingdom, but not the exaltation in that kingdom *until* they have complied with all the requirements of exaltation. For instance:

The crowning glory is marriage and this ordinance would have to be performed in their behalf before they could inherit the fullness of that kingdom. The Lord is just with all His children, and little children who die will not be penalized . . . simply because they happen to die. *The Lord will grant unto these children the privilege of all the sealing blessings which pertain to the exaltation. . . .*

All that we need do for children is to have them sealed to their parents. They need no baptism and never will, for our Lord has performed all the work necessary for them. . . .

Boys and girls who die after baptism may have the endowment work done for them in the temple. Children who die in infancy do not have to be endowed. So far as the ordinance of sealing is concerned, this may wait until the millennium.[12]

What will be the state or condition of a child after it has been resurrected?

The Prophet Joseph Smith asserted on several occasions that children would be resurrected as they were laid down in the grave but would not grow in stature after that point.[13] In several other instances, however, the Prophet declared that while children would be resurrected as they were at the time of their death they would grow afterward to the full stature of their spirit.[14] "President [Brigham] Young said he heard Joseph Smith say . . . that children would not grow after death and at another time that they would grow and he hardly knew how to reconcile it."[15]

Why did the Prophet teach two opposing views on this particular issue? A valuable insight was provided by President Brigham Young, who disclosed that Joseph Smith "never had any *revelation* upon the subject."[16] President Wilford Woodruff, in a letter he wrote to the recorder of the Logan Temple, indicated that the Prophet was offering his own personal opinion on children and the Resurrection.

> Now concerning what Joseph Smith the Prophet said about children: In the first place he said children would rise from the grave, as they were laid down, and their parents would receive [them] as they laid them away. This, I believe. He conveyed an idea in the first place, that they would not grow, but *after more mature reflection,* he conveyed the idea that they eventually would grow to the full stature of man. . . . [H]is views on the resurrection . . . enlarged before he got through, and he said children would grow to full stature.[17]

One of the occasions when the Prophet said that children would *not* grow after the Resurrection was during the King Follett discourse, delivered 7 April 1844. Elder Orson Pratt said this of the remarks that were made on that day:

> I very much doubt whether the Prophet Joseph, at the time he preached that sermon, had been *fully instructed by revelation* on that point, for the Lord has revealed a great many things to prophets and revelators, and among them to Joseph Smith, the fullness of which is not at first given. . . . [I]n regard to the resurrection, there may have been many things revealed to him that were true, and others upon which, *without having revelation, he would draw his own conclusions,* until it should please the Lord to give further revelation. . . . I have heard, whether it be true or not I do not know, that before Joseph was martyred, he had obtained further light and information on this subject, to the effect that there would be a growth after the resurrection.[18]

It is possible that the Prophet believed children would not grow after their redemption from the grave because of what he saw in a vision on 21 January 1836. During this revelatory experience, which is now published as section 137 of the Doctrine and Covenants, the Prophet "beheld that all children who die before they arrive at the years of accountability are saved in the celestial kingdom of heaven" (v. 10). In addition, the Prophet saw his "father" and "mother" (who were still alive) in the celestial realm (v. 5). Even though it is clear that this vision employed symbolic imagery, the Prophet may have taken the scene of children in the celestial kingdom literally and thus come to the conclusion that they would not grow after they received their resurrected bodies.

NOTES: APPENDIX I

1. Joseph F. Smith, *Gospel Doctrine* (Salt Lake City: Deseret Book, 1986), 455, hereafter cited as *GD*.

2. Bryant S. Hinckley, *Sermons and Missionary Services of Melvin Joseph Ballard* (Salt Lake City: Deseret Book, 1949), 247–48.

3. Andrew F. Ehat and Lyndon W. Cook, eds., *The Words of Joseph Smith: The Contemporary Accounts of the Nauvoo Discourses of the Prophet Joseph* (Orem, Utah: Grandin Book, 1991), 107, hereafter cited as *WJS*.

4. B. H. Roberts, ed., *History of the Church*, rev. ed. (Salt Lake City: The Church of Jesus Christ of Latter-day Saints, 1932–1951), 4:11, hereafter cited as *HC*.

5. *WJS*, 106–107.

6. Unpublished funeral address for Rebecca Adams, 28 October 1967, 2–3. For two stories that confirm this principle see L. Brent Goates, comp., *Harold B. Lee: Remembering the Miracles* (American Fork, Utah: Covenant Communications, 2001), 147–49; Duane S. Crowther, *Life Everlasting*, rev. ed. (Bountiful, Utah: Horizon Publishers, 1997), 169–70.

7. G. Homer Durham, ed., *The Discourses of Wilford Woodruff* (Salt Lake City: Bookcraft, 1969), 292.

8. *GD*, 455.

9. Hinckley, *Sermons and Missionary Services of Melvin Joseph Ballard*, 260.

10. Joseph Fielding Smith, *Answers to Gospel Questions* (Salt Lake City: Deseret Book, 1998), 1:54.

11. Ibid., 3:113. The following statement is found in an article published in the *Ensign.* "Precisely what the Lord will require in the form of ordinances, or other requirements, for spirits who died as infants or children on earth in order to receive exaltation has not been revealed. Certain it is that we do not currently endow children who die before accountability nor do we seal them to a spouse. But this does not mean that the blessings of these latter ordinances are unavailable to them" (*Ensign,* June 1981, 36). Elder Bruce R. McConkie asked, "Will children [who die before reaching the age of accountability] be married and live in the family unit?" He answered, "Certainly. There can be no question about this. If they gain . . . exaltation, it means that they are married and live in the family unit" (ibid., April 1977, 5).

12. Joseph Fielding Smith, *Doctrines of Salvation* (Salt Lake City: Bookcraft, 1999), 2:54–55, emphasis in original, hereafter cited as *DS.* Elder Melvin J. Ballard once said, "You mothers worry about your little children [who have passed away]. We do not perform [marriage] sealings for them. I lost a son six years of age, and I saw him a man in the spirit world after his death, and I saw how he had exercised his own freedom of choice and would obtain of his own will and volition a companionship . . . [I]n due time to him, and all those who are worthy of it, shall come all of the blessings and sealing privileges of the house of the Lord. Do not worry over it. They are safe; they are alright" (Hinckley, *Sermons and Missionary Services of Melvin Joseph Ballard,* 260).

13. For example, see the Prophet's comments made on 20 March 1842 (*WJS,* 109), 18 May 1843 (George D. Smith, ed., *An Intimate Chronicle: The Journals of William Clayton* [Salt Lake City: Signature Books, 1995], 104), 7 April 1844 (*WJS,* 342, 347, 354), and 12 May 1844 (ibid., 369, 372). It is interesting to note that during the 18 May 1843 statement just listed the Prophet taught that "children who are born dead will have full-grown bodies being made up by the resurrection." For further reading on the future status of stillborn children see Daniel H. Ludlow, ed., *Encyclopedia of Mormonism* (New York: Macmillan, 1992), 3:1419; *DS,* 2:280–81; Bruce R. McConkie, *Mormon Doctrine,* 2d ed. (Salt Lake City: Bookcraft, 1966), 768; Bruce R. McConkie, *Doctrinal New Testament Commentary* (Salt Lake City: Bookcraft, 1965), 1:84–85.

14. In October of 1843 Joseph Smith's niece, Sophrina Smith, died. The Prophet said to Agnes Smith, her mother, "You will have the joy, the pleasure, and satisfaction of nurturing this child, after its resurrection, until it reaches the full stature of its spirit" (*GD,* 456). Lorin Walker, a brother-in-law to President Joseph F. Smith, was present during Sophrina's funeral. He reported the

Prophet as saying that "the body remains undeveloped in the grave, but the spirit returns to God who gave it. Afterwards, in the resurrection, the spirit and body will be reunited; the body will develop and grow to the full stature of the spirit, and the resurrected soul will go on to perfection" (ibid.). Wilford Woodruff said that after the King Follett discourse (delivered on 7 April 1844) "he heard [the Prophet] modify [the] assertion" that children would not grow after they were resurrected (Abraham H. Cannon Journal, 6 April 1889, Special Collections, Harold B. Lee Library, Brigham Young University, Provo, Utah, 199). B. H. Roberts likewise reports that "President Woodruff very emphatically said . . . that the Prophet taught subsequently to his King Follett sermon that children while resurrected in the stature at which they died would develop to the full stature of men and women after the resurrection" (*HC*, 4:556). M. Isabella Horne reports that the following incident occurred "sometime after the King Follett funeral," which she attended. "In conversation with the Prophet Joseph Smith once in Nauvoo, the subject of children in the resurrection was broached. I believe it was in Sister Leonora Cannon Taylor's house. She had just lost one of her children, and I had also lost one previously. The Prophet wanted to comfort us, and he told us that we should receive those children in the morning of the resurrection just as we laid them down, in purity and innocence, and we should nourish and care for them as their mothers. He said that children would be raised in the resurrection just as they were laid down, and that they would obtain all the intelligence necessary to occupy thrones, principalities, and powers. The idea that I got from what he said was that the children would grow and develop in the millennium, and that the mothers would have the pleasure of training and caring for them, which they had been deprived of in this life." Isabella's husband, Joseph Horne likewise testified: "I heard the Prophet Joseph Smith say that mothers should receive their children just as they laid them down, and that they would have the privilege of doing for them what they could not do here. The Prophet remarked: 'How would you know them if you did not receive them as you laid them down?' I also got the idea that children would grow and develop after the resurrection and that the mothers would care for them and train them" (ibid., 4:556–57, ftnt.).

15. Scott G. Kenney, ed., *Wilford Woodruff's Journal* (Midvale, Utah: Signature Books, 1984), 6:363.

16. Ibid., 5:544, emphasis added.

17. Letter, Wilford Woodruff to Samuel Roskelley, 8 June 1887, Samuel Roskelley Papers, Special Collections, Merrill Library, Utah State University, Logan, Utah, emphasis added.

18. George D. Watt, comp., *Journal of Discourses* (London, England: F. D. and S. W. Richards and Sons, 1854–1886), 16:335–36, emphasis added. Benjamin F. Johnson, who was an acquaintance of the Prophet Joseph Smith, explained that "the gospel [was] . . . given to us by fragments, . . . and perfection here can only exist in parts or degrees." Since "the Holy Ghost may not always remain upon a man, may not even a prophet to whom [the gospel] was not yet all revealed, make mistakes, as in the [case of governing the practice of] baptism for the dead, and also in the [P]rophet['s] sermon[s] at the funerals of a child of Windsor Lyon and [also] King Follett, when he preached that children, 'even infants, would sit upon thrones with dominion,' which was published in the *Times and Seasons* at the time, but which, like President Woodruff, I am positive he afterwards reconsidered?" (E. Dale LeBaron, *Benjamin Franklin Johnson: Colonizer, Public Servant, and Church Leader*, master's thesis, Brigham Young University, 1966, 330). It should be remembered that the Prophet himself said, "I never told you I was perfect, but there is no error in the *revelations* which I have taught" (*WJS*, 369, emphasis added).

APPENDIX II

COVENANT STATUS AND SALVATION

On 13 August 1843 the Prophet Joseph Smith delivered the funeral sermon for Judge Elias Higbee. Some of the comments that the Prophet made on that day have been interpreted to mean that children who are (1) sealed to their parents or (2) sealed to parents who make their calling and election sure will be saved in the celestial kingdom of God regardless of how they live their mortal lives. The Prophet's remarks, as recorded in the *History of the Church*, are as follows:

> The world is reserved unto burning in the last days. [The Lord] shall send Elijah the prophet, and he shall reveal the covenants of the fathers in relation to the children, and the covenants of the children in relation to the fathers.
>
> Four destroying angels holding power over the four quarters of the earth [withhold their destruction] until the servants of God are sealed in their foreheads, which signifies sealing the blessing upon their heads, meaning the everlasting covenant, thereby making their calling and election sure. When a seal is put upon the father and mother, it secures their posterity, so that they cannot be lost, but will be saved by virtue of the covenant of their father and mother.[1]

The compilers of the *History of the Church* indicate at the beginning of the speech from which this quotation is taken that it is only a "synopsis" of what the Prophet said on 13 August 1843. It should also be noted that the statement under consideration does not come from a single source. Rather, these words are an amalgamation of incomplete notes taken from the Joseph Smith Diary (which was kept by Willard Richards) and also the journal of William Clayton. Fortunately, Howard Coray (who served as one of the Prophet's clerks) wrote down more of the details of this discourse. His transcription makes it clear that the Prophet did *not* teach the unconditional salvation of covenant children. The Coray notes read as follows:

> Malachi 4th ch[apter verse 1]: "Behold the day cometh that shall burn as an oven and all the proud and they that do wickedly shall be as stubble and [the day] that cometh shall burn them up." Although in the beginning God created the earth standing in the water and out of the water, still in the end it shall be burned and few men left. But before that God shall send unto them Elijah the prophet and he shall reveal unto them the covenants of the fathers with relation to the children and the covenants of the children in relation to the fathers that they may have the privilege of entering into the same in order to effect their mutual salvation.

> [Revelation 7:2–3 says,] "And I saw another angel ascending from the east having the seal of the living God and he cried . . . saying, 'Hurt not the earth nor [the] sea nor [the] trees till we have sealed the servants of our God in their foreheads.'"

> Now I would ask, Who know[s what] the seal of the living God [is]? Behold the ignorance of the world.

> A measure of this sealing is to confirm upon their head in common with Elijah the doctrine of election or the covenant with Abraham which when a father and mother of a family have entered into *their children who have not transgressed are secured by the seal wherewith the parents have been sealed.* And this is the oath of God unto our father Abraham and this doctrine shall stand forever.[2]

Andrew F. Ehat and Lyndon W. Cook, the editors of *The Words of Joseph Smith*, note that "the wording of the published version suggests that the children of parents who receive the fullness of the Priesthood can never fall." But, they point out, Howard Coray's "previously unpublished, more complete account of the Prophet's idea *does* contain a conditional. Clearly this a more reasonable and consistent doctrine: if it were not for such a conditional, the concept would contradict significant doctrines taught by Joseph Smith, not the least of which would be a contradiction of his Article of Faith [#2] that 'men will be punished for their own sins.'"[3]

Several of the leaders of The Church of Jesus Christ of Latter-day Saints have made comments that are relevant to this issue. For example, President Joseph Fielding Smith had the following to say about children who are born under the covenant:

> Those born under the covenant, throughout all eternity, are the children of their parents. Nothing except the unpardonable sin, or sin unto death, can break this tie. . . .
>
> *All children born under the covenant belong to their parents in eternity, but that does not mean that they, because of that birthright, will inherit celestial glory. The faith and faithfulness of fathers and mothers will not save disobedient children.*
>
> *Salvation is an individual matter, and if a person who has been born under the covenant rebels and denies the Lord, he will lose the blessings of exaltation.* Every soul will be judged according to *his works and the wicked cannot inherit eternal life. We cannot force salvation upon those who do not want it.* Even our Father's children had their agency before this life, and one-third of them rebelled.
>
> It is the duty of parents to teach their children so that they will *walk uprightly and thus obtain the blessings of their birthright.*
>
> But children born under the covenant, who drift away, are still the children of their parents; and the parents have a

claim upon them; and *if* the children have not sinned away all their rights, the parents *may* be able to bring them *through repentance,* into the celestial kingdom, but *not* to receive the exaltation. Of course, if children sin too grievously, they will have to enter the *telestial* kingdom, or they may even become sons of perdition.[4]

President Charles W. Penrose, who served as a counselor in the First Presidency of the LDS Church, taught that only those who conform to God's laws will enjoy perpetual family relationships in the celestial world. Men and women who obey the Lord's law pertaining to celestial marriage will come forth in the Resurrection as eternal companions, "and the children of that union, *if* [they are] fit to come into that family circle, will be there, sharing with the parents in the joys and the glories of the celestial world." But "*if not,*" said President Penrose, "then they will have to take that which justice shall deal out to them. . . . [T]hey must go into the condition for which they have fitted themselves."[5]

Finally, we should take the words of President Spencer W. Kimball into careful consideration. He acknowledged that he had "sometimes seen children of good families rebel, resist, stray, sin, and even actually fight God." Then he made this important observation. He said that "there is no guarantee, of course, that righteous parents will succeed always in holding their children, and certainly they may lose them if they do not do all in their power. *The children have their free agency.*"[6]

The clear message put forward by these Church leaders is that even children who are sealed to their parents for time and all eternity can forfeit an inheritance in the celestial kingdom of God because of the unwise choices that they make.[7] Their destiny lies in their own hands.

NOTES: APPENDIX II

1.   B. H. Roberts, ed., *History of the Church*, rev. ed. (Salt Lake City: The Church of Jesus Christ of Latter-day Saints, 1932–1951), 5:530. This quotation is also

found in Joseph Fielding Smith, comp., *Teachings of the Prophet Joseph Smith* (Salt Lake City: Deseret Book, 1976), 321. Some might argue from this quotation that those parents who make their "calling and election sure" will automatically be saved in the celestial kingdom. But Elder Bruce R. McConkie, after quoting the Prophet's 13 August 1843 statement, disagreed with such an interpretation. He taught instead that "if *both parents and children have their calling and election made sure,* none so involved shall be lost; all shall come forth to an inheritance of glory and exaltation in the kingdom of God" (Bruce R. McConkie, *Doctrinal New Testament Commentary* [Salt Lake City: Bookcraft, 1973], 3:492, emphasis added).

2. Andrew F. Ehat and Lyndon W. Cook, eds., *The Words of Joseph Smith: The Contemporary Accounts of the Nauvoo Discourses of the Prophet Joseph* (Orem, Utah: Grandin Book, 1994), 240–41, emphasis added.

3. Ibid., 300, n. #19.

4. Joseph Fielding Smith, *Doctrines of Salvation* (Salt Lake City: Bookcraft, 1999), 2:90–91, emphasis in original. President Smith made some other comments that are relevant to the topic under discussion. "*Question:* 'If a member of the Church has been sealed to his parents, but marries out of the Church, what kingdom will he inherit in the Resurrection?' *Answer:* No matter how a person is sealed he will be assigned to his proper place. If a person is sealed to his parents, or is born under the covenant, and then he lives a telestial law, to the telestial kingdom he will go, or to the terrestrial. Salvation is an individual responsibility. Only through living the gospel can we enter the celestial kingdom" (Joseph Fielding Smith, *Answers to Gospel Questions* [Salt Lake City: Deseret Book, 1998], 5:169).

5. Conference Report, October 1914, 42, emphasis added, hereafter cited as CR.

6. Edward L. Kimball, ed., *The Teachings of Spencer W. Kimball* (Salt Lake City: Bookcraft, 1982), 335, emphasis added.

7. An appeal is sometimes made to a statement by Orson F. Whitney in order to bolster the claim that children who are sealed to their parents will eventually make it to the celestial kingdom regardless of their probationary performance (see CR, April 1929, 110–11). It should be noted, however, that in these remarks Elder Whitney indicates that he is drawing from the teachings of the Prophet Joseph Smith. This raises the question of whether he was paraphrasing the amalgamated and incomplete statement that had been published in the

History of the Church. President Spencer W. Kimball's son, Edward L. Kimball, made the following point after referring to Elder Whitney's remarks. "The idea that the faithfulness of the parents will save their children is comforting, but it is, after all, in tension with principles of agency and individual responsibility. We are taught that we will not be punished for our parents' sins, nor will we be saved by our parents' righteousness. Alma the Elder's prayers brought an angel to confront his son, but it was still for young Alma to change his life" (Edward L. Kimball, "Staying Together Despite Not Praying Together: Families Dealing with Inactivity," in Dawn Hall Anderson, Susette Fletcher Green, and Marie Cornwall, eds., *Women and Christ: Living the Abundant Life* [Salt Lake City: Deseret Book, 1993], 170).

APPENDIX III

SALVATION AND GRACE

This appendix is designed to direct the reader to information on the LDS view of salvation and grace. Below are samples of quotations, books, articles, scriptures, and hymns that refer to and expound upon this important doctrine.

Quotations on Salvation and Grace

Ezra Taft Benson: "Grace consists of God's gift to His children wherein He gave His Only Begotten Son that whosoever would believe in Him and comply with His laws and ordinances would have everlasting life.

By grace, the Savior accomplished His atoning sacrifice so that all mankind will attain immortality. By His grace, and by our faith in His Atonement and repentance of our sins, we receive the strength to do the works necessary that we otherwise could not do by our own power. By His grace we receive an endowment of blessing and spiritual strength that may eventually lead us to eternal life if we endure to the end. By His grace we become more like His divine personality. Yes, it is 'by grace that we are saved, after all we can do' (2 Ne. 25:23)."[1]

Rulon S. Wells: "I rejoice in the gospel of repentance, because I know that it has within it the power of God unto salvation; and I know that it is necessary for us to make individual efforts to control the thinking powers of our minds, to control those elements of our nature that require our purification to fit and qualify us to dwell in the presence of God. That is the part of our salvation that is left to us. Through the grace of God we will be redeemed from the dead. Through the grace of God we will be relieved from the consequences of evil, not only from the original transgression of our first parents in the Garden of Eden, but also of all our own personal acts and short-comings, provided we will practice this great gospel of repentance from sin, and bring unto the Lord a broken heart and a contrite spirit, and manifest in our daily lives that we are determined to lead that perfect life and to resist evil in all of its forms, no matter how it may present itself to us."[2]

Spencer W. Kimball: "Some people not of our Church like to quote the following words of Paul: 'For by grace are ye saved through faith; and that not of yourselves: it is the gift of God: Not of works, lest any man should boast' (Eph. 2:8–9).

One of the most fallacious doctrines originated by Satan and propounded by man is that man is saved alone by the grace of God; that belief in Jesus Christ alone is all that is needed for salvation. . . . One passage in the Book of Mormon, written perhaps with the same intent as Paul's statement above—to stress and induce appreciation for the gracious gift of salvation offered on condition of obedience—is particularly enlightening: 'For we labor diligently to write, to persuade our children, and also our brethren, to believe in Christ, and to be reconciled to God; for we know that it is by grace that we are saved, after all we can do' (2 Ne. 25:23). . . .

However good a person's works, he could not be saved had Jesus not died for his and everyone else's sins. And however powerful the saving grace of Christ, it brings exaltation to no man who does not comply with the works of the gospel.

Of course we need to understand terms. If by the word *salvation* is meant the mere salvation or redemption from the grave, the 'grace of God' is sufficient. But if the term *salvation* means returning to the presence of God with eternal progression, eternal increase, and even-tual godhood, [then] for this one certainly must have the 'grace of God,' as it is generally defined, plus personal purity, overcoming of evil, and the good 'works' made so important in the exhortations of the Savior and His prophets and apostles."[3]

David O. McKay: "An outstanding doctrine of the Church is that each individual carries the responsibility to work out his own salvation and that this salvation is a process of gradual development. The Church does not accept the doctrine that a mere murmured belief in Jesus Christ is all that is essential to salvation. A man may say he believes, but if he does nothing to make that belief or faith a moving power to do, to accomplish, to produce soul growth, his protestation will avail him nothing.

To work out one's salvation is not to sit idly by, dreaming and yearning for God miraculously to thrust bounteous blessings into our laps. It is to perform daily, hourly, momentarily, if necessary, the immediate task or duty at hand, and to continue happily in such performance as the years come and go, leaving the fruits of such labors either to self or to others to be bestowed as a just and beneficent Father may determine.

I am not unmindful of the scripture that declares 'By grace are ye saved through faith, and that not of yourselves; it is a gift of God.' That is absolutely true, for man in his taking upon himself mortality was impotent to save himself. When left to grope in a natural state, he would have become, and did become 'carnal, sensual and devilish by nature.' But the Lord through His grace appeared to man, gave him the gospel or eternal plan whereby he might rise above the carnal and selfish things of life and obtain spiritual perfection. But he must rise by his own efforts and he must walk by faith."[4]

Orson F. Whitney: "Men must 'work out their salvation' (Philip. 2:12), and gain exaltation by continuous upward striving. Salvation and exaltation, while depending primarily upon the grace of God, are also the fruits of man's acceptance of the gospel, and his steadfast adherence thereto, until it shall have done for him its perfect work. There are degrees of glory—'many mansions' in the great house of God, and the highest are reserved for those who render to the Master of the house the fullness of their obedience."[5]

Bruce R. McConkie: "Salvation in all its forms, kinds, and degrees comes by the grace of God. That is, because of His love, mercy, and condescension, God our Father ordained the plan and system of salvation which would 'bring to pass the immortality and eternal life of man' (Moses 1:39). Pursuant to this plan He sent His Only Begotten Son into the world to work out the infinite and eternal atoning sacrifice.

Then our Lord, in turn, also because of His love, mercy, and condescension, performed the appointed labor so that all men are 'raised in immortality,' and those who believe and obey the gospel law inherit 'eternal life' (D&C 29:43–44). The faithful gain a forgiveness of their sins and are reconciled to God because they believe and obey His laws.

Men are thus saved by grace alone, in the sense of being resurrected; they are saved by grace coupled with obedience, in the sense of gaining eternal life. The gospel plan is to save men in the celestial kingdom, and hence Paul teaches salvation by grace through faith, through obedience, through accepting Christ, through keeping the commandments."[6]

Books and Articles on Salvation and Grace

- M. Russell Ballard, "Building Bridges of Understanding," *Ensign*, June 1998, 64–66.
- D. Todd Christofferson, "Justification and Sanctification," *Ensign*, June 2001, 18–25.
- Gene R. Cook, "Receiving Divine Assistance Through the Grace of the Lord," *Ensign*, May 1993, 79–81.
- Andrew F. Ehat and Lyndon W. Cook, eds., *The Words of Joseph Smith: The Contemporary Accounts of the Nauvoo Discourses of the Prophet Joseph* (Orem, Utah: Grandin Book, 1991), 330, 333–34.
- Bruce C. Hafen, "The Restored Doctrine of the Atonement," *Ensign*, December 1993, 7–13.
- Daniel H. Ludlow, ed., *Encyclopedia of Mormonism* (New York: Macmillan, 1992), 2:560–63.

- Daniel H. Ludlow, "The Relationship Between Grace and Works," in Daniel H. Ludlow, *Gospel Scholars Series: Selected Writings of Daniel H. Ludlow* (Salt Lake City: Deseret Book, 2000), 335–53.
- Gerald N. Lund, "Salvation: By Grace or By Works?" *Ensign*, April 1981, 16–23.
- Gerald N. Lund, "'Then Is His Grace Sufficient for You' (Moro. 10:32)," in Gerald N. Lund, *Gospel Scholars Series: Selected Writings of Gerald N. Lund* (Salt Lake City: Deseret Book, 1999), 208–19.
- Bruce R. McConkie, "What Think Ye of Salvation by Grace?" *Brigham Young University Fireside and Devotional Speeches 1983–84* (Provo, Utah: Brigham Young University Press, 1984), 44–50.
- Bruce R. McConkie, *Mormon Doctrine*, 2d ed. (Salt Lake City: Bookcraft, 1966), 338–39.
- Bruce R. McConkie, *A New Witness for the Articles of Faith* (Salt Lake City: Deseret Book, 1985), 99–100.
- Robert L. Millet, *By Grace Are We Saved* (Salt Lake City: Bookcraft, 1989), 128.
- Robert L. Millet, *The Mormon Faith: A New Look at Christianity* (Salt Lake City: Shadow Mountain, 1998), 69–79, 168–69.
- Dallin H. Oaks, "Have You Been Saved?" *Ensign*, May 1998, 55–57.
- Robert E. Parsons, "What Is the Role of Grace in LDS Theology?" *Ensign*, July 1989, 59–61.
- Daniel C. Peterson and Stephen D. Ricks, "Comparing LDS Beliefs with First-Century Christianity," *Ensign*, March 1988, 10.
- Stephen E. Robinson, *Believing Christ* (Salt Lake City: Deseret Book, 1992), 57–82.
- Joseph Fielding Smith, *Doctrines of Salvation* (Salt Lake City: Deseret Book, 1999), 2:306–11.
- Rodney Turner, "Grace, Mysteries, and Exaltation," in Robert L. Millet, ed., *Studies in Scripture: Volume 6, Acts to Revelation* (Salt Lake City: Deseret Book, 1987), 110–11.

Scriptures on Salvation and Grace

- The Father is full of grace (D&C 66:12).
- Jesus Christ is full of grace (2 Ne. 2:6; Alma 5:48; 9:26; 13:9; D&C 93:11).
- Salvation is only in and through the grace of God (2 Ne. 10:24).
- Justification and sanctification come through the grace of Jesus Christ (D&C 20:30–31).
- Individuals are saved by grace after all that they can do (2 Ne. 25:23).
- God's power is granted unto individuals because of His grace (Jacob 4:6–7).
- Perfection in Christ is possible because of God's grace (Moro. 10:32–33).
- No person can dwell in God's presence except it be through the grace of the Holy Messiah (2 Ne. 2:8).
- Those who keep God's commandments will receive grace (D&C 93:20).
- It is possible for an individual to fall from grace (D&C 20:32).
- Grace is restored to those who repent of their iniquities (Hel. 12:20–24).

LDS Hymns on Salvation and Grace

The first hymnal of The Church of Jesus Christ of Latter-day Saints was produced by divine directive (see D&C 25:11). The hymns that are listed below illustrate how Latter-day Saints regard the doctrine of grace and how they incorporate it into their weekly worship services.[7]

- Glory to God on High (67)
- Praise the Lord with Heart and Voice (73)
- How Firm a Foundation (85)
- Great God, Attend While Zion Sings (88)

- Father, Thy Children to Thee Now Raise (91)
- Did You Think to Pray? (140)
- Sweet Hour of Prayer (142)
- Gently Raise the Sacred Strain (146)
- Sweet Is the Work (147)
- Great God, to Thee My Evening Song (164)
- Abide with Me! (166)
- Come, Let Us Sing an Evening Hymn (167)
- As Now We Take the Sacrament (169)
- God, Our Father, Hear Us Pray (170)
- 'Tis Sweet to Sing the Matchless Love (176)
- O Lord of Hosts (178)
- Reverently and Meekly Now (185)
- I Stand All Amazed (193)

NOTES: APPENDIX III

1. Ezra Taft Benson, *The Teachings of Ezra Taft Benson* (Salt Lake City: Bookcraft, 1988), 353–54.

2. Conference Report, April 1910, 24, hereafter cited as CR.

3. Edward L. Kimball, ed., *The Teachings of Spencer W. Kimball* (Salt Lake City: Bookcraft, 1982), 70–71.

4. David O. McKay, *Pathways to Happiness* (Salt Lake City: Bookcraft, 1957), 129–30.

5. Orson F. Whitney, *Gospel Themes* (Salt Lake City: The Church of Jesus Christ of Latter-day Saints, 1914), 23–24.

6. Bruce R. McConkie, *Doctrinal New Testament Commentary* (Salt Lake City: Bookcraft, 1970), 2:498.

7. The hymns that are listed are referenced to *Hymns of The Church of Jesus Christ of Latter-day Saints* (Salt Lake City: The Church of Jesus Christ of Latter-day Saints), 1985.

SELECTED BIBLIOGRAPHY

Books

Ballard, Melvin R., ed., *Melvin J. Ballard: Crusader for Righteousness* (Salt Lake City: Bookcraft), 1966.

Benson, Ezra Taft. *Come Unto Christ* (Salt Lake City: Deseret Book), 1983.

_____. *The Teachings of Ezra Taft Benson* (Salt Lake City: Bookcraft), 1988.

Brewster, Hoyt W., Jr. *Doctrine and Covenants Encyclopedia* (Salt Lake City: Bookcraft), 1988.

Brown, Matthew B. *All Things Restored: Confirming the Authenticity of LDS Beliefs* (American Fork, Utah: Covenant Communications), 2000.

Cannon, Donald Q. and Larry E. Dahl. *The Prophet Joseph Smith's King Follett Discourse: A Six Column Comparison of Original Notes and Amalgamations* (Provo, Utah: BYU Religious Studies Center), 1983.

Clark, James R., comp., *Messages of the First Presidency of The Church of Jesus Christ of Latter-day Saints*, 6 vols. (Salt Lake City: Bookcraft), 1965–1975.

Cowan, Richard O. *Answers to Your Questions About the Doctrine and Covenants* (Salt Lake City: Deseret Book), 1996.

Doxey, Roy W. *The Doctrine and Covenants Speaks* (Salt Lake City: Deseret Book), 1964.

Durham, G. Homer, ed., *The Discourses of Wilford Woodruff* (Salt Lake City: Bookcraft), 1969.

Ehat, Andrew F. and Lyndon W. Cook, eds., *The Words of Joseph Smith: The Contemporary Accounts of the Nauvoo Discourses of the Prophet Joseph* (Orem, Utah: Grandin Book), 1991.

Featherstone, Vaughn J. *The Incomparable Christ: Our Master and Model* (Salt Lake City: Deseret Book), 1995.

Flake, Lawrence R. *Three Degrees of Glory: Joseph Smith's Insights on the Kingdoms of Heaven* (American Fork, Utah: Covenant Communications), 2000.

Goates, L. Brent, comp., *Harold B. Lee: Remembering the Miracles* (American Fork, Utah: Covenant Communications), 2001.

Haight, David B. *A Light Unto the World* (Salt Lake City: Deseret Book), 1997.

Hinckley, Bryant S. *Sermons and Missionary Services of Melvin Joseph Ballard* (Salt Lake City: Deseret Book), 1949.

Holland, Jeffrey R. *Christ and the New Covenant: The Messianic Message of the Book of Mormon* (Salt Lake City: Deseret Book), 1997.

Hunter, Milton R. *The Gospel Through the Ages* (Salt Lake City: Stevens and Wallis), 1945.

Hymns of The Church of Jesus Christ of Latter-day Saints (Salt Lake City: The Church of Jesus Christ of Latter-day Saints), 1985.

Jackson, Kent P. *From Apostasy to Restoration* (Salt Lake City: Deseret Book), 1996.

Kenney, Scott G., ed., *Wilford Woodruff's Journal*, 9 vols. (Midvale, Utah: Signature Books), 1983–1985.

Kimball, Edward L., ed., *The Teachings of Spencer W. Kimball* (Salt Lake City: Bookcraft), 1982.

Kimball, Spencer W. *The Miracle of Forgiveness* (Salt Lake City: Bookcraft), 1969.

Lee, Harold B. *Decisions for Successful Living* (Salt Lake City: Deseret Book), 1973.

Ludlow, Daniel H., ed., *Encyclopedia of Mormonism*, 4 vols. (New York: Macmillan), 1992.

Ludlow, Victor L. *Principles and Practices of the Restored Gospel* (Salt Lake City: Deseret Book), 1992.

Matthews, Robert J. *Behold the Messiah* (Salt Lake City: Bookcraft), 1994

_____. *A Bible! A Bible!* (Salt Lake City: Bookcraft), 1990.

Maxwell, Neal A. *All These Things Shall Give Thee Experience* (Salt Lake City: Deseret Book), 1979.

_____. *We Will Prove Them Herewith* (Salt Lake City: Deseret Book), 1982.

McConkie, Bruce R. *Doctrinal New Testament Commentary*, 3 vols. (Salt Lake City: Bookcraft), 1965–1973

_____. *Mormon Doctrine*, 2d ed. (Salt Lake City: Bookcraft), 1966.

_____. *A New Witness for the Articles of Faith* (Salt Lake City: Deseret Book), 1985.

McIntosh, Robert and Susan McIntosh, eds., *The Teachings of George Albert Smith* (Salt Lake City: Bookcraft), 1996.

_____. *The Promised Messiah* (Salt Lake City: Deseret Book), 1978.

McKay, David O. *Gospel Ideals* (Salt Lake City: Improvement Era), 1953.

_____. *Pathways to Happiness* (Salt Lake City: Bookcraft), 1957.

McKay, Llewelyn L. *Home Memories of President David O. McKay* (Salt Lake City: Deseret Book), 1956.

Millet, Robert L. *By Grace Are We Saved* (Salt Lake City: Bookcraft), 1989.

_____. *The Mormon Faith: A New Look at Christianity* (Salt Lake City: Shadow Mountain), 1998.

Monson, Thomas S. *An Invitation to Exaltation* (Salt Lake City: Deseret Book), 1997.

Nelson, Russell M. *Perfection Pending, and Other Favorite Discourses* (Salt Lake City: Deseret Book), 1998.

Newquist, Jerreld L., ed., *Gospel Truth: Discourses and Writings of President George Q. Cannon* (Salt Lake City: Deseret Book), 1987.

Petersen, Mark E. *Abraham: Friend of God* (Salt Lake City: Deseret Book), 1979.

Pratt, Parley P. *Key to the Science of Theology* (Salt Lake City: Deseret Book), 1978.

Richards, Franklin D. and James A. Little. *Compendium of the Doctrines of the Gospel* (Salt Lake City: Bookcraft), 1925.

Roberts, B. H. *A New Witness for God* (Salt Lake City: George Q. Cannon and Sons), 1895.

_____. *New Witnesses for God* (Salt Lake City: Deseret News Press), 1911.

_____. *Outlines of Ecclesiastical History* (Salt Lake City: Deseret Book), 1979.

_____. *The Seventy's Course in Theology: Fifth Year* (Salt Lake City: Deseret News Press), 1912.

_____. ed., *History of the Church*, rev. ed., 7 vols. (Salt Lake City: The Church of Jesus Christ of Latter-day Saints), 1932–1951.

Robinson, Stephen E. *Believing Christ* (Salt Lake City: Deseret Book), 1992.

Romney, Marion G. *Learning for the Eternities* (Salt Lake City: Deseret Book), 1977.

Smith, George D., ed., *An Intimate Chronicle: The Journals of William Clayton* (Salt Lake City: Signature Books), 1995.

Smith, Joseph F. *Gospel Doctrine* (Salt Lake City: Deseret Book), 1986.

Smith, Joseph Fielding. *Answers to Gospel Questions*, 5 vols. (Salt Lake City: Deseret Book), 1998.

_____. *Church History and Modern Revelation*, 4 vols. (Salt Lake City: The Church of Jesus Christ of Latter-day Saints), 1946–1949.

_____. *Doctrines of Salvation*, 3 vols. (Salt Lake City: Bookcraft), 1999.

_____. *Man, His Origin and Destiny* (Salt Lake City: Deseret Book), 1954.

_____. *The Progress of Man* (Salt Lake City: Deseret Book), 1973.

_____. *Seek Ye Earnestly* (Salt Lake City: Deseret Book), 1970.

_____. *The Way to Perfection* (Salt Lake City: Genealogical Society of Utah), 1949.

_____. comp., *Teachings of the Prophet Joseph Smith* (Salt Lake City: Deseret Book), 1976.

Sperry, Sidney B. *Answers to Book of Mormon Questions* (Salt Lake City: Bookcraft), 1967.

_____. *Book of Mormon Compendium* (Salt Lake City: Bookcraft), 1968.

_____. *Doctrine and Covenants Compendium*, 2d ed. (Salt Lake City: Bookcraft), 1960.

Stuy, Brian H., ed., *Collected Discourses*, 5 vols. (Burbank, California: B. H. S. Publishing), 1987–1992.

Talmage, James E. *Articles of Faith* (Salt Lake City: Deseret Book), 1984.

_____. *The Great Apostasy* (Salt Lake City: Deseret Book), 1994.

_____. *Jesus the Christ* (Salt Lake City: Deseret Book), 1979.

Taylor, John. *The Government of God* (London, England: S. W. Richards), 1852.

_____. *Mediation and Atonement* (Salt Lake City: Deseret News Press), 1882.

Watt, George D., comp., *Journal of Discourses*, 26 vols. (London, England: F. D. and S. W. Richards and Sons), 1854–1886.

Wells, Robert E. *The Mount and the Master* (Salt Lake City: Deseret Book), 1991.

Whitney, Orson F. *Gospel Themes* (Salt Lake City: The Church of Jesus Christ of Latter-day Saints), 1914.

_____. *Saturday Night Thoughts* (Salt Lake City: Deseret News Press), 1921.

Widtsoe, John A. *Evidences and Reconciliations* (Salt Lake City: Bookcraft), 1960.

_____. *Joseph Smith: Seeker After Truth, Prophet of God* (Salt Lake City: Deseret News Press), 1951.

_____. *The Message of the Doctrine and Covenants* (Salt Lake City: Bookcraft), 1969.

_____. *Priesthood and Church Government* (Salt Lake City: Deseret Book), 1939.

_____. *A Rational Theology* (Salt Lake City: Deseret Book), 1965.

Williams, Clyde J., ed., *The Teachings of Harold B. Lee* (Salt Lake City: Bookcraft), 1996.

_____. ed., *The Teachings of Howard W. Hunter* (Salt Lake City: Bookcraft), 1997.

_____. ed., *The Teachings of Lorenzo Snow* (Salt Lake City: Bookcraft), 1996.

Articles

Ballard, M. Russell. "Answers to Life's Questions," *Ensign*, May 1995, 22–24.

_____. "Building Bridges of Understanding," *Ensign*, June 1998, 64–66.

Christofferson, D. Todd. "Justification and Sanctification," *Ensign*, June 2001, 18–25.

Cook, Gene R. "Receiving Divine Assistance Through the Grace of the Lord," *Ensign*, May 1993, 79–81.

Dahl, Larry E. "The Concept of Hell," in *Doctrines of the Book of Mormon: 1991 Sperry Symposium on the Book of Mormon* (Salt Lake City: Deseret Book, 1992), 42–56.

_____. "The Vision of the Glories (D&C 76)," in Robert L. Millet and Kent P. Jackson, eds., *Studies in Scripture: Volume 1, The Doctrine and Covenants* (Salt Lake City: Deseret Book, 1989), 279–308.

Doxey, Roy W. "Accepted of the Lord: The Doctrine of Making Your Calling and Election Sure," *Ensign*, July 1976, 50–53.

Gillum, Gary P. "Repentance Also Means Rethinking," in John M. Lundquist and Stephen D. Ricks, eds., *By Study and Also By Faith* (Salt Lake City: Deseret Book and The Foundation for Ancient Research and Mormon Studies, 1990), 2:406–37.

Godfrey, Kenneth W. "The History of Intelligence in Latter-day Saint Thought," in H. Donl Peterson and Charles D. Tate, Jr., eds., *The Pearl of Great Price: Revelations from God* (Provo, Utah: BYU Religious Studies Center, 1989), 213–35.

Hafen, Bruce C. "The Restored Doctrine of the Atonement," *Ensign*, December 1993, 7–13.

Harrell, Charles R. "The Development of the Doctrine of Preexistence, 1830–1844," *BYU Studies*, vol. 28, no. 2, Spring 1988, 75–96.

Lane, Jennifer Clark. "The Lord Will Redeem His People: Adoptive Covenant and Redemption in the Old Testament and Book of Mormon," *Journal of Book of Mormon Studies*, vol. 2, no. 2, Fall 1993, 39–62.

Lee, Robert England. "Teaching Our Children the Plan of Salvation," *Ensign*, September 2001, 32–39.

Ludlow, Daniel H. "The Relationship Between Grace and Works," in Daniel H. Ludlow, *Gospel Scholars Series: Selected Writings of Daniel H. Ludlow* (Salt Lake City: Deseret Book, 2000), 335–53.

Lund, Gerald N. "The Fall of Man and His Redemption," in Monte S. Nyman and Charles D. Tate, Jr., eds., *The Book of Mormon: Second Nephi, The Doctrinal Structure* (Provo, Utah: BYU Religious Studies Center, 1989), 83–106.

_____. "Salvation: By Grace or By Works?" *Ensign*, April 1981, 16–23.

_____. "'Then Is His Grace Sufficient for You' (Moro. 10:32)," in Gerald N. Lund, *Gospel Scholars Series: Selected Writings of Gerald N. Lund* (Salt Lake City: Deseret Book, 1999), 208–19.

Matthews, Robert J. "The Doctrine of the Atonement: The Revelation of the Gospel to Adam," in Robert L. Millet and Kent P. Jackson, eds., *Studies in Scripture: Volume 2, The Pearl of Great Price* (Salt Lake City: Randall Book, 1985), 111–29.

Maxwell, Neal A. "The Great Plan of the Eternal God," *Ensign*, May 1984, 21–23.

McConkie, Bruce R. "Making Our Calling and Election Sure," in *Brigham Young University Speeches of the Year 1968–69* (Provo, Utah: Brigham Young University Press, 1969), 1–11.

_____. "The Salvation of Little Children," *Ensign*, April 1977, 3–7.

_____. "The Seven Deadly Heresies," in *Brigham Young University Devotional and Fireside Addresses 1980* (Provo, Utah: Brigham Young University Press, 1981), 74–80.

_____. "What Think Ye of Salvation by Grace?" *Brigham Young University Fireside and Devotional Speeches 1983–84* (Provo, Utah: Brigham Young University Press, 1984), 44–50.

Millet, Robert L. "A New and Everlasting Covenant (D&C 132)," in Robert L. Millet and Kent P. Jackson, eds., *Studies in Scripture: Volume 1, The Doctrine and Covenants* (Salt Lake City: Deseret Book, 1989), 512–25.

Nelson, Russell M. "Is It Necessary to Take the Sacrament with One's Right Hand? Does It Really Make Any Difference Which Hand Is Used?" *Ensign*, March 1983, 68–69.

Nyman, Monte S. "The State of the Soul Between Death and the Resurrection," in Charles D. Tate and Monte S. Nyman, eds., *The Book of Mormon: Alma, The Testimony of the Word* (Provo, Utah: BYU Religious Studies Center, 1992), 173–94.

Oaks, Dallin H. "The Great Plan of Happiness," *Ensign*, November 1993, 72–75.

_____. "Have You Been Saved?" *Ensign*, May 1998, 55–57.

Packer, Boyd K. "The Brilliant Morning of Forgiveness," *Ensign*, November 1995, 18–21.

_____. "The Law and the Light," in Monte S. Nyman and Charles D. Tate, Jr., eds., *The Book of Mormon: Jacob Through Words of Mormon* (Provo, Utah: BYU Religious Studies Center, 1990), 1–31.

Parsons, Robert E. "What Is the Role of Grace in LDS Theology?" *Ensign*, July 1989, 59–61.

Peterson, Daniel C. and Stephen D. Ricks. "Comparing LDS Beliefs with First-Century Christianity," *Ensign*, March 1988, 6–11.

Peterson, H. Donl. "What Is the Meaning of the Book of Mormon Sscriptures on Eternal Hell for the Wicked?" *Ensign*, April 1986, 36–38.

Pratt, Parley P. "Four Kinds of Salvation," *Millennial Star*, vol. 2, no. 2, June 1841, 21–22.

Romney, Marion G. "Making Our Calling and Election Sure," *Improvement Era*, December 1965, 1115–16.

Scott, Richard G. "The Plan for Happiness and Exaltation," *Ensign*, November 1981, 11–12.

Todd, Jay M. "Salvation for the Dead," *Ensign*, February 1995, 46–51.

Turner, Rodney. "Grace, Mysteries, and Exaltation," in Robert L. Millet, ed., *Studies in Scripture: Volume 6, Acts to Revelation* (Salt Lake City: Deseret Book, 1987), 110–11.

INDEX

Adam, is Michael the archangel, 59; helped to create the earth, 59; brought seeds and animals to the earth during the creation, 59; was created temporally by the Father, 60–62, 79 (n. 13); was created outside of the Garden of Eden, 80 (n. 16); reasons why, was not created as a telestial being, 62–63; did not have blood before the Fall, 62, 65, 80 (n. 14); received the Priesthood in premortal times, 20; died within the day of the Lord, 81 (n. 21)

Adversity, purposes of, 96–98; has a purifying effect on human nature, 101 (n. 39)

Age of Accountability, is eight years old, 105–106 status of children before they reach, 235–36

Agency, granted by God during premortal life, 18, 29 (n. 40); granted by God on the earth, 63–64; is exercised in the postmortal spirit world, 155, 168 (n. 50); is necessary for building character, 36

Angels, are the same species as God and man, 21 (n. 2); do not reside on a planet like the earth, 18; are sent among mortals to declare the plan of salvation, 72; serve as sentinels, 123, 214; are assigned to keep records, 187, 198 (n. 52); and temple work during the Millennium, 157, 169 (ns. 53–54)

Atonement, meaning of the word, 72–73; rules of operation, 73–74; application of the, to individuals who sin, 76–78, 85 (n. 48); provides power to cleanse, 83 (n. 41)

Attitudes, a person's, do not automatically change after death, 152–53

Baptism, was ordained before the foundation of the world, 48 (n. 16); is connected with personal salvation, 105; must be by immersion to be valid, 106–107; proper authority is needed to perform, 103–104, 128 (n. 6), 164 (n. 25); by water is incomplete without the gift of the Holy Ghost, 130 (n. 19); symbolism associated with, 107–109; and entrance into paradise, 148–49, 164 (n. 26); is needed for entrance into the celestial kingdom, 228 (n. 41); pertains to the celestial kingdom only, 109, 129 (n. 16), 130 (n. 17), 229 (n. 42); and the application of Jesus Christ's atonement, 85 (n. 48)

Blasphemy Against the Holy Ghost, nature of, 203–204, 219 (n. 12); there is no forgiveness for, 203; and murder, 219 (n. 14); is a sin against all three members of the Godhead, 221 (n. 18); Lucifer said he could save even those who committed, 50 (n. 31)

Blood, need for the shedding of Jesus Christ's, 75–76; was not in the bodies of Adam and Eve before the Fall, 62, 65, 80 (n. 14); is not found in resurrected bodies, 179, 191 (n. 24); flesh and, cannot dwell in God's presence, 228 (n. 38); making garments white in the, of Jesus Christ, 77, 108

Body, is necessary to be like God, 11; relationship between the, and the spirit, 88–89; is a reward for premortal faithfulness, 99 (n. 3); a being with a, has more power than a spirit, 33; Satan uses the, against mortals, 90, 100 (n. 11); deficiencies, deformities, and handicaps of the, 128 (n. 9), 179, 192 (n. 29); a resurrected telestial or terrestrial, will have limitations, 231 (n. 47); some individuals with a resurrected celestial, will have limitations, 231 (n. 47); should be presented pure before God in the celestial kingdom, 99 (n. 3)

Born Again, being, comes by the Spirit of God through ordinances, 131 (n. 25)

Born Under the Covenant, parental claim on children who are, 247–48; being, does not assure a celestial inheritance, 247–48, 249 (n. 4)

Calling and Election Sure, can be accomplished in this life, 126; Joseph Smith exhorted Latter-day Saints to make their, 137 (n. 87); the Melchizedek Priesthood is necessary for, 118; is in addition to temple marriage, 124; comes through the fullness of temple ordinances, 126; is bestowed by a sealing, 245; and being sealed with the Holy Spirit of Promise, 123; and the more sure word of prophecy, 126–27; kings and priests have their, 215; and being sealed up unto eternal life, 126–27

Celestial Kingdom, criteria for entering into, 211–12; must be clean to enter, 77, 189, 229 (n. 43); must become as children to enter, 18, 95; must sacrifice to enter, 95; must repent to enter, 84 (n. 44); baptism and gift of the Holy Ghost are necessary for entrance into, 211, 228 (n. 41), 229 (n. 42); sealing to parents does not guarantee entrance into, 249 (n. 4); trials are necessary before entrance into, is granted, 95–96, 212; three degrees within, 211–15, 230 (n. 46); there is no family organization outside of, 125; varied levels of salvation within, 134 (n. 56); ritual qualifications for the three degrees within, 229 (n. 45); white stone given to the inheritors of, 211; and heavenly fire, 228 (n. 38)

Character, is the crowning glory of mortals, 92–93; trials and tribulations build, 98

Children, nature of, before birth, 235; nature of, after death, 238; condition of, after the resurrection, 192 (n. 29), 239–41, 242 (n. 14); and the age of accountability, 235–36; the gospel is taught to, who die, 238; ordinances and, who die, 238–39, 242 (ns. 11–12); stillborn, 242 (n. 13); creation of terrestrial, 79 (n. 11); all people must become as, in order to inherit the kingdom of heaven, 18, 95; reasons that some, die, 236–37; cannot inherit celestial glory because of their parents' righteousness, 249 (n. 7)

Church of the Firstborn, relationship of the temple endowment to, 222 (n. 19); and temple marriage, 215; male members of, are kings and priests, 119; and the fullness of the oath and covenant of the Melchizedek Priesthood, 224 (n. 26)

Confirmation, nature of, 109–110

Covenant(s), the Godhead was formed by, 40; and salvation, 119; and the uplifted right hand, 129 (n. 14); oath and, of the Melchizedek Priesthood, 224 (n. 26); and the temple endowment, 120, 122

Creation, was accomplished by Elohim, Jehovah, and Michael, 59; was executed by delegation of authority, 59; human knowledge of, is limited, 78 (n. 6)

Damnation, scope of, 127 (n. 4); is not predes-

tined, 40, 46; those who will not obey God will reap, 103; those who will not believe and be baptized will receive, 105; partaking of the sacrament unworthily can result in, 114; resurrection of, 175

Daughters of Perdition, First Presidency statements on, 217 (n. 8)

Day, of the Lord and the length of Adam's life, 81 (n. 21)

Degrees of Glory, prerequisites for inheriting each of the, 207–215; no progression between, after resurrection, 180–83, 192 (n. 33), 192 (n. 35) 193 (n. 36), 194 (n. 38); those in higher, may visit those in lower, 227 (n. 31)

Descending Below All Things, and the veil of forgetfulness, 82 (n. 32); is necessary for achieving exaltation, 48 (n. 18), 69

Devil, forfeited his right to a physical body and its blessings, 90, 99 (n. 7), temptations of the, are necessary for the exercise of agency, 64; has power over those who have a carnal nature, 76; reincarnation is a doctrine of the, 192 (n. 25)

Dispensation, of the fullness of times and the salvation of mankind, 165 (n. 27)

Earth, was created from chaotic matter, 50 (n. 31), 60; will eventually become a celestial kingdom, 216 (n. 4)

Elements, eternal nature of, 23 (n. 10); the universe is filled with, 16, 23 (n. 10), 27 (n. 30); are utilized in spiritual and temporal creations, 15–16, 23 (n. 10), 60

Elijah, restored the sealing power, 123; power of, and the Holy Spirit of Promise, 123; sealing by the power of, and making one's calling and election sure, 123; sealing on earth and in heaven by the keys of, 123

Elohim, is the God of all other gods, 50 (n. 31)

Endowment, meaning of the word, 122; was foreordained in premortal times as an earthly ordinance, 34; components of the, 122–23; pertains to exaltation in the celestial kingdom, 120; is connected with heirship 120, 135 (n. 66)

Eternal Progression, within each degree of glory, 194 (n. 38); comes by obedience to divine laws, 22 (n. 3)

Eternity, meaning of, 10, 23 (n. 11); Priesthood existed with God from, 19–20; mortal life is to prepare a person for, 95; the posterity of gods will never cease in, 137 (n. 89); God the Father's existence in, 10, 13, 23 (n. 12);

compliance with heavenly laws brings a legal claim on blessings in, 167 (n. 46); Gods, worlds, and mortal life have existed from all, 9; the mysteries of, are unlocked by keys, 205

Eve, scriptural account of the creation of, is figurative, 62, 79 (n. 12), 122; was created in the same manner as was Adam, 79 (n. 12); was created temporally outside of the Garden of Eden, 80 (n. 16)

Exaltation, the Lord desires that His children receive, 124; can only be achieved by keeping God's commandments, 124; criteria for receiving, 212–15; will not be denied to the faithful regardless of earthly circumstances, 136 (n. 77); cannot be attained without ordinances, 103; and the higher ordinances of the Priesthood, 137 (n. 86); is only granted to sealed husbands and wives, 118, 124; there is no, without the fullness of the Priesthood, 118; those who reach, hold the keys of the kingdom of heaven, 214; plural marriage is not necessary for, 136 (n. 78)

Fall, was a foreordained event, 65–66, 81 (n. 22); was the deliberate use of a law, 82 (n. 31); did not entail sin, 67–68; was a step downward but forward, 68; reasons why God did not cause, 69–70; effects of, on Adam and Eve, 70–71; and descending below all things, 69

Fallen Angels, lost their innocence when they rebelled against God, 18; forfeited their right to a physical body, 90; are destitute of love, 202–203

Foreordination, is a conditional preappointment, 40; to earthly leadership positions, 40–41; to earthly circumstances, 41–43; and earthly relationships, 43–44; of earthly events, 44

Forgiveness, the Lord's declarations on obtaining, 77; and different levels of salvation, 85 (n. 47)

Foreknowledge, nature of God's, 45, 53 (n. 55)

Garden of Eden, reasons for Adam's and Eve's removal from, 71, 83 (n. 35)

Gift of the Holy Ghost, is sealed upon a person, 131 (n. 27); and adoption into the Abrahamic lineage, 131 (n. 23); enjoyment of, 132 (n. 29); is needed for entrance into the celestial kingdom, 228 (n. 41); pertains only to the celestial kingdom, 229 (n. 42)

God, is an exalted Man of Holiness, 8, 22 (n. 6); had a progenitor, 9–10; has experienced mortality, 10–12, 23 (n. 12), 24 (n. 14); has received temple ordinances, 12; has been resurrected, 13–14, 25 (ns. 22, 25); is a Being of agency, 24 (n. 17); has created innumerable worlds, 58; desires to exalt His children, 24 (n. 17), 47 (n. 12), 87, 98 (n. 2); has a divine Spouse, 13; power of, is connected with His knowledge, 91; work and glory of, is to bring about immortality and eternal life, 12; men and women must become like, in order to dwell with Him, 95, 101 (n. 32); planet where, resides is a great Urim and Thummim, 210; being assimilated into the likeness of, 91

Godhead, was formed by covenant, 40; obedience to the laws of the, brings eternal progression, 22 (n. 3)

Godhood, children of God may achieve, 8; the Father designed that His children should rise to, 87, 98 (n. 2), 137 (n. 89); doctrine of, is taught throughout the scriptures, 8; mortal experience is necessary for achieving, 36; means joint-heirship with Jesus Christ, 222 (n. 20); nature of, 212–15, 232 (n. 48); means receiving the Lord's own fullness and glory, 12; those who attain, are still subject to the Savior, 232 (n. 49)

Gospel, is older than the earth, 31–32; will be utilized on future worlds, 31, the Father is the author of, 32, 46 (n. 4); pertains to the celestial kingdom only, 130 (n. 18), 229 (n. 42); will eventually be taught to everyone, 149–51, 167 (n. 45); must be heard by everyone before their final judgment takes place, 151; women preach the, to women in the spirit world, 165 (n. 36)

Grace, quotations on, and its relationship to salvation, 251–54; books and articles regarding, 254–55; scriptures about, 256; hymns that refer to, 256–57

Grand Council, was convened by God the Father, 32–33; took place on Kolob 32–33; creation of the heavens, earth, animals, and mankind discussed during, 33; bounds of planets and stars set during, 58; earthly laws and ordinances established during, 33–34; dispensation heads and apostles foreordained during, 40

Heavenly Mother, every man and woman has a literal, 15; women are made in the image of, 13, 15; women have the potential to become like, 48 (n. 18), 98; and the creation of Adam, 79 (n. 13); it is inappropriate to pray to, 25 (n. 21)

Hell, was created by God for the fallen spirits, 39; Latter-day Saints who do not repent are sent to, 164 (n. 24); damnation of, awaits those who disobey God, 103; is temporarily located in the earth's vicinity, 216 (n. 4)

Holy Ghost, gift of the, 109–113; gift of the, is sealed upon a person, 131 (n. 27); cleanses a person from sin, 112–13; and grafting into the lineage of Abraham, 131 (n. 23)

Holy Spirit of Promise, being sealed with, 123, 213, 220 (n. 15), 223 (n. 22), 229 (n. 45)

Humans, are the same race as God and the angels, 21 (n. 2); are the literal children of God, 7–8, 14; are gods in embryo, 22 (n. 3); make a record of themselves that will be used in their judgment, 198 (n. 54); and the theory of evolution, 80 (n. 15)

Jesus Christ, was the firstborn of the spirits, 15, 21, 30 (n. 51), 49 (n. 28); was chosen as the Redeemer in premortal times, 37–38; is the only name whereby salvation comes, 46 (n. 4); became the Savior by right of inheritance, 37, was assigned by the Father to create worlds, 59; was born in mortality with power over death, 84 (n. 42), 190 (n. 6); was the Only Begotten of the Father in mortal flesh, 79 (n. 13); atonement of, 71–78; mortals are commanded to emulate, 87; is the Second Comforter, 220 (n. 15); could have become a son of perdition by disobeying God, 44

Joseph Smith, was foreordained as a prophet in the Grand Council, 52 (n. 41); said there were no errors in God's revelations, 244 (n. 18)

Judgment, is one of the first principles of the gospel, 171–72, necessity of, 183–84, persons who will carry out, 184–85, 195 (n. 45); administration of, 185–86; criteria for, 186–88; of the righteous, 188–89; of the wicked, 189; will be fair, 198 (n. 54); part played by mercy during, 196 (n. 47)

Kingdom of God, identified as the celestial kingdom, 129 (n. 16)

Kings and Priests, becoming, is the ultimate objective of mortality, 87; have been endowed, married for eternity, and sealed up unto eternal life, 215; belong to the Church of the Firstborn, 119, 215; have the fullness

of the Priesthood, 118, 134 (n. 56); will participate in the resurrection, 175; become gods, 222 (n. 19)

Knowledge, relationship of, to salvation, 91; and the power of God, 91, 100 (n. 15); revealed, unlocks the glories and mysteries of God's kingdom, 91; secular, 91–92

Law(s), the Father is a God of, 167 (n. 46), the Father instituted, in premortal times, 33–34; the Father established, for the advancement of His children, 47 (n. 12); sanctification comes by obedience to divine, 201; of adoption, 124–25; of the Lord in regard to parents and their children, 105; ignorance of, and judgment, 197 (n. 48); those who die without, 227 (n. 33); those who cannot understand, 105–106; sons of perdition seek to a become a, unto themselves, 202

Laying On of Hands, bestowal of authority through, 104, 128 (n. 6); gift of the Holy Ghost is sealed upon a person by, 111, 128 (n. 6), 131 (n. 27), 171, 211; confirmation is accomplished through, 110; is a tangible link of transmittal, 111; is a vicarious act, 111

Lucifer, had a high status before his rebellion, 36–37, 49 (n. 28); volunteered to be the Redeemer, 37; desired to modify the Father's plan, 37–38, 49 (n. 30); wanted to save people in their sins, 38, 50 (n. 32); sought for that which was unlawful, 50 (n. 31); tried to destroy the agency of man, 38; wanted to usurp the Priesthood power of God, 38; lost his chance to receive a body, 39–40, 89–90, 99 (n. 7); boasted that he could save even blasphemers against the Holy Ghost, 50 (n. 31); temptation by, is necessary for the exercise of agency, 64; targets mortal bodies, 90

Marriage, temple, is essential to exaltation, 124; temple, sealing is broken by a husband and wife inheriting different kingdoms, 136 (n. 77); plural, is not essential to salvation or exaltation, 136 (n. 78)

Mercy, access to God's presence comes through the, of the Messiah, 72; the repentant are claimed by, 73; the Savior possesses the rights of, 74; deficiencies will be corrected through God's, 128 (n. 9); cannot rob justice, 196 (n. 47); sons of perdition cannot be sanctified by, 202; idea of predestination robs God of, 53 (n. 55); God's, does not overcome the requirements of His law, 228 (n. 41); every person will hear the gospel through the Father's, 238; God ordained the plan of salvation because of His, 254

More Sure Word of Prophecy, is evidence that one's calling and election is sure, 126–27; is God's promise of eternal life, 137 (n. 88); Joseph Smith admonished the Saints to ask God for, 137 (n. 87)

Mortality, purpose of, 87; risk involved in, 34–36; developing spirituality during, 93–94; trials to be overcome during, 94–98; prepares a person for eternity, 95

One Eternal Round, relation of God and man to, 22 (n. 4)

Ordinances, of God's kingdom were instituted in the Grand Council, 34, are necessary for the fullness of salvation, 103, 127 (n. 3); must be attended to in the mortal sphere, 166 (n. 43); power of godliness is manifested through, 104; must be administered by legitimate Priesthood authority, 103–104; ensure a legal claim on the blessings of eternity, 167 (n. 46); being born again comes through, 104; reception of, demonstrates a willingness to obey divine commands, 166 (n. 43)

Paradise, spirits in, are organized in family capacities, 143; ordinary buildings in, are superior to Solomon's Temple, 143–44; numerous flowers found in, 144; tree of life is planted in, 142; is a state of peace and rest, 142; government, organization, and grades within, 143

Perdition, meaning of the word, 39; sons of, 202–206; daughters of, 217 (n. 8)

Perfection, mortals can achieve, in their sphere, 100 (n. 14); comes by obedience to divine law, 201; body and spirit are both necessary for, in time and eternity, 177; and vicarious temple work, 167 (n. 48); and family sealings, 126, exalted beings achieve, through Jesus Christ's atoning blood, 213; achieving, in Jesus Christ through God's grace, 232 (n. 49)

Pillars of Eternity, are listed in the Book of Mormon, 57

Plan of Salvation, general articles on, 4 (n. 3); applies to every son and daughter of Adam, 215 (n. 1); ultimate objective of, is celestial heirship, 98 (n. 1); is a system of laws and ordinances, 1; eternal nature of, 31–32, 46 (n. 3); is the same today as in the days of Adam, 32

Predestination, is not a genuine doctrine of the gospel, 40, 46, 53 (n. 55)

Premortal Life, environment during, 17–18; organization in, 19, 30 (n. 47); authority was given to spirits during, 19–20; achievement by spirits during, 20–21; activities during, affect mortal circumstances, 42; house of Israel during, 42–43

Priesthood, was held by individuals during premortal times, 19–20, 34; spirits are organized according to the everlasting, 30 (n. 41); makes its bearer a proxy for the Lord, 104, 111, 128 (n. 6); is required for the performance of ordinances, 128 (n. 6); makes ordinances binding in heaven, 118; Melchizedek, is the channel through which knowledge, doctrine, and the plan of salvation are revealed from heaven, 134 (n. 48); fullness of, is necessary for exaltation, 118, 134 (n. 56); fullness of, makes a man a king and priest, 134 (n. 56), 224 (n. 26); oath and covenant of the Melchizedek, 224 (n. 26); women and the, 217 (n. 8); men cannot be sealed up unto eternal life without the Melchizedek, 118; the highest honor of the, 224 (n. 25)

Procreation, is one the purposes of mortal life, 89, 99 (n. 8)

Proxy Ordinances, list of, performed in the temple, 153; will not be performed for all of the dead, 156–57; are not forced upon the dead, 155, 168 (n. 50); are not efficacious for everyone, 155; pertain only to the celestial kingdom, 154–55; are not a second chance at celestial salvation, 155–56, 168 (n. 51); bring release from the spirit prison, 135 (n. 62), 154; during the Millennium, 157, 169 (ns. 53–54); neglect of, by the living will affect their salvation, 166 (n. 41)

Redeemer, meaning of the word, 74–75; reasons why Jesus Christ acted as, 75

Repentance, meaning of the word, 76–77; is a commandment, 76

Resurrection, meaning of the word, 173; is one of the first principles of the gospel, 171–72; every mortal will receive, 173; necessity of, 173–74; methods of accomplishing, 174–75, 191 (n. 24); keys of, to be delegated to certain individuals, 191 (n. 15); the body is quickened by glory at the time of, 175; four categories of, 175–77; nature of bodies after, 177–80, 192 (n. 29); children and the, 180; brings glory, honor, power, and dominion, 47 (n. 10); gives a person ascendancy over disembodied spirits, 33; morning of the first, 177; Joseph Smith was shown a vision of the, 191 (n. 18); Wilford Woodruff was shown a vision of the, 191 (n. 24)

Right Hand, use of, during the sacrament, 116; uplifted, 108–109, 129 (n. 14)

Sacrament, is an ordinance of salvation, 132 (n. 32; and personal worthiness, 114–15; difference in prayers on, 115–16; renews the baptismal covenant, 115; taking of, with the right hand, 116–17; does not remit sins, 116, 133 (n. 45); water used in, instead of wine, 132 (n. 33)

Salvation, universal nature of, 215 (n. 1); personal, is an individual responsibility, 249 (n. 4); fullness of, comes only through ordinances, 127 (n. 3); of children, 235–41, covenant status and, 245–48; and the grace of God, 251–57

Salvation for the Dead, was planned by the Lord in premortal times, 149, 165 (n. 27); was inaugurated by Jesus Christ, 149–50; is connected with the salvation of the living, 121

Saviors on Mount Zion, prophecy of Obadiah concerning, 121; are those who perform proxy temple work, 134 (n. 61), 135 (n. 62)

Sealing Power, is the power of Elijah, 123; and marriage sealing, 124; and family sealing, 124–26, 136 (n. 84); and sealing to eternal life, 126–27, 137 (n. 86), 213

Second Comforter, identification of the, 220 (n. 15)

Second Death, meaning of, 224 (n. 27)

Sin, and knowledge of law, 197 (n. 48); is remitted on condition of repentance, 75; service helps to recompense for, 85 (n. 45); unto death, 247

Sons of Perdition, seek to become a law unto themselves, 202; are destitute of love, 202–203; criteria for becoming, 203–206; eternal punishment of, 206; steps whereby Cain became one of the, 216 (n. 6); only members of the true Church can become, 217 (n. 7); gospel is not preached in the

spirit world to, 151; mortals who become, must first receive the fullness of gospel blessings, 222 (n. 19)

Spirit of God, will replace blood in resurrected bodies, 178–79, 191 (n. 24); will play a role during judgment, 187–88

Spirit Prison, is separate from hell, 147–49, 160 (n. 19), 164 (n. 23); those who never heard the true gospel in mortality go to, 148, 167 (n. 45); those who hear but reject the true gospel go to, 148, 167 (n. 45); those who reject the true gospel on earth but then accept it in, inherit the terrestrial kingdom at most, 151, 168 (n. 51), 210; means of release from, were foreordained in premortal times, 165 (n. 27); proxy ordinance work is required for release from, 135 (n. 62)

Spirits, inhabit mortal bodies, 14; are brought into existence by an act of creation, 14; are begotten and born of Heavenly Parents, 14–15, 25 (n. 26); Jesus Christ was the first-born among premortal, 15, 21, 30 (n. 51), 49 (n. 28); no conscious existence before the creation of, 16, 28 (n. 32); are made of matter, 15–16, 25 (n. 28); are created on a celestial world, 18; are male and female, 29 (n. 35); premortal, have emotions and character traits, 28 (n. 33); can only be created by exalted beings, 232 (n. 48); premortal, live in a sphere governed by law, 21, 30 (n. 41), 33, 47 (n. 12), 50 (n. 31); are tangible to other spirits, 16; resemble mortal bodies, 16–17, 28 (n. 34); Joseph Smith's comments on the eternal nature of, 25 (n. 28); premortal, are endowed with agency, 18; some, with power seek to subjugate other, 47 (n. 10); enhanced capabilities of righteous, 144–46; progress by knowledge, 20, 159 (n. 9); premortal, live in an organized society, 19; do not return to God's immediate presence after death, 158 (n. 1); are separated from translated and resurrected beings, 147, 158 (n. 1); three groups of, that the devil has power over, 163 (n. 21); cannot receive ordinances that pertain to mortality, 166 (n. 43); intellectual and moral condition of, does not automatically change after death, 166 (n. 37)

Spirituality, is developed over time, 93–94; suggestions for increasing, 94

Spirit World, is not the same place as heaven, 141; partial judgment as one enters, 142;

divisions within, 142–49, 158 (n. 1), 160 (n. 19); location of, 142, 158 (n. 3); learning process continues in, 145, 159 (n. 9); is separate from the world of resurrected beings, 158 (n. 1); those in the, are aware of earthly events, 159 (n. 8)

Stewardship, an account of, in both time and eternity to be given at the judgment, 186

Telestial, meaning of the word, 227 (n. 28)

Telestial Kingdom, criteria for inheriting, 207–208; inheritors of, are thrust down to hell after death, 208

Temple Marriage, is necessary to receive the fullness of God's glory, 12

Temple Ordinances, are eternal in nature, 24 (n. 18), teach the ways of salvation, 34; are related to heirship in God's kingdom, 121, 135 (n. 66)

Terrestrial Kingdom, criteria for inheriting, 209–210; includes those who are without law, 227 (n. 33); Latter-day Saints who are not valiant will inherit, 210; there are several degrees within the, 228 (n. 36); those who rejected the gospel in Noah's day can only inherit the, at most, 151, 168 (n. 51)

Theology, Latter-day Saints should become experts in, 100 (n. 22)

Trials, purposes of, 96–97; burn the dross out of human nature, 101 (n. 39); veil of forgetfulness is necessary for, 34–35, 82 (n. 32)

Unpardonable Sin, nature of, 203–206, 218 (ns. 10–11), 219 (ns. 13–14); Cain was guilty of committing, 216 (n. 6); can only be committed by members of the true Church, 217 (n. 7); cannot be committed until the Holy Ghost is received, 219 (n. 12); and calling and election sure, 223 (n. 22); high degree of knowledge needed to commit, 221 (n. 18); cannot be committed after death, 221 (n. 16); breaks the covenant tie, 247

Veil of Forgetfulness, is necessary for testing agency, 34–35, 80 (n. 18); and descending below all things, 82 (n. 32); will be removed in the future, 35–36, 80 (n. 18)

War in Heaven, began over the subject of redemption, 37; there were no neutral spirits during, 51 (n. 35); Orson Pratt's thoughts on, 38–39

Washings and Anointings, are connected with heirship in God's kingdom, 121